Just Around The Matterhorn

Just Around The Matterhorn

Book Two in the Alpine Thru-Hiking series

Dan Colegate

Copyright © 2019 Dan Colegate

All rights reserved. This edition produced in January 2020.

Thank purchasing this book. This book remains the copyrighted property of the author and may not be redistributed to others for commercial or non-commercial purposes. This book or any portion thereof may not be reproduced or used in any manner whatsoever without the express written permission of the author except for the use of brief quotations in a book review.

If you enjoy this book, please leave a review and encourage your friends to purchase their own copy.

Thank you for your support

www.estheranddan.com

www.instagram.com/estheranddan

www.facebook.com/estheranddan

To my parents

To my mum, for your inspiration in caring for the strays of the world and showing that every dog deserves as many chances as it takes.

And to my dad, for showing that it's never too late to discover the abundance and joy of the Great Outdoors.

Contents

Where Did It All Go Wrong 1
Furry Friends 9
Preparation 16
Setting Forth 26
New Heights 32
Mr Grumpy 41
The Cabin 50
Rain 63
Icefall 74
Schön 86
To Glacier Or Not To Glacier 94
Suspended 107
Nude 119
Lost In Fog 125
Benvenuto in Italia 131
How Much Higher? 141
Ski Slopes 148
The Dude 155
Sick 166
Sicker 177
Risking It 182
Woozy 190
Thieving Marmot Bastard 198
Hot and Bothered 208
Verbier 218

Tomato Sauce	227
The Glacier	235
Ice Climb	244
Are We Nearly There Yet?	255
Glorious	262
Epilogue	264
Thank You	265
Acknowledgements	266
Photos	267
Also By The Author	275
A Note On Names, Altitudes And Distances	281

Where Did It All Go Wrong

We all face challenges in life. We never wish for them but, if we're lucky, those challenges can redirect us down some of the most exciting roads we'll ever take.

It was 3 a.m. in the middle of a sleeting January night when a serious-faced young surgeon gently suggested that Esther and I might want to say a 'proper goodbye' to each other, just in case. Yet now, five and a bit years later, at 3 p.m. on a drizzly August afternoon in the Alps, we're luxuriating together in the dry heat of an Alpine sauna. Outside, beyond the glass wall and just visible beneath the low clouds, is a postcard-worthy collection of wooden lodges set against the dark green sides of the valley, a typically idyllic outlook for this beautiful region. At the moment, however, what's mostly holding my attention and the attention of others around me, is the sight of two young French ladies in striped bikinis who have, inexplicably, decided to wrestle each other on the damp grass in front of the spa. They seem to be taking it quite seriously. It's at times like this that I can't help but chuckle to myself, 'where did it all go wrong?'

The fact that the decisions which led us to this point all grew from the spark that was ignited on that terrifying winter night is not lost on me. The decision to cancel our wedding. The decision to change our lives instead. The decision to leave our jobs for good. The decision to drive away from our home, our friends and our illusions of security in a rattling second-hand motorhome that looked like a big mushroom on wheels. All of the thousands of major and minor decisions that we've taken (or not taken) since our departure that have somehow led me to this moment, sitting in a ludicrously hot pine box and watching two barely-dressed ladies try and sit on each other's heads. Where did it all go wrong indeed?

For us, I suppose the truth was that life had been at least a little bit wrong for a long time, it just took an especially shocking event to wake us up to the fact that the only people keeping it that way was us.

All of our life Esther and I had been apparently high-achievers, climbing the ladder of life with the top always seeming just one or two more rungs away. We'd met at Oxford University, the first in our families to go to university at all, and had both left with first class degrees to do further study at Durham University. Research jobs at Cambridge University came next, followed shortly afterwards by securing investment to launch our own venture capital backed online business. Gala dinners, young entrepreneur awards and conference calls with excitable Silicon Valley types occupied the next few years. All around us were people who'd 'made it' themselves and who wanted to tell us how great it was that we were doing the same. "People like you two", they would say, "are the future of business".

There was just one problem. We hated it. Yes, the dinners were nice and the awards were shiny, but the awards couldn't reply to emails or make phone calls for us. No matter how many dust-gathering, decorative paperweights we accumulated, our inboxes still continued to fill up faster than we could empty them. We felt in a constant state of high-alert, rushing from one overdue and must-do task to the next.

Our many and varied 'contacts' may have been kind and generous with their advice and ideas for bigger and faster growth, but in the cold light of dawn our lives, our health and our relationship were slowly falling apart. We didn't want to be hard-nosed business people, sashaying into breakfast meetings with an agenda in mind. We didn't want to see friends as contacts. To approach every new face wondering "what can we get out of this interaction?" We weren't natural schmoozers. We'd only started the business as a way of spending more time together and because we thought our initial idea could genuinely help people. After a few years, however, with all the changes that securing investment had required and with business demands consuming almost every waking hour, all we really wanted was to make our website popular enough that someone would buy it and we could stop.

Then there was the fact that like the good little capitalists we'd become, we'd also decided to invest in property by taking on a level of personal debt that the banks really should have known better than to lend us. We had a total of fifteen bedrooms to fill, decorating and furnishing each one ourselves during overnight decorating sessions. Like the proverbial house of cards, if just two rooms had stood empty for a couple of months, the whole complicated financial web we'd built around ourselves would have collapsed, which was enough to deprive me of the little sleep I occasionally had time for. That said, repainting windowsills, unblocking shower-trays or repairing shelves at midnight while eating supermarket donuts were sometimes the happiest parts of my week.

Frequently I found myself recalling a t-shirt my dad used to wear while I was a kid with a blunt and colourful slogan proclaiming it to be "Another Shitty Day In Paradise". It seemed the perfect description of our lives. This was it. This was 'making it'. We were fully paid up members of the capitalist club, so deeply immersed in interest rates, convertible loans and the promise of future wealth that we couldn't even tell the difference between swimming and drowning any more. We were almost there. Any moment now it would all work out for the best. It simply had to. So why were we more miserable than we'd ever known?

It all sounds very melodramatic in hindsight, which is because it was very melodramatic. There's nothing like prolonged sleep deprivation, non-stop tension within a previously loving relationship and the feeling that the best part of a day is going to bed at the end of it to make you feel sorry for yourself, which is partly what we were doing. Yet there was also a truth in the unhappiness, a message that something really wasn't right. We had genuinely overstretched, overtired and overwhelmed ourselves in the pursuit of some bastardised version of success, a version which we'd somehow convinced ourselves was a suitable goal for our lives. Dreams be damned, it was time to push through and wait for the pay off.

It was almost a mercy when the business folded and we had to sell most of the property to reduce our debt. If it weren't for the fact other people lost their jobs, I think I would have jumped for joy.

At first, life slowed down dramatically. I got a job as a business development manager at another university, one of the few things I seemed qualified to do as a lapsed academic who'd dabbled in business. Dividing my time between assessing possible inventions arising from the chemistry and chemical engineering departments and playing email ping-pong with invisible colleagues, I swiftly developed my 90-10 theory of large organisation employment: that each new employee will spend around 90 percent of their time dealing with internal, institutional issues, with only 10 percent of their time available to actually do anything useful. Not that I minded, I was just pleased to have a boss, a salary and my weekends back.

Esther took a different approach, retraining as a personal trainer. Pretty soon she had enough clients to ensure a decent and stable income and, like me, she enjoyed having more free time. Unfortunately, unlike me, her free time was rarely at evenings and weekends so there was no guarantee we'd get to enjoy it together.

Still, life was pleasant enough and certainly less stressful. There just wasn't any spark to it, no zest, especially after the first few months when the novelty of the change began to wear off. We didn't seem to have any dreams any more.

At first, we were annoyed at ourselves for our apparent inability to enjoy all we had. "We're being ungrateful wankers" we berated ourselves, "we have a good life and we're so much more fortunate than others", which was completely true. For weeks on end we'd alternate between which one of us was being the cheerful one, trying to buoy the other up before sliding back ourselves and finding our roles had reversed. It was only a matter of time before we both slid back together. That's when we decided to finally get married.

Depression isn't one of the most famous catalysts for marriage, at least as far as I know, but in our case a wedding was just one part of an ingeniously cunning plan. Here's how it went. Since we still had some savings and a lot less debt than before, we'd decided to take a 'career break' for six months. At the time, a career break seemed like a much more professionally acceptable way of stopping working, for a while, without the risks and stigma of quitting and becoming deliberately unemployed.

However, simply saying to friends, family and colleagues that "we're going on a six month holiday" also felt far too irresponsible to our work-conditioned minds, so we decided that our career break should become an 'extended honeymoon' instead. Hence, setting a date for a wedding.

Finally, and this was the real stroke of genius, rather than buying a round the world plane ticket so we could sip cocktails on a Vietnamese beach, our extended honeymoon would be a six-month hiking challenge. Surely nobody could accuse us of being workshy, lazy spongers if we were hiking all the way from Holland to the Mediterranean along the GR5 hiking trail, passing through five different countries and including a month-long section through the French Alps. Hell, we'd probably be even *more* employable after our time off. Stupid really, but for two people who'd always derived their self-esteem from visible achievements, we just didn't feel comfortable with simply kicking back. Without a project, we felt, we'd have no purpose.

Which is why the first few weeks of 2014 found us making travel-themed wedding decorations on our living room floor, chasing up 50-odd dinner choices, disagreeing over whether it was worth forking out for some faux-marble columns at the front of the wedding venue, arguing with parents about champagne versus prosecco, downloading GPS coordinates, accumulating hiking gear and preparing resupply boxes for our family to ship out to us along the way. My final day at work was in mid-Feburary, our wedding would happen a few days later and our hike would start just a week after that. A perfectly stress-free way of doing things really, as I'm sure you can imagine.

Then the wheels came off. I'd first noticed a little lump on my stomach on Boxing Day and in early January the doctor confirmed what I already knew, that I had a minor incisional hernia. Throughout the preceding few years I'd undergone multiple surgeries related to a birth defect, a defect that had left me with lifelong bowel incontinence. It was a problem I'd largely hidden for the first thirty years of my life, coping as best as I could to appear normal and only finally seeking medical help at the age of twenty eight, which is far too long a story to say much about here. Needless to say, the surgeries hadn't exactly helped during our times of greatest stress and, unfortunately, they hadn't helped much with my incontinence either.

All of the surgical interventions had been reversed in the end, leaving me with little more than a patchwork of scars that Chuck Norris would have been proud of and a lifelong, unshakeable respect for the nursing staff of the NHS. It was one of those old scars that had opened up in my abdominal wall and through which my intestines were bulging, like a lost mole that couldn't quite break through the surface.

The idea that I could ignore it and take off on a six-month hiking challenge with a hole in my stomach muscles was a non-starter, so it felt like a minor miracle when a sympathetic consultant offered me a last-minute NHS surgery slot just a few weeks after the hernia appeared. I got a short absence cleared at work and showed up at the hospital the very next morning ready to be cut open, stitched up and, fingers crossed, ready to carry a heavy pack in line with our original schedule, or at most with just a week or two delay.

Seven days later I was back in hospital with a serious post-operative infection. Educated fool that I was, I'd ignored the initial redness and swelling, shrugged off the feverish sweats and chills and willingly believed the home-visit GP Esther had insisted on calling out when she told me that a short course of antibiotics would make it all better again. If Esther hadn't met a friend at the gym and heard a story about a lady who'd almost died of an infection after an appendix removal, I probably would have even refused to go to the out of hours doctor completely. I've never liked a fuss when I feel ill, preferring to retreat into my cave and be left alone until it goes away.

As it was, the out of hours doctor had taken one look at the redness encircling my midriff, from belly button to spine, and the grapefruit sized yellow-pink swelling beneath the surgery wound and driven me to accident and emergency herself. A surgeon came, cut me open immediately (without anaesthetic), poked around in the oozing hole and declared that I was in more trouble than I realised. He then called in two more senior colleagues to have a rummage themselves.

They used the phrase 'necrotising fasciitis' a lot. Sometimes known as the 'flesh-eating disease', it's a condition that results in the death of the body's soft tissues and spreads rapidly. Treated by aggressively cutting out infected tissue and starting intravenous antibiotics as soon as possible, that's why I was in so much trouble. There's only so much 'middle' you can cut out and they had no idea how far inside of me it had already spread. The plan was to take me in to surgery, cut out as much as they needed to (or could) and then keep me sedated in intensive care so that I could go in for further cutting as required. It was just a short while later that we were told to say a proper goodbye, just in case. I was wheeled away to be knocked out and carved up while Esther had to go home to a cold apartment full of hiking gear and butterfly-shaped confetti that we'd hole-punched out of old maps. I've always thought I got the better deal out of that one.

Just over three months later we drove south from Durham, riding Homer the mushroom-shaped motorhome towards our search for a new life. I had a single, much larger scar in place of a collection of smaller ones, but thankfully the infection hadn't spread quite as far as the surgeons had feared. It was far enough though. Far enough for me to wake up with a chunk of my tummy in the shape of a slice of watermelon missing. Enough to make us see that tinkering around the edges wasn't going to work any more. Enough to know that, if we got through this, life was going to change significantly. Life had to change significantly, because we were going to change it ourselves. Life had finally gone wrong enough for us to want to find out what 'right' might look like again.

Furry Friends

Five and a half years of nomadic motorhome wanderings, after a life of school, work, mortgages, kitchen cleaning and lawnmowing, was a pretty major life change, and we'd done our best to fill our time with new experiences. We'd hiked up so many mountains we couldn't remember them all and cycled up almost as many high road passes. We'd worked on organic farms. Danced at festivals. Tried house-sitting in rural France. Looked after swimming pools and driven sit-on lawnmowers (a life ambition fulfilled – eat your heart out Forrest Gump). Visited Egypt. Been back to the UK to give away all of the stuff we'd left in a friend's attic. Changed our motorhome three times. Built sandcastles all along the Mediterranean coast. Been skinny-dipping. Written some books. And we'd made friends with people from all over the world.

But more than all of that, we'd changed as people. It would be wrong to imply that there was some design or direction in the change, and certainly it would be misleading to suggest that any changes were somehow 'finished'. Yet there was no denying that we just weren't the same people who had excitedly rattled south into the great unknown.

All of the unplanned, unforeseen and uncontrollable events that had buffeted us around Europe, drifting from one whim to the next, had opened our eyes to the endless ways that different people make their lives. Our previous images of 'success' and beliefs about how to 'get by' had been so narrow, constricting and judgemental. In a very real sense, our experiences had opened our minds and shown us that joy was not dependent on material circumstances and achievements after all. Quite the opposite in fact. Provided our basic needs for food and shelter were met, the less we had the happier we seemed to become. But against all of the many experiences that showed us the most about ourselves, none were more powerful than the events that started with a single cheese toastie and ended with a pregnant dog. It wasn't even our cheese toastie.

It began in mid-December 2016, towards the end of our third year on the road. Esther's parents were visiting us as we travelled through Spain, so we'd gone out for the morning to enjoy the sunshine together. Easing ourselves into the white plastic garden chairs of a shoreside café, we'd used pretty much the full range of our Spanish vocabulary at the time to order some drinks. "Dos café con leche, una Polio Menthe y una agua con gas, por favor".

The waiter nodded, smiled to confirm we hadn't bodged the Spanish too badly and then meandered slowly back inside to fetch the drinks. So far, so good. All we had to do now was sit back, bask in the morning sun and watch those colourful boats bobbing around on the shimmering sea.

A few moments of quiet reverie slipped by when Esther's dad suddenly added "Hmm, I think I'll have a cheese and ham toastie as well. Would anyone else like anything?"

A quick round of head shaking confirmed that, since we'd all only just enjoyed breakfast, we were quite happy to wait for our drinks and enjoy the morning warmth with a little companionable chatter. Esther's dad, however, was undeterred. We were 'out', and going 'out' meant toasties, breakfast or not. "Just me then" he said with a smile, getting up and heading inside to add a toastie to his order.

A few minutes later the drinks arrived along with an alarmingly large length of steaming baguette, liberally smothered in melted cheese and surprisingly pink strips of ham that had Esther's dad grinning from ear to ear. Ten minutes later, however, his pace had slowly significantly.

"I'm not sure I'm going to be able to manage all this on my own you know, are you sure you no-one else wants any?"

We were all shaking our heads again when a new voice suddenly joined the conversation to say "Give it to the dog".

We looked down and there she was, the dog I mean, not the voice. A small, sleek, ginger cylinder of fur with a white nose and a tufty Mohican running the length of her upper back. I could say that she was wagging her tail expectantly in the general direction of the toastie, but that wouldn't be wholly accurate. Better to say that she was wagging her entire body in excited ripples that extended right from the end of her shaking nose to the white tip of her beating tail, her front paws padding quickly from side to side as though she was only just managing to restrain the explosion of excitement that the mere existence of "toastie" was creating in her mind.

This being southern Spain, the presence of several street dogs wandering around a café or perusing the nearby dustbins was not an unfamiliar sight. Nor was it uncommon for other dog owners to simply allow their pets to roam at leisure while they supped and chatted somewhere in the vicinity. Sort of zoning out and accepting their usually benign presence was an easy habit to fall into. Occasionally you might reach down to provide an ear scratching service or complement a nearby owner on their "lovely dog", but certainly, being British, actually feeding somebody else's pet wasn't usually on the agenda, not without permission anyway.

The owner of the pleasant Mexican-sounding voice turned out to be a lady named Blanca, well-tanned with a shock of white frizzy hair, who was sitting just across the café from us with a friend. Quite naturally, since she was dishing out permission so freely, we assumed she must be the owner of the cute excited dog. It was wearing a collar after all.

Quarter of an hour later, when we stood up to leave, Esther reached down to give the expectant, happy face a final fuss. She really was a lovely dog. Gentle, soft, quiet and persistent but without being a pushy nuisance. In fact, as much as the melted cheese had clearly delighted her, fuss and cuddles seemed to invoke just as much response. The slightest touch had her rolling on her back for a tummy rub and, if we had the nerve to try and stop, she would jump up and push her snout back into our hand to remind us that there was still more rubbing to do.

"She's really lovely" said Esther to Blanca as we made to step away.

"You want her?" was the unexpected response. "She was only found in our village last week. I've taken her in for now and tried to find an owner but we can't keep her. We already have several cats and another dog of our own, Lily". She nodded towards a large Alsatian-type dog that had been running back and forth on the nearby beach for the past quarter of an hour, barking like a nutter at the indifferent seagulls.

"We call this one Chiquita."

I half-heartedly dialled Blanca's number so it was stored in my recent call list, although I didn't bother to save it as a contact. For the next two weeks we went back and forth, discussing and debating, dismissing and delaying on the issue of whether we could, or should, offer the little dog a home. It was undeniable that we led a fairly interesting life and also had the resources to offer a dog a home, plus we definitely both loved animals, but was it a commitment we wanted to make?

After much soul searching, we eventually decided that it was. Incredibly, Blanca's unsaved number was just clinging on at the very bottom of the 'recently dialled' list in my archaic handset. One more phone call and we'd have had no way to get in touch at all. Yes, the dog was still with her and yes, she'd be delighted if we could try taking her home. "If it doesn't work out" she assured us, "you can bring her back to me and I'll keep looking."

We collected Chiquita on a Friday. By the end of the day she had become Leela, a name she instantly responded to, and for the next four days we couldn't believe our luck. She followed us around, did as we asked her and generally made life a lot more fun. She was attentive, quiet, gentle with strangers and small children and seemed the ideal companion for a young couple living in a van.

It wasn't until the following Tuesday we found out she was pregnant. We never doubted Blanca, who was as genuinely shocked as we were. The idea that this compact, lean to the point of being underweight dog could be pregnant seemed absurd. But she was, and we'd seen the ultrasound to prove it. Leela wasn't just pregnant, she was very pregnant! Yet the idea of handing her back to Blanca didn't seriously cross our minds either. We'd made a commitment to Leela and that meant we'd do what needed to be done.

Less than a fortnight later, six more dogs entered the world. "Don't name them" friends told us, "it'll just make it harder when you rehome them". They were right. Within a week Bella, Rose, Jess, Teddy, Pati and George had become part of our family as we felt blessed to watched them grow, open their eyes, take their first steps and fill the world with a little more happiness than before they'd appeared.

After eight weeks or so Jess and Teddy left the band to join their new forever homes, and we really couldn't have wished for better families for them to become part of. Yet for one reason or another the others didn't leave. There was always a sensible reason at the time, but before we knew it six months had gone by and we were exchanging our little van for a bigger motorhome. At least Leela was a small dog and her offspring were all under ten kilograms, so at least we weren't drowning in Great Danes!

The next two and half years of touring were more frantic, fur-filled, fast-paced and fun than anything that came before. It required a fair bit of planning and compromise to make sure we all got what we needed, but although it felt like madness at times there was always plenty to remind us why we loved them so much. For me, afternoon cuddles were the best. Having developed a siesta habit in Spain, most afternoons we'd toss the furballs up onto our bed, climb into the pile and doze off in a hairy heap as the gang used different parts of us as pillows and snout rests. It was awesome. Seven loved-up souls in totally companionable chaos.

Still, after the two and a half years of lead-juggling, bum-fur trimming, six-times a day sweeping and nocturnal toilet trips (who could forget the five-dog-diarrhoea incident in Liege!), we both agreed that a few weeks of dog-free time would be rather nice, if possible. Not too long, we'd miss them too much. But a month, perhaps, or even a little longer?

Maybe we'd go thru-hiking again? We hadn't done that since the summer before adopting Leela when we'd spent a month wandering in the Alps around Mont Blanc. That adventure had become so much more than just a long walk in the mountains that I was moved to write about it in my first book, *Turn Left At Mont Blanc*. Yes, going hiking again for longer than half a day would be a real gift.

Throughout our meanderings, we'd never lost sight of how fortunate we were to be leading the roaming lifestyle we'd fallen into, and we knew it could be taken away at any time by all manner of unimaginable circumstances related to health, finances, politics or family needs. We wanted to make the most of the opportunities that came our way, always remembering that tomorrow shouldn't be taken for granted.

Which is why I was so grateful when Esther made the arrangements that made it possible for us to lose ourselves in the hills once again. Bella and Rose would stay with friends in the south of France, while Leela, George and Pati would get their holidays with Esther's parents back in sunny England. The exact dates were a little vague, nobody wanted to commit to anything too firmly, but if all went well we'd have at least six or seven weeks entirely to ourselves.

All we had to do now was deliver 'Team Ginger Bums' and decided where us humans were going?

Preparation

Living in a van opens up a whole world of possibilities. It's hard to describe the sensation of waking up each morning and knowing that, within reason, many thousands of square kilometres lay open for exploration, adventure and new experiences. Over the years we'd worked hard to try and manage the near infinite possibilities by imposing a sort of structure on our days, a structure intended to minimise the time spent weighing up options in favour of actually getting on and 'doing stuff'. Still, we always seemed to be much better at thinking up new ideas than ruling them out.

Which probably explains why it wasn't until we'd dropped off the gang and were rolling off the ferry back into Calais that we eventually made up our minds. In the preceding weeks we'd discussed everywhere from the Julian Alps of Slovenia to the Jotunheim mountains of Norway, but in the end, of all the wild places of Europe to lose ourselves in, it was the high Alps of Switzerland that won out.

It was a region we'd visited in our motorhome, several times, which is part of the reason we decided to go back there. Of all the many beautiful mountains and valleys we'd had the good fortune to see over the years, it was always the snow-topped, glacier-decorated enormity of the Swiss 4000's that most captured our imagination. At the same time, we also felt we had some unfinished business to take care of.

In the final week of our *Turn Left At Mont Blanc* adventure, we'd been just hours away from setting out on the Chamonix-to-Zermatt Haute Route, a 225 kilometre trail across some Switzerland's highest passes. We'd only changed our minds at the last moment, after receiving an unexpected offer that we just couldn't refuse, but we'd never forgotten our excitement at the prospect of thru-hiking in the shadow of some of Europe's loftiest summits. And it wasn't only the Haute Route that excited us, but a handful of other high altitude, multiday treks in the region that we'd heard about and seen in leaflets over the years. Itineraries such as the Tour of the Matterhorn, the Tour of Monte Rosa and the Tour des Combins, to name a few.

With up to six or seven weeks available to us and a veritable feast of well signed hiking trails criss-crossing the slopes, we both agreed that it was the mountains clustered against the Swiss-Italian watershed that would be the ideal place for our odyssey back into nature.

Our exact starting point, the mountain village of Zinal in the Val d'Anniviers, was the perfect balance of practicality and beauty. The Val d'Anniviers is one of many gigantic, glacial cuts which funnel down into the main Rhone valley, which runs east to west between Martigny and Brig. Some of the most famous resorts in Switzerland are nearby, such as Zermatt and Saas-Fee located in other similar valleys, but while the Val d'Anniviers can rival them for scenic spectacle it isn't nearly as heavily developed. Yes, there are cable cars and yes, there are roads. There are even a few hydroelectric stations. But compared to the tourist hotspots nearby, it's the ideal place to enjoy a dose of Alpine tranquillity with just enough civilisation to make it comfortable.

We arrived in Zinal on the very last day of July, having spent the previous six days delivering dogs and visiting family all over Europe and the UK. We'd covered over 3000 kilometres in a total of 40 hours of motorway time and I swear I was starting to have nightmares of rolling tarmac and weaving trucks.

Just prior to that, I'd been busy injuring myself in a fantastic, yet foolish, birthday attempt to run a very, very long way. I'd first heard about the Ultra-Trail du Mont Blanc, or UTMB, five years earlier. As possibly the world's most famous ultra-running race, with over 2500 competitors each year, it involves a continuous loop around the entire Mont Blanc massif. That's 171 kilometres with ten thousand metres of vertical ascent.

I didn't enter the race though, which wouldn't happen until September. Nor had I even done any ultra-running before, though I'd long thought it seemed like a cool thing to try. However, when Esther turned to me a few days after my 37th birthday during our drive back to the UK and said "Dan, you know we're driving past Mont Blanc on the way up to Calais. Well, I know you've always wanted to have a go at the UTMB...."

Needless to say, I liked her thinking. I left Esther parked in La Peuty, a little hamlet on the Swiss portion of the loop, and told her I'd be back within 48 hours, probably. Armed with a tiny rucksack containing a water bladder, lots of dried fruit and not many extra clothes, I marched into the night wearing a head torch, some skimpy shorts and an overly ambitious ego.

At this point I should probably add that I don't have the body of an ultra-runner. Back when I used to lift weights, friends likened me to a short wardrobe with feet. I've tried a handful of half marathons over the years and they've all followed the same pattern. I tear across the start line at semi-pro pace, which I maintain for a handful of kilometres, before spending the bulk of the distance slowly fading into a blistered, gibbering, slobbery mess. In finish line photos I invariably look 106 years old. Strange really that I felt so chirpy setting out to try and cover more than 100 mountainous miles. We'd done a lot of cycling in the months beforehand, so I was in decent shape, but nothing at all like this.

Twenty hours, sixty five miles and 6000 vertical metres later, I hobbled into Courmayeur. I was caked in dirt from head to toe, having smothered my pasty skin in dust to protect against the blazing sun, leaving just two white circles behind my sun-glasses. My left knee had threatened strike action some thirty miles earlier and was now refusing to bend at all. My emotions were screwed up, flitting from tearfulness to elation. Everything was intensified, from the smiles of strangers to the colour of butterflies. Life was so indelibly real in that moment. I loved it, regardless of the agony.

Esther rescued me, as usual. She was proud of me for not doing my usual trick of carrying on regardless and utterly crippling myself. Yet I was still sore and limping slightly when we pulled up in Zinal less than a week later. Needless to say, we were both feeling fairly exhausted when we finally turned off the engine, took a deep breath and looked out of the window at the Alpine beauty that we'd driven back into.

Incredibly, we parked next to a mini bus full of British Army soldiers that Esther had met in La Peuty while I was attempting to solo around Mont Blanc. They were hiking the Haute Route themselves, in customised stages, and recognised Esther the instant we pulled up.

"Oi oi" they called out, "I thought you were going back to Britain?!"

Over the years we've almost become accustomed to such crazy coincidences, bumping into people over and over again, sometimes years after first meeting them. It's one of the delights of travelling, that you meet so many kind and kindred spirits also roaming through the world.

We had a nice chat before the soldiers drove off in search of food, leaving us to take stock and think about our own adventure. We'd arrived in the mountains, but we still had a few decision to make, like which way we'd set out?

Both the Chamonix-to-Zermatt Haute Route and the Tour of the Matterhorn pass directly through Zinal and actually follow very similar (though not identical) routes for some distance. As a result, it was somewhat academic for us which we decided to follow. We already had a copy of the

Cicerone guidebook to the Haute Route on Esther's unreliable smartphone, but as the battery had a tendency to flake out every twenty minutes, we knew we'd need a hardcopy map as well.

I know that many hikers nowadays use electronic devices for navigation, but I still prefer a map and compass. Not because it's rustic or traditional, or because I'm a technophobe, I just like knowing it can't run out of batteries. As luck would have it, the most suitable map for the surrounding area available in the Zinal tourist office was a 1:50000 'Edition spéciale! Tour du Cervin', complete with a suggested itinerary traced out in orange and estimated timings between various landmarks. It was like a guidebook, but without detailed descriptions of which fenceposts to turn at.

Which is basically how we decided our initial route, because of the best map available and because it looked really exciting, a 145 kilometre tour, almost 10,000 metres of vertical climbing and two glacier crossings. We'd never crossed a glacier before, but we imagined it would be thrilling. Not to mention the chance to circle what is arguably Europe's most iconic peak and skirt beneath a raft of other stunning summits as well. Whether we mentally thought of it as the Tour of the Matterhorn, or a Haute Route variant, or just a long walk in the Alps, was almost arbitrary. We'd set out from Zinal towards Zermatt and see what came up. We didn't have a fixed plan beyond that. Perhaps we'd be gone for a week, or perhaps it would be a month? Maybe even longer? Who knew what adventures were lying in store for us just across the mountains?

First though, we decided to take a full day in Zinal to pack and relax, sort of. In the morning we tried a fast hike up to the Corne de Sorebois some 1300 metres above the village, ostensibly to stretch our legs after all the driving and to test my knee out. However, all we proved was that it still hurt. In the afternoon, we visited the spa, the one with the wrestling French ladies, to get clean and loosen our tight muscles. It wasn't until the evening that we got around to packing anything.

During our *Turn Left At Mont Blanc* adventure it had taken us three days of suffering before we'd admitted to ourselves that our packs were massively overladen. We'd then emptied them out and easily posted home 4 kg of unnecessary bumph we'd foolishly thought useful from the comfort of a living room floor. Even then, we still finished the tour with bruised hips and lumpy collarbone swellings. This time around, we wanted to get down to the bare minimum.

Fortunately for us, over the years we'd invested in some pretty decent trekking kit. Our rucksacks, for example, were both Osprey Exos models and weighed just over 1 kg each, which is not a lot for a 46 and 58 litre pack with a solid internal frame and comfortable hip straps. Most large rucksacks weigh more than double that and even the lightest of the ultralight models that we'd seen online (of similar size) still weighed half a kilogram, even without an internal frame to help transfer the load from the shoulders to the hips. We each had Rab Infinity 300 down sleeping bags, which weighed just 650 grams but were still graded down to a 0°C comfort temperature. To put that in context, an entry level sleeping bag from Decathlon with a similar comfort rating (at the time of writing this anyway) was advertised as weighing 1.7 kg. Our air mattresses were Thermarest NeoAir (300 g), our saucepan was made of titanium, our Black Diamond headtorches could shine like car headlights when required, our Leki hiking poles were carbon fibre, our Mountain Equipment waterproofs had Gore-Tex lining, our Rab down jackets were on an Everest base camp recommended kit list once upon a time. I could go on, but I'm sure you get the picture by now.

Most of our core camping and hiking equipment was high-end stuff, some of it from specifically lightweight product lines. It wasn't cutting edge any more since it was all at least 5 or 6 years old, but it did the job and after many excursions we trusted it to stand up to the trials of the outdoors. A decade earlier we'd tried all sorts of budget options, but once we'd been able to afford the better stuff (via eBay mostly) we'd never regretted the investment. It just kept on going and kept on working, year after year. Until it broke, we had no intention of replacing any of it.

  The only new thing we were taking with us was our tent. For years we'd used a battered 2 kg Vango tent which was simple and not too heavy, but which had a tiny doorway and sharply sloping sides that meant we couldn't really sit up inside it. After travelling with us for over a decade, we'd accepted the fact it was no longer up to the job for two people.

  Which is why we'd picked up a new tent from Decathlon as we driven through France, choosing a model which had an almost identical design to a far more expensive brand of tent but which we had no way of getting our hands on in time. The trade-off was that it weighed more than our old tent at 2.8 kg, but we were willing to carry the extra weight in return for having a doorway each and extra porch space. It's incredible what becomes important when your home is made of canvas and you have to carry it all day.

  On top of this were some things that we had little wriggle room on. The weight of a propane gas canister, for instance, was unavoidable, as was my irrigation kit. This is the equipment I have to use to self-administer enemas, controlling when I go to the loo and so managing my bowel incontinence. Consisting of a water bag, various bits of tubing, a squeezy hand pump and disposable catheters, it's not an especially heavy item although it is an awkward shape.

  When I wrote *Turn Left At Mont Blanc*, the fact I'd been using this kit in the great outdoors was a big deal for me, so I wrote about it. I mentioned some of the places I'd used it, the challenges of doing so and the occasional unexpected gifts, such as seeing the stars in the dead of night or getting a mountain sunrise to myself.

Still, three years later, the fact that this adventure also involved day-time and night-time enemas, enemas in the rain, on rocks, in forests, in holes, surrounded by flies, mosquitoes, sheep and goats, and even in some of those terrible squatting toilets they have in Italy, this is the most I'm going to say about it in this book. It was just less of a big deal for me this time around. Plus, I'd also matured regarding my willingness to ask for help, so in addition to the outdoor enemas, I was able to benefit from the facilities and kindness on offer in the many mountain refuges and hotels along our route.

Some people, I understand, would find it off-putting having to heat up water, find a place to shelter (or at least hide) and then hang around semi-naked for half an hour surrounded by the elements, beasts and bugs. I know I did at first, but now I'm more used to it I'm mostly just grateful that in return for those less comfortable moments, I get the rest of my day back. I get to camp and hike and thrive in the wilderness.

Back to packing and cutting out the non-essentials. Our spare clothes amounted to just one pair of spare pants each (wear one, wash one), two spare pairs of socks and a single set of base layers for sleeping in or for emergency weather scenarios. Our first aid kit was pared down to a few painkillers, diarrhoea medication, plasters, a single bandage and a pair of scissors and tweezers. For years we'd hauled an almost military-grade field dressing kit with us and hardly used a single safety pin. This time, we decided that if we got into trouble we'd just have to manage or call for help.

As on previous trips we would share a toothbrush, although we extravagantly decided not to cut the shaft in half this time around. We'd also share an ultralight pack towel (which looked more like a dishcloth), a tiny pot of homemade toothpaste and no other toiletries at all.

Some people might find the idea of existing in the wild without shower gel, deodorant and moisturising cream (as a bare minimum) to be bordering on savagery. I have noticed that some outdoor stores even sell "lightweight wash bags". For us, however, deodorant and minty shower gel just didn't make the "essentials" list. We were more than happy to go a few days without a shower in return for a hefty dose of nature, knowing there would always be waterfalls and mountains streams to rinse off the worst of the dried sweat if it got bad enough. The idea of polluting them with some sort of zesty soap was sacrilege.

With the addition of passports, credit cards, a bit of cash and a few other odds and ends, my pack came in at around 10 kg and Esther's at about 7 kg. To some ultralight trekkers this would still be far too much, but we reckoned we'd either have to spend a lot more money on new kit or shave off a significant amount of comfort to make drastic a reduction on that. Some people might use a 300 gram poncho tarp as a waterproof *and* overnight shelter, but we weren't at that stage just yet. We were satisfied with the balance we'd achieved, which is really what thru-hiking is about, making your own personal compromises.

We then added in a 2-litre water bladder each plus a couple of stainless-steel drinking bottles for extra fluids, our usual quota. I always like to carry lots of water on hikes, possibly too much, but since you can't always guarantee a regular supply I always like to have a litre in reserve in case I need to use the loo.

Food-wise, we tried to pack for about four days-worth of wilderness, with a couple of kilos of oat bran, a couple of kilos of lentil pasta, some couscous and lots of nuts and dried fruit. We've taken a look at pre-made, calorie-specific freeze-dried meals in the past, but they're very expensive and we prefer simpler, whole food options. We kind of expect to under-eat a little out on the trail, because carrying enough calories to fuel days and days of full time outdoor living is a heavy business. However, in a region with plenty of valleys, villages and mountain refuges, it was unlikely we'd get into serious trouble. We've never bothered with detailed food calculations, preferring to listen to our bodies as we go along. If we find we're struggling, we simply adjust at the next shopping opportunity.

All in all, our packs hefted in at about 15 kg for me and 10 kg for Esther. Not too bad really considering that was full water and full food plus camping and cooking equipment, waterproofs, down jackets and toiletries. We had a fully self-sufficient home on our backs. All we had to do now was take it for a walk.

As though to mark the occasion, the sky above Zinal erupted that night into a glittering, thundering display of pyrotechnic glory. There were even glowing paragliders cutting across the heavens and trailing sparks. Of course, the fireworks weren't really for us. The first of August is the National Day of Switzerland, commemorating the 'founding' of the nation over 700 years earlier, when three Alpine cantons swore "the oath of federation". Still, it was nice to pretend.

Everywhere around us were locals and holidaymakers waving flags, drinking, singing and marvelling at the sky-filling umbrellas of colour bursting above us. Everyone was smiling. Everyone was relaxed. Tomorrow, we'd be leaving it all behind, but for now it was time to dance.

Setting Forth

It was half past eleven on a roasting hot Saturday morning when we finally hoisted our well packed bags onto our semi-well-rested shoulders. We had intended to get going earlier in the day, like good, well-behaved hikers who are mindful of afternoon thunderstorms should do, but we hadn't. Early starts from a tent on a hillside are one thing, but when we're nervous and saying farewell to home comforts for an unknown length of time, we do have a tendency to dawdle.

We'd woken slowly, lingered over breakfast in the softness of our motorhome, taken a final warm shower because we could and then simply sat in silence for half an hour to reflect on the moment. This was it, more than three years after our previous life-changing journey into nature and we were striking out onto the trail once again. With the sun beating down on the high summits which ring the head of the Val de Zinal, it felt like something special was about to happen, as though there was a charge lingering in the air around us that would spark at any moment.

We'd parked our motorhome right at the end of the road beyond the village, so our first steps were back down the tarmac into Zinal, heading towards the trail markers we knew were tucked away at the back of the swimming pool. From there we would pick up the track snaking upwards towards our first col, the 2874 metre Forcletta Furggilti, some 1200 metres above us and around 10 kilometres of hiking away.

I confess, I was nervous. I liked the idea that we would make up our route as we went along, but it scared me too. Would we be back in a week, or three? How far were we going? How high? How would my knee respond? I couldn't ignore the fact that it still wasn't in great shape.

After the previous day's painful jaunt up to the Corne de Sorebois, I'd wound a heavy bandage tightly around it along with an even tighter knee support over the top of the bandage, which I could now feel constricting the blood flow to my lower leg. Already my left foot was feeling a little tingly and I knew that wasn't exactly ideal, but without it my knee just hurt too much when I moved.

Esther told me a week later that as we first started up the trail and she saw me dragging my left leg as though it were made of wood, she was tempted to veto the whole trip there and then. "What the hell are we doing" she'd thought "going off hiking when he can hardly walk?!" At the time, however, I'd shut down all enquiries on the subject.

"Just ignore it and let me deal with it" was my response when she'd tried to ask. I joked "it's not like I don't have another one", though in seriousness I was a little worried. If it got any worse I couldn't see us making it very far at all. On the other hand, if it stayed the same or somehow improved, then I'd regret not trying. So we carried on, one step and one limp at a time.

The initial trail out of Zinal was steep, switch-backing through pines on wide and well-made paths that had been churned to dust by weeks of sunshine and the tread of many feet. In only a week's time this exact route would be the final run-in for competitors completing the annual Sierre-Zinal trail run, a 31 km sky running event with over 2000 metres of vertical ascent. The winning athlete would complete the course in just under two and a half hours and would fly down this section at a pace approaching gravity-speed freefall. For now, however, it was just us, trudging uphill like ponderous snails with overly large shells on.

Despite all of our careful packing and "essentials only" policy, it was still a shock to the system to feel so much extra weight being transmitted through our feet. There was nothing that could be called pain, chafing or even rubbing yet, just an all-pervading sense of heaviness as our toes gripped into the soles of our boots and mini dust clouds mushroomed up with each slow step.

    Still, progress was happening, progress and lots of sweat. As is often true when zig-zagging up a switchback climb, the mini-target of each approaching corner made the mental challenge that much easier. It seemed like no time at all before we were rising out of the trees to look back on a magnificent sight. Even with the relatively small height gain we'd achieved so far, about 400 metres, the opening up of the view towards the head of the Val de Zinal was marvellous. The lofty summits of Dent Blanche (4357 m), Obergabelhorn (4063 m) and the Zinalrothorn (4221 m) were all framed against the bright blue sky, while the Matterhorn itself (4476 m) was just visible in the very centre of the panorama, poking out just above the ridgeline connecting those other enormous summits. Not the iconic angle but still an instantly recognisable peak, its steep sides shining in the early afternoon sun. It was a wonderful reminder of just why we loved this place so very much. We'd only been walking for just over an hour and were already being spoiled by some of the finest scenery the Alps has to offer!

    From here the trail flattened into a high balcony route, traversing northwards on the eastern flank of the Val d'Anniviers. Across the valley we could see Grimentz village, one of the most beautiful destinations in all of Switzerland, where sun-blackened wooden houses are decorated with countless bright red geraniums.

    Before we knew it two hours had flown by, so we picked a grassy patch at the side of the trail to settle down for a spot of lunch. We had a few leftovers from last night's dinner with us, cold roast potatoes all the way from my mum's Nottinghamshire allotment, which we enjoyed before an afternoon doze in the sun. Our hope was that by taking it easy like this, resting often and not going too far in a single day, we'd be able to make our exertions more sustainable. As it would later turn out, our desire to go ever higher and further would still get the better of us in the end. But for now, pulling my wide-brim hat over my face in the manner of Indiana Jones, I invited Esther into the crook of my arm as we drifted away into a light snooze.

    It took us another two hours after lunch to reach the Forcletta Furggilti, climbing away from the balcony route and crossing the Tsahélet plateau alongside a herd of inquisitive black cows, their jumbo bells clanging chaotically as they swung their heavy heads in search of juicy cud. Looking west, beyond the pastures and rocky ridges of the Val d'Anniviers, the vast bulk of both the Grand Combin and the Mont Blanc massifs were visible in the distance. Had it not been for a chilly breeze and the fact it was now five o'clock, I expect we might have lingered for much longer than we did.

    As it was, given the time and the falling temperature, I was mindful that we should probably start thinking of where we might pitch our brand new tent. Generally speaking, wild camping in Switzerland is not allowed and for good reason. We'd personally seen too many abuses while hiking to question why it's discouraged in country with so much natural beauty to protect. That said, Switzerland also has a very devolved system of government and laws vary between regions and even local authorities. As a result, wild camping is more tolerated in some places than in others, so it's always worth asking locally if you are thinking of pitching a tent somewhere.

    For us, having asked at various tourist offices, we'd been advised that provided we were above 2500 metres and not in a grazing space, we would "probably" be okay. That we intended to leave no trace of our presence, take all of our rubbish with us (including toilet paper) and only pitch our tent from evening until morning went without saying. This is basically what the French would call bivouacking and at such high altitude I suppose it becomes self-regulating, in that the kind of people that want to do it are most likely to be the kind of people that do respect their surroundings. Or at least that's what I hope.

The very first time we wild camped was in the Lake District, many years earlier, as part of a mountain leader training course. Neither of us had any intention of leading large groups, we were just a pair of novice hikers that hoped the course would boost our self-confidence and safety out on the hills. Back then, even for just that one night trip, I had a completely full 85 litre rucksack overflowing with fleeces and spares. It must have weighed a good twenty kilograms, despite the fact we were never more than a couple of hours away from the course base at Borrowdale youth hostel.

After meandering around all day with twenty other participants from the Durham University Hill Walkers Society, we eventually pitched our tents in the shadow of Great End before heading out to practice night navigation on the fells around Sprinkling Tarn. It had felt so wild and dangerous at the time, so treacherous, even with instructors on hand. Now, almost a decade later, we were planning to pitch our tent above 2500 metres, higher than we'd ever camped before and miles from anybody. I could still feel that same frisson of excitement in my tummy at the prospect of it.

The pitch we settled on was a small rocky shelf 100 metres to the side of the trail at an altitude of around 2700 metres. Invisible from both the path and the rest of the hanging valley below us, it was also close to a small trickle of water that would give us enough to cook and drink from.

It took just quarter of an hour to go from walking to sitting alongside our shiny new tent with our little saucepan simmering away in the evening sunshine. It helped we had so little stuff with us, so there really wasn't a lot to think about. Tent up, airbeds inflated, sleeping bags unrolled, headtorches handy and base layers warming against our chests. There really wasn't anything else to do.

While I'm not sure I'll ever be able to say that I enjoy sleeping in a tent (I enjoy my duvet far too much for that), I can't deny how amazing the absolute freedom that camping in the wilderness provides feels to me. Wrapped in our down jackets, we sat on a rock alongside our portable home to watch the shadow of the mountain behind us creep up the face of the opposite valley. We had warm food in our tummies and no TV, WiFi or even traffic noise to disturb the total tranquillity of the moment. It's a difficult sensation to reproduce in any other way.

I don't want to say it's 'simple', because in many ways it requires a lot of thought and energy, but in that moment when the essentials of survival are taken care of, when you have warmth, shelter and nourishment sorted for the night, it is blissfully uncomplicated. We had nowhere else to be. No deadlines to chase. We didn't even have a fixed route plan for the next day. All we had to do, all we could do, was sit, watch and lose ourselves in nature's grandeur.

The temperature began to drop when the shade arrived. Less than an hour later we were in the tent for a quick game of cards before tucking ourselves into our lime green sleeping bags. Shortly before we went to bed, a couple of curious sheep had appeared to stare at us, but they didn't stay long. Other than them, we hadn't seen a single other living being since the cows in mid-afternoon.

Vital Statistics – Day 1
Start Point: Zinal
End Point: Blüomattälli Valley
Distance Hiked: 11 km
Hiking Time: 4 ½ hours
Ascent: 1200 metres
Descent: 100 metres

New Heights

"What adventures will we have today?" we said in unison, rolling over to look into each other's eyes and smile at the prospect of whatever might unfold for us.

After a comfortingly good night's sleep, we'd woken up just as the morning light began casting its soft illumination through the yellow walls of our inner tent. Just as we'd hoped, each having our own exit in the night and extra headroom had proved to be a huge improvement over our previous tent. Neither of us had kneeled on each other's face or covered our backs in condensation on our way out for a pee. Such luxury! We'd also been a little concerned that we might be cold at such a high altitude, but even with a clear sky we'd felt warm all night long.

All in all, we were very pleased with our new canvas home, which I began rolling away while Esther did a few stretches nearby. This being early August and because we were on a high, east-facing slope, the sun had risen especially early for us and by eight o'clock everything around us was already warm and dry. Because we'd anticipated needing to get a brisk start to stay warm, Esther had made our breakfast the night before, a mixture of water, oat bran, chia seeds and raisins that would become a mainstay of our diet for the weeks ahead. We called it 'Esther's overnight oat bran', a crumbly, calorie dense, tasty stodge that would sustain us throughout a morning of hiking. This time around we were able to have a more leisurely start to our day, but having breakfast prepared in advance would prove a useful strategy for some of the less fine weather we'd encounter later on.

Sitting together on the warm stones, passing our shared pot of overnight oat bran back and forth between us, we perused our map and discussed the day ahead. More than three years earlier, during a previous visit to the Val d'Anniviers, we'd met a Swiss hiker who'd recommended a visit to the valley directly below us, the Turtmanntal. His specific suggestion was that we hike to the summit of the Barrhorn at over 3600 metres, a peak generally considered as the highest snow-free summit in the Alps! Not that it doesn't get covered in snow in winter of course, or that it can't be covered in snow year-round if the weather dictates, but there are no permanent glaciers to cross and it's usually clear come high summer. The climb was by no means 'on the way' in terms of a Matterhorn loop, but that didn't really matter to us given our 'suck it and see' approach to our hike. All we knew was that 3600 metres would be a whole new level of altitude for us.

We'd been fortunate during our years of travelling to hike to a couple of cols and summits at around 3000 to 3100 metres, most of them in Switzerland, but it was a threshold that still held a great deal of magic and excitement for us. Coming from the UK, where the highest peak is Ben Nevis at 1345 metres, and having done most of our walking in the Lake District which tops out on Scafell Pike at 978 metres, the idea that we could walk so high was staggering.

It was Esther who had remembered the recommendation (like she does most things), so we decided to name it "Esther's magical mystery detour". The plan was to walk partway down into the Turtmanntal, turn south to traverse a balcony route and then ascend towards the Turtmannhütte refuge at 2519 metres. We'd then leave most of our stuff at the refuge, taking just a few essentials to the summit of the Barrhorn and back and then hopefully camping somewhere near the refuge with the guardian's permission at the end of the day. If not, we'd just have to keep walking, although we hoped that wouldn't be necessary after such a big climb. It was an exciting plan and an ambitious one, with around 1500 metres of ascent and descent, but we still had fresh legs and my knee (thankfully) hadn't gotten any worse during our hike the previous day. We reckoned we could make it.

We quickly descended down the hanging valley in which we'd camped, passing a large herd of cows and negotiating a network of electrified fencing that made us feel lost in a TV game show for a while, a little like a bovine Crystal Maze. At around 2200 metres we began traversing south, skirting right on the uppermost fringe of the treeline. Although the trail itself was dry, dusty and easy to follow, all around us the vegetation was thick and green, already buzzing with insects and grasshoppers making the most of the now hot sun.

In the distance, across the southern skyline, the summit of the 4135 metre Bishorn was framed perfectly by the rocky sides of the Turtmanntal, with the tongues of two separate glaciers flowing towards each other in the centre of the scene. From the right side, as we saw it, came the Turtmanngletscher while from the left came the tip of the larger Brunegggletscher (which is the spelling on the map, not a sticky 'g' key). In the expanse of smooth bare rock between the two tongues was written the history of the valley, when these two ice giants had once merged into one.

It took us just over an hour to reach the end of the balcony route at the Turtmannsee lake, from where we began a 350 metre climb on a much rockier trail towards the refuge. After spending much of the last twenty four hours in a bubble of solitude, it was a strange sensation to suddenly see other hikers around, albeit only a couple of dozen of them. Despite its relatively high altitude, the Turtmannhütte is a reasonably easy to reach mountain refuge due to a small road which runs right up to 1900 metres in the valley below.

For anyone not familiar with mountain refuges, they're buildings usually located in areas of natural beauty where people might be able to stay, shelter and often get a hot meal while walking in the wilderness. However, within that deliberately vague description is an infinity of variation between different refuges in different mountain ranges in different countries. Some are in valleys; some are on peaks. Some have live-in guardians; some are unstaffed. Some offer food; some don't. Some are privately owned; some are owned by national Alpine clubs. Some can be strolled to; others must be climbed to. Some are big; some are tiny. Some are open all year; some open only for limited dates. I could on, but you get the idea.

The Turtmannhütte, for example, is a moderately sized, stone-built refuge owned by the Swiss Alpine Club. Built in 1945 and expanded a couple of times since, it can provide dormitory beds for up to 50 people in summer and 24 in a winter room the rest of the time. Location wise, it's built on a rocky shoulder overlooking the two glacier tongues we'd been hiking towards all morning, which makes it a stunning place to spend a night.

When we arrived after two and half hours of hiking and asked about whether we could camp nearby that evening, they smiled and told us that since they were already fully booked for most of summer, we were welcome to camp nearby. All they asked was that did so out of sight of the refuge. They even pointed us in the right direction and invited us to use the refuge facilities if we wanted to.

Although there's no guarantee that a mountain refuge will tolerate camping nearby (except in some cases where they state it on their website), if they're full and the refuge is remote, we'd read that they usually say yes to small groups. They were originally created as refuges after all, places where weary and hungry mountaineers could find safety as opposed to simply being prettily-positioned restaurants. Our experience is that it's the refuge guardians, the seasonal workers who spend weeks or months living in the refuge to prepare meals, clean up and generally be on hand to help, that have the greatest influence over the mood inside, much more than the location and facilities.

Fortunately, they are usually very kind people who love the outdoors themselves.

Even though it wasn't even midday yet, with our plan to hike another 1000 metres uphill and back down again, it was reassuring to know that we could stay nearby when we got back. It meant we didn't have to rush. So, after an early spot of lunch in the sunshine, we left my larger pack with our tent, most of our food, cooking equipment and sleeping gear in the boot room and set off uphill with just a single pack containing a few extra layers, water and enough food for the afternoon.

After a short flat section from the refuge, we tackled a steep series of switchbacks with some chain-assisted steps up through a narrow ravine. Although it was an ascent of only 100 metres or so, when we saw the gentleman behind us pause to put on a helmet it did make us wonder if we were perhaps underestimating the climb ahead of us? Certainly as we scrambled and skidded up the loose paths, with small stones tumbling down behind us, we could fully understand why he had taken the precaution.

Fortunately, the immediate risk of falling rocks only lasted for a short while until the path emerged onto a much more solid area marked by an impressive cairn, with excellent views of the Bruneggglestscher which we were now climbing alongside. Although we were still less than 200 metres higher than the refuge, it was already possible to see much more of the vast ice sheet that was pushing behind the tongue we'd been looking at all morning.

The trail continued along the tip of a hard-packed glacial moraine, rising steadily as we picked our way across the uneven surface to leave any last remnants of greenery or soil far behind. It was a dry, bare and barren landscape that we had entered, with stones of all shapes, sizes and shades of grey surrounding us. Sometimes we were stood on dust while at others we were striding up steep, bare rock that appeared bone white in the afternoon sun. It was as though we were climbing the very spine of the mountain.

The higher we climbed, the more the sheer scale of the Bruneggglestscher was revealed, sweeping across the view and dominating the landscape falling away beneath us. As a relatively flat glacier, descending just 600 metres over a distance of 4 kilometres, the ice appeared quite smooth on first glance and the waves appeared gentle, yet we knew from experience the real scale of those undulations. Up close, it would be like a heaving sea frozen in time.

Clouds had been slowly building all day and just as we reached the final approach to the summit they seemed to darken, while a cold wind began to whip across the mountainside. We were well above 3000 metres now, looking down across miles and miles of ice-bound Alpine scenery, and the conditions seemed to be conspiring to hammer home just how tiny we were in this gargantuan place. What had started out sunny and jovial had grown dark and foreboding. Even the shape of the summit, a steep slope on one side with a sheer drop on the other, seemed to scream "stay away".

The solid rock of the climb had also given way to a loose, shale-like surface which our feet sank into with each step, further enhancing the challenge of this final quarter of an hour. Yet it also made it that much more exciting. Almost everything we could see was now below us, from glaciers to all but the highest, whitest summits. The wind was biting, the surface was unstable and apart from a single other hiker we could some distance below us, there wasn't another soul around. We were higher than we'd ever hiked before. This felt like real adventuring.

We held hands for the final few steps, reaching the three metre high metal crucifix bolted to the very top of the mountain before hugging and jumping (carefully) for joy. At 3610 metres, all the world seemed laid out before us. Snow-capped peaks rose up in all directions, separated by deep valleys into which countless glaciers were sliding, carving them deeper with each passing year. To the south, framed in the void between the summits of the Brunegghorn and the Bishorn, was the Matterhorn itself, while away to the north was a long stretch of the Aletsch Glacier, the longest glacier in Europe at over 20 km long.

In our more immediate location, the contours on our map confirmed that on its eastern side the summit of the Barrhorn fell away pretty much vertically. Unable to stop myself, crawling on my hands and knees I edged past the crucifix and peered over the edge. Usually, I consider myself fairly comfortable with heights and, more specifically, drops. Yet what I looked down into from the Barrhorn made even my normally robust stomach turn. The pinnacle we were sitting on was just a few metres away from hundreds of metres of vertical oblivion. It was terrifying and it was awesome. I wanted to look again, yet I also wanted to run away. I couldn't remember the last time I'd felt queasy with a height, but that view down the Barrhorn still makes me twitch now when I imagine it.

Creeping away from the edge, we decided to put on our extra layers so that we could linger a while and absorb as much of this amazing experience as we could. Unfortunately, when we reached into our pack for the orange dry bag that contained our tightly stuffed down jackets, we discovered that I had, in fact, just carried the wrong orange dry bag up the mountain. The spare pants and socks I had been carrying would probably have helped a little, but we doubted they would be quite as warm as the jackets we'd been hoping for. Still, despite the chill and cutting wind, we didn't want to leave immediately after arriving, so we hunkered down onto the exposed rock to appreciate it for as long as we could.

We lasted about twenty minutes before the throbbing in our cold limbs and chattering teeth forced us off the summit. The now threatening sky further motivated us to keep moving, so we paused only once during the descent to snatch another brief respite from the cold wind behind a handy boulder. We were physically tired but emotionally we were on cloud nine at what we had just experienced, so it only felt like a matter of minutes before we were negotiating the steep ravine for a second time and plodding back towards the refuge. Our watch told us we'd been gone for over five hours but it was difficult to believe it had been that long.

Retrieving our gear from the boot room, we settled down on the grassy bank in front the refuge with the few dozen other folks waiting for their dinner to be ready. These were the overnight guests, we assumed, an eclectic mix of people temporarily bought together by their shared desire to spend a night sleeping among the mountains.

After a while we relocated ourselves to one of the refuge benches to cook up our own dinner, the same meal we'd had twenty four hours earlier, lentil pasta with garlic, tomato puree and stem ginger. Very nice! After that, we spoiled ourselves with some lovely fresh fruit that Esther had bought from the refuge kitchen. At around 1 Swiss franc per piece, it was really quite good value considering that it had been delivered by helicopter!

Bellies full, we sat in the delightfully warm evening sun to continue savouring the glacial views and sawtooth skyline. The forbidding afternoon clouds had abruptly parted during our meal to make way for a fine summer's evening, and since everyone else had gone inside to eat we temporarily had it all to ourselves.

We made use of the dying rays of sun to take a short uphill walk away from the refuge to pitch our tent in a little grassy recess on the hillside, before heading back in the twilight to enjoy the post-dinner warmth of the refuge common area. Joining the other residents, we smiled at strangers and held hands in an atmosphere of companionship set against the music of soft, multilingual chatter. A couple of card games were happening next to a game of monopoly. Some people were reading books, some were looking at maps and others, like us, were just sitting quietly to appreciate the moment.

    We spent the final part of the evening back outside, sitting in the gathering darkness outside of our tent to watch the last shreds of colour drain from the few remaining wispy clouds. It was another magical evening after an even more beautiful day, with the solitude of the previous night replaced by a sense of camaraderie and kindness. If this was just two days in, what more adventures could this summer possibly have in store for us?

Vital Statistics – Day 2
Start Point: Blüomattälli Valley
End Point: Turtmanhütte
Distance Hiked: 13 km
Hiking Time: 7 ½ hours
Ascent: 1400 metres
Descent: 1550 metres

Mr Grumpy

A series of heavy rain showers accompanied by storm-force winds gave our tent a thorough test during the night, flapping it about like a sail ship lost in a tropical tempest. Personally, I quite enjoyed it. There's something fundamentally exciting about lying in the arms of a loved one, feeling mostly safe, while cocooned in a warm sleeping bag. Outside, the 'whop-whop-whop' sound of canvas beating in the wind was backed by the lunatic drum beat of several thousand rain drops per second hitting canvas, but inside it was dry and warm. A stark but gratifying contrast.

Thankfully, the storm had eased by morning. Although it remained damp and overcast, it wasn't actually raining as we rubbed our bleary eyes and leaned in for our morning half-hug moment, like two lime green slugs stuck together. "What adventures will we have today?" we asked each other once again, repeating what we'd said the day before in what had apparently and quite naturally become a little daily ritual, before reaching over our shoulders to unscrew the caps from our air mattresses.

Continuing to look into each other eyes and smiling, we said a little countdown, "3, 2, 1…", before opening the valve and starting to sing "We're going down, we're yelling timber…..", which are the only words we remember from Pitbull's dance hit "Timber", but which for no good reason had also suddenly become part of our cute little morning routine.

We then emerged from our sleeping bags together, rushing to pull on our single set of cold and smelly hiking clothes, popped outside to take care of immediate needs and then, while Esther started rolling and stuffing away our sleeping gear, I stayed out in the damp air to pull out tent pegs, tie up guy ropes and find a dry(ish) surface for our bags, jamming things away as Esther passed them to me.

We were like a well-oiled machine, going from snuggling in our sleeping bags to nipping up our hip belts and scanning the floor for anything we'd dropped in under ten minutes. A routine we'd repeat many times in the weeks ahead.

On this, the start of day three, we didn't need to be quite so careful about getting things well packed straightaway. We only intended to cover the short distance to the Turtmannhütte, where we'd have breakfast in the warm before doing any hiking. We got there just after half past seven to find that most of the overnight guests had already left. Early starts in mountain refuges are very much the norm, especially in the really high, climber-orientated ones, but it was surprising to find the Turtmannhütte as empty as it was. Still, it meant we had the facilities almost to ourselves.

We left just after nine, retracing our steps back down towards the Turtmannsee where we resumed our trek along the balcony route. We were now hiking pretty much due north, directly away from the amazing scenery that we'd been immersed in for the past twenty-four hours. The sky remained dark and cloudy, but the trail was wide and undemanding as it gently undulated across the green hillside.

For no good reason that I could articulate at the time, I began to feel a heavy melancholy coming over me as we walked. We'd been chatting about politics for a short while, mostly about Britain's recent change of prime minister and the government's continued determination to leave the European Union (despite so many of the claims made for doing so unravelling), when I found myself becoming not just sad, but angry. And not just a bit miffed, but angry to a degree that didn't seem justified by the blatant duplicity of many prominent politicians.

Pretty soon I was muttering under my breath like a storm cloud fit to burst, which is precisely what happened next, in both a literal and figurative sense. Yanking my waterproofs angrily up my legs, I began shouting about "this is all we're going to do isn't it. Walk, eat, shit and sleep. Day after bloody day. The world's going to hell and we're out here hiding, doing the same pointless things over and over again…."

Thankfully, Esther knew me well enough not to say anything while the wave passed, which it soon did. Having a bit of a vent was precisely what I needed to let all that pent-up negativity out of my head. The bare essentials of life were just so obvious and raw up here in the drizzle and mist, that even thinking about the frenetic world below had thrown me into an almost existential crisis. What was the point of it all? Why do humans manage to screw things up so fucking much? From neighbours waging legal battles over an inch of garden to CEOs enthusiastically encouraging actions that pollute, sicken and kill in the name of a better third quarter, what the hell was going on?

I believe this an angst most people feel to some extent a lot of the time, but in the whirlwind of daily life it becomes a sort of background buzz, drowned out by other more immediate demands. But in a tent on a hillside in the rain, it was as though the lunacy of the world we'd left behind had been slowly overwhelming me. Why couldn't people just accept that we're all basically the same, humans and animals, each of us just trying to stay safe and warm on a lump of rock flying through the cold void of space? How can we be so cruel to each other sometimes? I'd been so happy in those opening 48 hours and our chat about politics had thrown me right out of balance.

As though it was symbolic, the rain stopped just as my own internal storm ran out of energy. In the muggy air left behind I smiled, took a deep breath and apologised for my outburst. A few minutes later I was once again losing myself in the immediacy of hiking, reminding myself that people are essentially good natured (a fact we'd experience time and again in the weeks ahead) while simultaneously trying to find my way out of a boggy 'short cut' I'd led us into. I'd been trying to shave a little time off our climb towards the 2893 metre Augstbordpass, but it seemed my confidence exceeded my path finding skills.

By the time we found the path again and had shed our overly hot waterproof layers, it turned out to be a straightforward climb to the Augstbordpass, a somewhat grim looking grey saddle separating the quiet Turtmanntal from the much larger and heavily developed Mattertal. Above us, negotiating the gentle, stony switchbacks were a series of multi-coloured dots which turned out to be a large group of elderly French ladies also walking the Tour of the Matterhorn. We passed them just before the top and said our bonjours at around the same time we started adding layers again, this time against the biting wind whipping across the austere pinnacle of the climb.

Stood on the saddle, we were now looking down into a seeming rocky wasteland, with several large snow patches still clinging on and little in the way of greenery to break up the bleakness. Beyond that, we could make out the tail end of the enormous ridge sometimes referred to as the Mischabel Wall, a gargantuan slice of rock that separates the Mattertal from the equally popular Saastal (home of the resort town of Saas-Fee), while looking further still towards the eastern horizon an intricate tangle of snow-capped peaks were just visible in the gloom. All in all an enticing prospect as we began making our way down into the stone-littered bowl beneath us.

By now we'd been hiking continuously for about four hours and were definitely ready for some food and rest. After about twenty minutes of descending we found a flattish spot just to the left of the trail to dump our bags on, kick off our boots and lie back in a small wind shelter created by a few nearby boulders. Lunch was a little oat bran with nuts and dried fruit, which tasted incredible given the circumstances, and a short time later we found ourselves drifting away into dreamland. From time to time we were aware of other hikers passing by as we lay prone on the grass, but we didn't mind if we looked a little silly, open-mouthed and snoring in the breeze.

By the time we'd been static for over an hour, the persistent cold was starting to seep into our core so we knew we had to start moving again soon. We could see the trail ahead of us, dipping a little further to around 2400 metres before traversing around a craggy shoulder to enter the mouth of the adjacent Jungtal valley, which we intended to hike up and camp in. There were various other routes we could have taken and still been heading towards Zermatt, but we chose the Jungtal because it struck us as the most exciting, involving a 3114 metre pass with the peculiar name 'Wasulicke'. I wasn't sure what a 'wasu' was, or how you licked one, although I had a few silly guesses in mind.

The only spanner in the works was that after three days we were almost out of food, but Esther assured me we could eke out our single pack of bean pasta, handful of almonds, chia seeds and a few raisins for a dinner and a breakfast. As long as we definitely made it over the Wasulicke the next morning and reached the next refuge on the trail by lunchtime, we should be okay.

So that's what we decided, and thirty seconds later Esther snapped her hiking pole. It wasn't her fault, just a small stumble next to an unlucky crack in a rock. Our Leki carbon fibre hiking poles had covered thousands of kilometres with us during the six years we'd owned them, helping us on countless day hikes and several thru-hiking trips, so we couldn't complain we hadn't had good use from the broken one. However, it did put another spin on our immediate plans.

Some people don't use hiking poles at all and for many years we hadn't either. Esther's first pair cost just £10 in a Keswick outdoor store and felt more like iron bars than a piece of sports equipment. Our mountain leader course instructor picked one up once and asked Esther what she used them for, "walking or beating sheep to death?" But once she'd started using them she didn't want to stop and I slowly became a convert myself, which is why we eventually bought ourselves a decent pair.

For short day hikes we don't always bother, but for steep mountain trails with a heavy pack, we find that being able to use our arms takes a little pressure off of our knees, especially downhill, plus the extra stability they can provide is invaluable for staying upright on some of the more precarious routes.

"Use one of mine" I urged Esther, "I can manage with one for a few days"

"No, your pack's heavier. I'll be fine."

"Should we head down then? Take a different route? That Wasulicke crossing looks a high one. And steep. Why struggle?"

"No. I'll be fine. Let's go".

And that was that. Snapped pole to shrugging it off in about ten seconds. Considering that when we'd tried our first ever hike together in the Lake District, more than fifteen years earlier, Esther had experienced overwhelming vertigo on a path that can be most accurately described as a shallow staircase, this was like hiking with another person entirely.

"You're amazing, do you know that?" I said. In response, I got a hug. A big one. Walking with a life partner is a very different experience than walking with a group of friends. It's an intense test for any relationship and knowing when to appreciate each other, be close or give space is a delicate balance. We don't always get it right, but when we do the all-pervading sense of connection is magical.

We only made it another two minutes down the trail before we stopped again, this time to say hello to a Danish mother-daughter pair who were hiking the Haute route.

Incredibly, in another fantastic coincidence, Esther had met them as well during my Mont Blanc attempt.

"Oh, you're the dog lady" exclaimed the daughter, turning to her mum to say something in Danish before recognition dawned. It's always the dogs people remember first! Not that I mind. Since living with five dogs I haven't farted once, which is a small price to pay for becoming an anonymous face behind a pack of ginger dogs. The dogs fart all the time of course, sometimes even claiming that I did it, the cheeky sods.

It was at the mouth of the hanging Jungtal valley that we were treated to our first view south along the main Mattertal cut, a deep and narrow slice in the Earth leading towards some of Switzerland's highest mountains. Although we couldn't see the Matterhorn itself, we could see much more of the glacier-decorated, snow-capped hugeness of the Mischabel Wall extending towards the lower slopes of the Monte Rosa massif on the cloudy southern horizon. We were also treated to another little wave from the Aletsch Glacier, its mighty length appearing like a vast white swathe away to the north. This truly was a landscape of giant proportions.

Our ascent of the Jungtal started easily enough, heading up a gently sloping green valley towards yet another sheer rock face, this one extending up to the 3278 metre Rothorn. With our intention to climb almost as high the next day, the sheer scale of it was quite startling, even in a land cluttered with such huge features.

Our priority at this point was to find a place to pitch out tent for the night. Aiming to get above 2500 metres, we moved slowly past a small Alpage to be greeted by a herd of heavy-uddered cows being driven even more slowly towards us. Giving them a wide berth so as not to startle them, we picked our way around boulders and cow-pats before returning to follow a barely visible groove in the grass. After quarter of an hour, however, even that vanished and we found ourselves wondering where we'd gone wrong.

"This can't be the path" I said, turning to face Esther. "I reckon we missed a turn when we followed that electric fencing. I think the trail kinked ever so slightly and we didn't notice".

We soon agreed that we'd missed the path. In all likelihood, the actual trail was at least 100 metres higher than us by now, probably atop a grass-covered ancient moraine on our right hand side. That left us with two options. Walk directly up a 75% gradient smothered in dense spiky bushes or just keep going along the gentle valley and hope to meet up with the trail several kilometres further along. If it had been earlier in the day I'm sure we would have done the latter, however, we could see that if we did continue straight on we'd soon be in a world of scree that wouldn't exactly make for comfortable camping. As it was, we'd just have to tackle the hill.

Twenty minutes of sweating, slipping, scratching and swearing later, I stepped back onto a welcome, wide and obvious trail. "Found it" I called down happily to Esther, who was still about thirty metres below me and doing just fine with her single hiking pole. Just twenty more minutes after that and we were unrolling our wet tent in the warmth of the early evening sun. The clouds on the western horizon had parted just in time to help us dry our tent and enjoy a comfortable warmth at the end of another long hiking day.

"I'm going to go and get some water and give my top a rinse. It stinks." I announced. "There's just enough sun that it might dry before dark. Would you like me to do yours?"

"No" Esther replied, "it's not too bad. I'll just do some stretching". Esther does Yoga most days in normal life, so I knew how important stretching was for her, not just to keep her body supple but as a form of relaxing and unwinding at the end of a long day. I also knew how important it could be for my own body, since I'd done yoga regularly myself once upon a time. Yet at the time of this adventure I'd fallen out of the habit and always seemed to find something else to do instead. This time, I pottered a few hundred metres away from the tent towards a shallow stream. The next time Esther flexed into a cobra pose, she found herself looking straight at my bare white bottom.

Reasoning that it was really quite warm and that I was really quite smelly, as I was taking off my shirt it suddenly struck me that I might as well wash everything, myself included. So I did, and most liberating it was as well. There's nothing like trying to dip your danglies into a 2-inch-deep, bitingly cold stream to make you feel alive.

Enticingly wearing nothing but my sweaty boots, I struggled back up the hill to our now dry tent, gritted my teeth as I slipped into my wet pants and trousers and stood around waiting for dryness to reach my private regions. Thankfully, it did, just as the sun dipped below the mountains and we fired up our stove for our small but reassuringly warm late evening meal of lentil pasta.

It was a magnificent sunset that night, with just enough clouds in the sky to create a dazzling display of pinks, purples and reds above the Mischabel Wall. We sat out as late as we could to take it in, watching the sky fade an ever deeper blue until stars began to emerge and the grass around us grew wet with evening dew.

Vital Statistics – Day 3
Start Point: Turtmanhütte
End Point: Jungtal
Distance Hiked: 15 km
Hiking Time: 6 hours
Ascent: 1100 metres
Descent: 800 metres

The Cabin

We sat huddled together on the damp and breezy hillside, taking turns to suck down mouthfuls of watery chia gel and raisins. Ahead of us was another 600 metres of climbing to reach the intriguingly named Wasulicke and we were now totally out of food. We estimated it would take us about 4 hours to reach the Topalihütte on the other side of the pass, but as long as we kept moving we were optimistic that we'd manage somehow. All being well we'd be there shortly after midday, just as our bodies would be threatening strike action. Our gear was packed, my knee was tightly strapped and the sky looked like it might rain at any moment. It was time to get moving.

An initially grassy climb soon gave way to stones and rocks as we began to cut across the head of the Jungtal. Immediately ahead of us was an enormous grey moraine slanting towards a bare rock face, while the remnants of the Junggletscher that must have created this huge heap of debris could only just be seen much higher up the mountainside. It was up this moraine that we had to climb, weaving through a chaos of sharp rocks and constantly scanning for the next red and white trail marker among the otherwise disorientating tangle.

In Switzerland, the colour of the trail marker can tell you a little about what to expect on the route ahead. Swiss hiking trails are divided into six levels of difficulty as defined by the Swiss Alpine Club. Level T1, "recreational", is the easiest. These are marked with a yellow diamond or arrow and indicate features such as a "flat or gentle slope", "little or no risk of falling" and "no special skills" being necessary. The next two levels are "mountain hiking" (T2) and "demanding mountain hiking" (T3) and both are marked with red and white stripes. While T2 trails are "generally well-marked" but may be "steep in parts with a possible risk of falling", T3 is "almost certainly steep in parts", with "exposed areas" and "difficult sections that may include chains or ropes".

Above these mountain hiking levels are three levels of Alpine routes, T4, T5 and T6 which are marked with blue and white stripes. Even at T4 there is no guarantee that a marked trail exists, while by T6 there is definitely no established trail at all and it is unlikely there will be markings either, with often very exposed and steep drops.

The fact that we were following red and white markers, therefore, was actually reassuring since we were approaching an almost sheer-sided cliff that our map implied we needed to ascend. Usually, even in the high mountains, it's possible to make out at least a few bits of trail from below, yet as we reached 2800 metres and skirted a small tarn on a barren plateau, we still couldn't see anything resembling a trail above us. All we could see was dark grey slabs of rock interspersed with equally forbidding patches of scree.

"Well, there must be a way up it somewhere" we told each other, doing our best to feel reassured as we began to slide our way across a steeply angled slope of loose stone above a dirty patch of snow.

Of course, there was a way up and it turned out to be the closest thing to rock climbing we'd ever experienced, at least until a few days later anyway. About fifty metres to our right we could see a series of blue and white markers signalling an alternative Alpine route to the top, crossing some remnants of rubble-strewn glacial ice and using a sequence of ladders to negotiate the smooth cliffs.

"How the hell is that a blue and white, and this is a red and white" we grumbled as we dragged our way up dusty, loose slopes that were angled sharply down towards the glacier below. There were few places where we could actually place our feet and one false move would have meant a painful tumble down onto the ice. "I bet those metal ladders don't bloody well shift the moment people tread on them" I grumbled.

I've said before that I consider myself fortunate to have been born with a decent head for heights and I usually feel reasonably confident on unstable surfaces. Yet on this climb there were sections that made me nervous. For Esther, who was still prone to occasional vertigo and wobbly knees, I was honestly flabbergasted at how no-nonsense she remained while plugging away at the vertical metres with her single hiking pole. At one point the ground was so loose that we practically had to run on the spot to stop ourselves sliding backwards.

It was frightening and tense at times, but all the tension evaporated the moment we reached the top, stepping up onto a pointed saddle just a few metres across at its widest point and less than ten metres long. Positioned as it was, almost at the same level as most of the peaklets and spires ringing the head of the valley, it was as though we had now entered the realm of the eagles.

To the north, the direction we'd climbed from, we could now fully appreciate the sweeping, graceful patterns in the detritus lining the valley, suggesting that much more of the Jungglestscher than we'd originally thought still remained buried under all that rubble. With most of the landscape coloured grey, some might have described it with words like desolate or barren, but that wasn't what we saw at all. To us it was elegant. A display of nature's power on a monumental scale.

On the other side of the col, looking south into the Mattertal once again, there was a marginally more colourful view but only because of the addition of white glaciers on the flanks of the Mischabel Wall. With the floor of the Mattertal hidden from our view by another hanging valley immediately below us, there was mostly a lot more grey stone on display, further cementing the sensation of wildness and excitement at being in such a precarious place.

It took us a few minutes to work out exactly which of the sharp drops from the col marked the start of the descent, but we got there in the end, entering into yet another steeply-angled bank of scree. Thankfully, the trail itself was much more hard-packed on this southern side and we were able to lose height quickly without a constant fear of sliding away.

Rounding a right-hand bend in the trail, we were suddenly confronted by a gigantic bowl of rubble and ice beneath hundreds of metres of vertical rock. We stopped in our tracks, our eyes scanning up and down the lined rock face until we noticed the diminutive cross on top and realised exactly what we were looking at. This was the eastern face of the Barrhorn, the same 3600 metre peak we'd sat on top of just two days earlier, and that vertical rock face was the one I had felt queasy looking over the edge of. I felt even more queasy now imagining my little head poking out over that deathly void.

"Bloody hell" I exclaimed as we gave each other a big hug. "I can't believe we actually sat on that! No wonder it gave me the willies."

This wasn't long after I'd first watched the 2018 documentary Free Solo, the one about Alex Honnold climbing the 900 metre vertical face of El Capitan in the Yosemite National Park without any safety equipment. It was at this moment that I finally knew without any shadow of doubt that I would never, ever do anything like that! Not even for a billion pounds and a key to the Playboy mansion.

Carrying on, we headed down into the lower reaches of that gigantic bowl, waving hello to a herd of two-tone goats that were staring at us disdainfully. With short horns, long coats and a mop of hair hanging over their eyes, they looked like a bunch of hippy llamas after a rough night out. Their hair was pure black from their head to their belly but then bright white from their belly to tail. In an almost monotone landscape, with hardly any greenery on display, it was a remarkable sight to see, with dozens of identical goats all chewing and looking at us in that special unimpressed way that goats have. For want of a better name at the time we decided to call them the chocolate and vanilla gang, although we'd later find out they were called blackneck goats.

In the 1970s, the blackneck goat was actually close to extinction, but today there are around 2700 of them grazing in the mountains again. How they count them so precisely I haven't a clue, since they all look identical. Apparently, to be a recognised blackneck strict criteria need to apply regarding the colour mixing of the coat and also the body shape. What we were seeing, therefore, wasn't just a herd of goats but an exclusive goat club. No wonder they were looking at us with such disinterest.

We left the pompous goats behind to reach the Topalihütte after four hours of hiking, parking ourselves on the sun-warmed terrace alongside just two other hikers. Positioned as it is, high above the Mattertal, the Topalihütte has the same sort of magnificent Alpine outlook characteristic of most refuges in the area. The original was built in 1926, a twenty bed hut donated by the alpinist Topali to commemorate his son who had been fatally injured on a nearby glacier. That original masonry hut was destroyed in a fire in 1998 and the current hut opened its doors five years later in 2003. It's not an especially large hut with just 44 beds available, which helps it to maintain a comfortable homely feel despite looking like an oversized tin box on the outside. However, when we arrived, it was mostly their kitchen that we were interested in.

It took Esther just a few minutes to return from the refuge interior carrying two big bowls of dry muesli, two fresh apples and a handful of dried apple chips. I'd like to say we then sat and savoured our food in the sunshine while taking in the view, but mostly we just inhaled the food without it touching the sides on the way down. Esther then went straight back inside to buy the same again.

Just as we'd experienced at the Turtmannhütte, the refuge guardians couldn't do enough to help us. When Esther told them of our route and just happened to mention she'd snapped a hiking pole, they even went into a cupboard and pulled one out that had been left behind by a day-hiker more than a year before. "It's a little bent, but it seems strong. Any good for you?" they asked. They didn't even want anything for it and had only charged us a few francs each for the muesli, apples and all the fistfuls of apple chips Esther could manage.

We sat a while longer, chatting amiably with the other two hikers, two Swiss friends who were doing a seven day tour and planned to spend the night at the Topalihütte because a storm was forecast that evening.

"Do you know what time it's supposed to arrive?" we asked.

"Our forecast said at 5 p.m., but who knows? It's the mountains." He then got his phone out and showed us their route on the SwissMap app he was using.

"I see you still have a paper map and compass" he smiled. "That's old school. I'm impressed."

"It doesn't need batteries" I smiled back, as we mentioned some of our route ideas and received some recommendations in return. Talking to people, we've found, is the absolute best way to get ideas for future adventures, especially when you have someone like Esther who remembers everything (so I don't have to).

Having learned that there was a storm coming, the sign at the refuge informing us that part of the trail ahead of us was closed due to rock slides suddenly became a little more concerning. Although we hadn't thought about it too much before crossing the Wasulicke, the traverse we were about to make of the western flank of the Mattertal would have ultimately taken us down to the village of Randa, which was still more than five hours of hiking away. Probably, we'd have wanted to carry on and then wild camp somewhere before going into Randa the next morning, but the thought of a storm *and* a rock slide made high altitude camping in the immediate area seem like a bad idea. Probably, there's be some safe places, but we didn't want to push our luck when we didn't have to.

Ultimately, we decided we had two options. We could either stay at the refuge (which still had plenty of spaces for the night) or hike briskly along the portion of the traverse that was still open and then descend for over a mile into the village of Herbriggen to look for a room.

A trail marker told us it was about 4 hours to Herbriggen and it now one o'clock, four hours before the storm was forecast to begin. The question was, did we want to spend our afternoon racing the weather or lounging on a terrace?

We set off a few minutes later, cracking on at a solid pace along the sturdy but narrow and undulating trail. Hovering at around 2800 metres, we went up a bit, then down a bit, then up again, passing through two small hanging valleys as we made our way south above the Mattertal. Every now and then a handy ladder was hammered into the mountainside in order to make a five or six metre crag passable. It was at just such a ladder that we had our first meeting with a herd of walking pom-poms. They were sheep really, but with rounded bodies buried within an explosion of off-white wool and only a small portion of black snout visible, it was hard not to want to hug one despite the ribbed, curving horns.

We'd later find out this was another named breed of Alpine livestock. We'd already seen blackneck goats today and these, we'd later learn, were blacknose sheep. We couldn't wait to meet a blackarse cow. Some tourist offices even organise hikes specifically to see such sheep and goats, so we were lucky really that over the coming few days we'd get to see so many of them. They never looked any less cute though, especially when a few dozen were trotting nose-to-tail like a dinosaur-sized fluffy caterpillar.

Although we were flitting quickly through the scenery, mindful of the impending weather that we could see gathering into dark clouds on the southern horizon, we were not unaware of how impressive the hanging valleys we were skirting across were. Hiking on the uppermost reaches of green, at the transition from still chewable cud to bare scree and ice, we had a marvellous perspective from which to appreciate all aspects of the titanic Alpine canvas we were moving through.

Our vertical mile of descent towards Herbriggen began with a few dusty switchbacks, followed by a single goat from another herd of regular, multicolour goats that we'd just walked past. We guessed they didn't see too many humans up here, which is probably why the entire herd had approached us at first expecting food. Yet when we didn't stop, this lone little lady clearly decided she needed to keep trying and so began following us down. Bleating mournfully and occasionally looking back up towards the faces of her friends, she continued to trot five metres behind us for the next ten minutes. It seemed we'd acquired a pet goat. We even began to worry about how far she might come. There was no way a hotel would let us have her in a room. And besides, it's not like we needed any more hairy travel companions.

Thankfully, she gave up in the end, just before we reached a green plateau at 2100 metres. Pausing for a brief rest and some refuge-acquired apple chips, we looked south at the unmistakable sight of rain sweeping towards us along the Mattertal. Like a moving wall of mist, landmarks in the valley floor slowly vanished as the first wave of weather made its inevitable way towards us.

Glancing around, we spotted a log cabin just fifty metres below us. Hoping for a doorway to shelter in, or possibly even a cow shed if we were lucky, we hoisted our foodless packs and made a short dash to the building just as the first spots of rain arrived. But it turned out this was no ramshackle cow shed or half-ruined farmhouse. Instead, it looked to be a private cabin of some kind with a solid exterior and a rather new-looking roof. Unfortunately, it was also locked.

    We huddled against each other in the doorway as the first short shower passed through. When the dry skies returned we had a little look around, discovering an outdoor dry-toilet and an unlocked storage area below the main building. With another cluster of black clouds already approaching from the south, we briefly considered pitching our tent in this dark, damp and somewhat chemical smelling cellar rather than descend another 1000 metres, possibly in a storm. Eventually, however, we decided to stick with our original plan and make the dash downhill. But just as we set out, less than fifty metres away from the cabin, something pulled us back.

    "I really think we should try the door again" Esther said. "It just doesn't look like someone's holiday home and there wasn't a keyhole. There must be a way of getting inside."

    So we headed back, armed with a bagful of prestigious university degrees between us to try and work out how to open a door.

    "Well, there's a chain but we've unhooked that. It feels unlocked, but it's like there's something jamming it from inside."

    "Maybe they wedged it from inside and went out a window?"

    So, we checked the windows.

    "Nope, locked. How about a trapdoor from the storage space downstairs?"

    So we got out our headtorches and had a ferret around in the dark.

"Still no. Unless Harry Potter lives here, there must be a way in."

It wasn't until we'd been poking around for a good ten minutes that we finally noticed the eight inch length of two inch diameter stick protruding from a hole in the door.

"Try giving that a wiggle" Esther suggested, so I did. It didn't want to budge at first, but after a few firm yanks with both hands it finally gave way, sliding out to reveal the 2-foot length of solid wood that had been holding the door closed all along.

"What a good idea" we laughed at ourselves. "And it only took a couple of Oxford graduates ten minutes to figure it out."

What we discovered inside was like finding buried treasure. This was no private cabin or cow shed, but what looked to be a basic, unmanned shelter complete with eight wooden bunks, foam mattresses and blankets stored in the rafters, a table, wood-burning stove and a plentiful supply of timber. We'd seen such things in France before, stone or log huts in the wilderness where wanderers can take shelter, but we had no idea that they existed in Switzerland alongside the extensive refuge system.

With the next band of rain imminent, this was like a dream come true in more ways than one. Many years earlier, even in the first few months of our relationship, Esther and I had dreamed of one day living in a log cabin together in the wilderness. Something small and simple, possibly on the edge of a forest or alongside a river. It was a dream that had never been forgotten and although we'd camped in many such places and even stayed in mountain refuges with other people, we'd never had the luxury of our own little cabin, even just for one night.

"Do you think we can just stay here?" we questioned each other. "It might just be for local shepherds or something?" Certainly there was all the evidence that the place was often used, with candles, matches, pots and pans and even a memorial on the wall to a gentleman pictured with a couple of blacknose sheep who had passed away a few years earlier.

"It's a shelter on a mountain at over 2000 metres and there's bad weather coming. Even if someone came, it's not like we're doing anything 'wrong' by sheltering. That's what these places exist *for*" I reasoned. "I hope they don't though. Wouldn't it be wonderful if we had this to ourselves for a night? A real dream come true!"

There was just one final problem, our total lack of food. Poking around in the ancient kitchen cabinets fixed roughly to the walls, we discovered various ingredients that had been left behind over the years, stock cubes mostly, but also a few cup-a-soups and instant noodles. Then, right at the back, an unopened 1 kg bag of rice with a 2006 use by date. We know from experience that many winter refuges have an emergency food box, and given that this was thirteen years out of date we didn't expect it would be missed very soon, though we made a resolution to leave something at the next winter room we passed. It's good to keep karma in mind when benefitting from the kindness of strangers.

"That'll do" I said. "I'll light the stove to warm the place up and then we can cook on it as well".

It was exciting to make fire and indulge my inner caveman. I even had Esther take a photo of me holding an axe as I chopped up some of the larger chunks of wood (even though there were enough smaller ones). As a five-foot-seven lightweight with a receding hairline and freckles, it's not often I get to be so manly. Quite possibly, even holding an axe I still wasn't very manly. The jury's out. But it still felt macho at the time.

Twenty minutes later we had fire and a cabin full of smoke. Although the rain had stopped for now, the gusting wind was blowing the smoke straight back down the chimney and into the room to the extent that we could no longer see the walls. "Let's sit outside while it calms down" I suggested.

It was early evening now and other than another optimistic herd of multicolour goats who had appeared for a while, we still hadn't seen another soul. The sky had also brightened up with little suggestion there would be more rain in the near future. Esther decided to do some yoga on a handy flat rock outside the cabin while I got an enormous pan of water boiling to cook up our thirteen year old dinner. Every now and then a solitary ibex would appear to watch Esther stretching and then drift away again.

Despite the smoke, the fire was burning well and the cabin had warmed up to a cosy temperature as I patiently watched three litres of water take almost an hour to boil, and the same time again to cook the rice to satisfaction. Not that a quiet, secluded log cabin in the Alps is a difficult place to pass the time, especially after four tiring days of walking. Simply sitting in the warm or getting some fresh air on the step was enough to feel totally and utterly satisfied with life, especially with the relative security of knowing we had a roof over our heads for the night.

We ate as much rice as we could stomach that evening, with an indulgent amount left for breakfast and probably lunch the next day as well. Despite the age, it tasted entirely normal. As the sky darkened, we got ready to turn in by placing a couple of foam mattresses on the wooden platforms and unfurling our sleeping bags. The available blankets smelled only of washing powder, but they were also somewhat itchy. Not that we would need much in the way of covering for a while since I'd kept the fire going and it had grown positively sauna-like in the cabin.

We loosely propped the door shut, in case any other lost travellers might need shelter that night, and lay down. The foam pads felt instantly luxurious after three nights on eighty centimetre wide air mattresses. We still didn't fall straight to sleep though, instead holding each other close as we revelled in the realisation of our mutual dream. We'd woken up in a tent, crossed a pass like no other we'd crossed before, been given a hiking pole and then, just when we'd been without food in the rain, we'd found a cabin offering shelter, food and warmth. What more could we possibly wish for.

Vital Statistics – Day 4
Start Point: Jungtal
End Point: Guggini
Distance Hiked: 12 km
Hiking Time: 6 hours
Ascent: 900 metres
Descent: 1450 metres

Rain

No other hikers arrived in the night but the forecast thunderstorm did, lighting up the inside of the cabin and shaking it with ear-splitting thunderclaps. From our low palette-like bunk, we could see some of the lightning trails spark briefly across the sky and even stood for a time at the window to see the silhouette of the Mattertal momentarily illuminated. It was a little intimidating, but it was also thrilling, not to mention rather romantic. To be in an exposed mountain cabin in an Alpine storm, with the fading warmth of the wood-burning stove still infusing the thick wooden walls and the sound of the rain hammering above us. It was a very special moment.

By the time morning dawned the storm had blown itself out but the rain continued, with a thick layer of cloud above us and another filling much of the valley beneath us. In the narrow sandwich between these two misty barriers were occasional snippets of scenery, mostly of wet trees and distant glaciers, but there were also patches of mist passing directly across the hillside as well which blocked out everything more than ten metres away. All in all, a rather different day to the previous four.

Breakfast was as much cold rice as we could manage, and we lingered over it as we waited for a promising break in the frequent showers. Re-stowing our foam mattresses into the rafters and packing away our gear, we were almost ready to depart when a couple of dripping figures appeared from the mist. The figures turned out to be the same Swiss hikers who had warned us about the weather at Topalihütte the previous lunchtime. They'd had a fine afternoon and evening at the refuge, the only guests to stay there as it turned out, and were now also heading down to Herbriggen to find another room for the night. They didn't want to walk too far in the rain, they explained, and it was forecast to basically rain all day long.

We described our own experience in the cabin and even suggested they stay there since we were just leaving, but they were eager to keep moving and so we said farewell for a second and final time. There was just one more job to do before we left ourselves, which was to carve our initials into the cabin's interior. Normally, we'd never consider such a seemingly heinous act. Even as a child I never even wrote a swear word in a toilet cubicle. However, the several thousand other carved initials and dates decorating the inside walls made us feel it was not so much an act of vandalism as an enhancement to the obvious history of this beacon of safety.

The earliest date we found on the walls was 1933 and there were hundreds of others from each subsequent decade. Some, mostly the early ones, were ornate affairs with letters several inches high in almost gothic script. However, any aspirations I had towards an artistic legacy were blunted (literally) by the fact that my tiny pen knife could hardly make an impression on the dense wooden walls. It took me ten minutes, two blisters and one small cut to create a two centimetre high version of our initials plus a skewed attempt at '2019'. It was time to go.

Fully-waterproofed, we made our way quickly through the soggy pine forest separating our dream home from the valley floor. Scenery-wise, we mostly saw the trunks of pine trees vanishing upwards into the mist, but that was enough. There's an enchanting quality about being in a misty forest thick with the scent of damp pine. It's also unbelievably invigorating and it took us only just over an hour to descend the vertical kilometre, emerging from beneath the low clouds into a steady drizzle on the outskirts of Herbriggen.

"Do you realise" I asked Esther, "that this is the first time we've come below 2000 metres since we climbed out of Zinal 4 days ago?"

Initially, we'd intended to seek a room in Herbriggen to shelter from the weather, as those Swiss hikers we'd met were doing, but now that we were out and about we felt differently. Yes, it was wet. Yes, we couldn't see very much scenery. But it wasn't very cold, we weren't on a dangerous section of trail and we were rather enjoying the change. Hopefully there'd be a lot more scenery and sunshine in the days to come, but a little rain seemed no reason to spend a day hiding in a hotel room now that we'd gotten going

Ultimately, we were heading towards Zermatt and a glance at our map showed us that it was only about 12 kilometres away with just a gentle 350 metres uphill. We could easily do that by following the wide and undemanding trail the valley floor had to offer.

It took us another hour of marching, mostly along an easy riverside path, to reach the village of Randa, the point at which the landslide-blocked route above would have delivered us to. We hadn't left the cabin until almost eleven o'clock, so it was now well past our usual lunchtime. We still had a little cooked rice left so we weren't going to starve, but our bodies were urging us to seek out fresh food if it was at all available? After a brief search in Randa, we did eventually manage to find a small grocery store but it had closed just half an hour before we arrived. Deciding that we'd at least rest for a little while, eat our rice and shelter from the latest deluge, we began to offload our packs into the shop doorway when a round, moustachioed gentleman appeared, pulled out a key and pointed at the shop with an inquisitive look.

"I think he's the owner offering to open up for us?" guessed Esther, although we couldn't ask directly as we'd crossed an invisible language barrier since the last time anybody had said anything to us.

    Switzerland has four national languages (German, French, Italian and Romansch) and their history and interaction is a fascinating subject in itself. For personal interest I decided to look up the numbers, so on the off chance you also want to know what they are, here you go. If not, feel free to skip the next paragraph.

    German is the most common 'first language' (62.6% in 2017), followed by French (22.9%), then Italian (11.1%) and finally Romansch (0.5%). Geographically speaking, the German-speaking parts are in the north, east and centre, the French parts in the west and the Italian parts in the south. Of the 26 Swiss Cantons, 22 have only one official language (17 German, 4 French, 1 Italian), while 3 others are officially bilingual (French and German) and one canton is even officially trilingual (French, German and Romansch). However, even within the officially multilingual regions, different areas still have different primary languages.

    In our case, although we hadn't left the Valais canton which officially uses French and German, we had left a French-speaking area and entered a German-speaking one. There hadn't been any markers or any physical boundaries, other than the mountains of course, it was a change arising from purely traditional and historic reasons. It was almost like arriving into a different country. Luckily for me, Esther speaks fairly good German, she just hadn't needed to practice for a long time.

    "Danke Schön" we both offered as he eased past us and opened the gateway to food heaven. Some small stores in remote places, understandably, don't stock a lot of fresh produce. It makes more sense for them to focus on cheese, vacuum-packed meat and other long-life products. In this case, however, he had it all and after four days of pasta, oat bran and dried fruit, it was fresh fruit and vegetables we were craving more than anything. We bought tomatoes, juicy nectarines, peaches, plums, sauerkraut, cooked beetroot and a red pepper, plus a few other longer-term supplies.

As he was checking us out the smiling shopkeeper was gently dancing to some oompah-oompah style music on his radio, complete with background yodelling, and his smile and enthusiasm were so infectious that we found ourselves bobbing along with him. Our joining in made him laugh and his eyes sparkle even more. It was exactly what two damp hikers needed on a drizzly mountain day.

Stepping outside, we gestured to the doorway of the bank next door and asked, or at least we hoped we asked, if we could sit there to eat while it was closed. The answer was 'Ja', and to underline the fact our dancing, smiling shop friend even fetched an empty crate from his store, slipped an empty box over it and placed it in front of us to make a little table. What a wonderful man. As he drove away in his van we couldn't believe he had opened up just for us and made us feel so welcome.

Half an hour of happy eating followed, savouring the juicy freshness of our vegetables and fruit one by one until our bellies were in danger of cancelling any hiking for the rest of the afternoon. Every now and then a walker or family would stroll past and smile at our homely little setup. We even kept smiling at it ourselves. It reminded us of the scene in Disney's animated version of Lady and the Tramp (1955), where Lady and Tramp share a bowl of spaghetti courtesy of Tony, who plays the accordion nearby.

As we were letting our feast go down our shopkeeper friend even came back, sang 'Hallo Hallo' to us, and headed back into his food cave. Seconds later the happy, trombone-dominated music returned, allowing us to lay back and continue smiling as we made up lyrics to fit the bombastic beat. You may not have heard the Valaisan hit songs "Have you seen my cow? She has a black arse" or

"My trombone has a funny bulge in it" just yet, but I've posted the lyrics to Ed Sheeran so it can only be a matter of time.

Thoroughly well fed and entertained, we did eventually start walking again, continuing south towards the next village of Täsch which was signposted to be another hour away. It was now mid-afternoon and the weather was hovering in that uncomfortably wet but warm zone which makes waterproofs necessary but awkwardly humid. Which is why, by the time we reached Täsch, we felt soaked both inside and out.

Although we'd visited Täsch once before, in our motorhome, we'd forgotten quite how busy and bustling it is. Zermatt is a hugely popular destination and, as a result, it's closed to all but a handful of local vehicles which are only allowed to park on the outskirts of town with a special permit. All other vehicles in the centre are battery-powered in an attempt to reduce air pollution and so ensure an unhindered view of the famous peak people travel so far to see. As a result, all outside visitors either have to walk the four kilometres from Täsch or take the train, which is also what all freight and deliveries into Zermatt have to do as well.

For us, walking was the only option we considered. We knew there was a campsite in Zermatt, so we left the ugly grey concrete train station in Täsch behind and continued following the river upvalley.

Refreshingly, although much of the scenery for our final hour of hiking into Zermatt was still veiled behind clouds, we did find plentiful patches of wild raspberries to gorge on as we walked. Well, I say scenery, but the valley is quite steeply sided at this point and follows the railway line closely, so mostly what we got to see was people waving at us from the frequently passing trains. Despite the weather, every train was crowded with happy faces returning to their accommodation in Täsch, their car or possibly even Geneva airport. Swiss transport is often referenced as a paradigm of efficiency and that's certainly the case with such popular destinations as Zermatt. Basically, you can get from your aeroplane to a 3000 metre high cable car station without walking more than a few hundred metres and with very little waiting time.

Of course, the price of the popularity is expansion and our final approach into Zermatt quite literally stopped us in our tracks for a while. After four days of near complete wilderness and even after a wet day alongside roads and trains, the sight of piles and piles of apartment buildings and hotels bounded by cranes and building sites was still somewhat jarring. I'm not saying Zermatt is 'ugly' in the grand scheme of things, just that it is a lot of human impact in an otherwise spectacular glacial valley.

Then again, who were we to complain as we joined the throngs of camera-toting tourists browsing the souvenir and luxury-item stores along Zermatt's main thoroughfare. We were visiting the place every bit as much as they were and for similar reasons, albeit with less interest in the Rolex and Gucci shop windows (we didn't need the added weight in our packs).

After a trip to a heaving Coop store to get some salad things for our dinner, we went and pitched our tent on the campsite directly adjacent to the train station. We'd arrived too late for reception, but a sign encouraged us to pitch our tent and either pay in the morning or leave the fee in an honesty box on the wall. We liked that. Some campsites in busy areas can feel 'hard', as though you're an inconvenience, but this system was immediately welcoming. And of course, when you trust people most tend to respond by being trustworthy. That's not an attitude you often find in a big city, but in the mountains where gear is often left lying around in refuges and people have to depend more on each other, it works.

It had stopped raining by now and we were able to get an apparently nice spot towards the back of the site, slightly away from the main groups of tents clustered against the toilet blocks. I popped up the tent and began unpacking our sleeping gear while Esther prepared a tasty and simple tofu salad with nuts and seeds, which we ate sitting on slightly damp garden chairs with our bare feet drying in the breeze.

Unfortunately, my much-loved hiking boots, which had already been showing signs of splitting when we left Zinal, had revealed just how knackered they really were. Although they were Gore-Tex lined and still had reasonable tread, my feet had been soaked for most of the day due to two large splits which had opened up either side of my toes and clearly went right through the waterproof lining. When I'd first taken my boots off my feet looked like I'd just had a six hour bath.

It had been a little uncomfortable but mostly I'd just been disappointed. I'd really hoped these boots would survive one more trip. They were the same boots I'd worn for our *Turn Left At Mont Blanc* adventure and for countless day trips before and since. They were also the second pair of this particular model I'd owned, Salomon Comet 3D GTX, which were wonderfully comfortable on my feet and lightweight. I would have much preferred to have the same again and to have bought them at online prices rather than here in Zermatt. "Will they last just a few more days if it brightens up?" I optimistically wondered.

Oh well, that was going to be a problem for the morning. After food we decided to take a stroll around Zermatt. Although the busyness and commercial focus of the centre had been unsettling, and still was, there was a part of us that felt we were perhaps being unfairly judgemental. I mean, we'd only really seen the high street up close, so of course that would be shoulder to shoulder with tourists on an August afternoon. What about the rest of Zermatt?

As it turned out, there was indeed a pretty church, while among the mostly more modern stuff was Zermatt's 'Old Village', a collection of thirty or so buildings dating from the 16th to the 18th century. The traditional technique of building barns on flat stone slabs balanced on top of wooden stilts, to keep out mice, was one we'd seen before in places like Grimentz, but it was odd to see it here among Zermatt's commercial centre.

Until the mid-1800's, Zermatt was an agricultural community like most mountain settlements. It was only after the famous first ascent of the Matterhorn in 1865, which drew a lot of publicity due to the controversy surrounding the tragic deaths of four team members, that tourists began flooding into the region. Today, most of the local economy is tourism based and the town has a permanent population of under 6000 people, not a lot considering it receives almost 2 million visitors a year!

Still, after half an hour of passing mostly shops, pubs and restaurants, shoulder-bumping on the still busy streets and dodging the electric shuttles ferrying people between their hotel and the train station, we'd had enough sightseeing and were ready to get back to our tent.

Completely by chance, just as we were reaching the campsite, we bumped into the Danish mother-daughter pair we'd seen a couple of days earlier beneath the Augstbordpass. They'd now finished their three-week version of the Haute Route and had just one more night in Zermatt before catching the train back to Geneva. Although we knew they'd been camping most of the way, they were looking especially glamorous this evening, with shining straight hair and make-up, so we guessed they'd treated themselves to a hotel for their last night.

"Oh yes" the daughter, Isabelle, explained. "We stayed on the campsite last night and it was horrible.

Construction noise all night long. It was crazy. So loud. We didn't sleep for a minute."

"Terrible!" exclaimed the mother, Ásdis, who didn't speak very much English but clearly understood what her daughter was telling us.

"The noise started about 11 p.m. when the trains stopped, then they worked on the tracks all night until the trains started again" Isabelle continued.

"No sleep. No sleep." added Ásdis, pulling a face that looked like someone had just kicked her in the shins and stolen her purse.

"So, where are you staying tonight?" asked Isabelle brightly.

"Erm, the camping" we replied sheepishly.

"Noooooo!" said Ásdis.

"You have to move" said Isabelle matter-of-factly.

Since it's basically just a small field surrounded by hotels, a supermarket and the trainline, Zermatt's only campsite is totally open to its surroundings. We could understand that if any building work was happening nearby then there'd be no sound reduction at all. In response to what they'd said, we first asked in their hotel directly across the street from the campsite, but they were fully booked for the next four days. We also had a quick look on Booking.com, but there were no rooms left for less than 500 francs in the whole of Zermatt that evening. In other words, too expensive for us.

Resolving to stay put and risk a noisy night, we continued enjoying a nice chat for another half an hour, Isabelle telling us about her college course and plans to try and get a refuge guardian job next summer.

"I want to work at the Cabane des Dix" she told us. "It's the best refuge on the route. You just have to go there".

Eventually, as darkness closed in around us, we said good night and dashed back to our tent. We moved it as far from the train line as we could (so that's why the area next to the toilet block was so crowded) before taking our first hot shower in five days and then trying to get to sleep before any noise began. We didn't, though I'm not sure it would have made much difference if we had.

Sure enough, at about half past ten a generator was fired up, followed shortly afterwards by a JCB and a pneumatic drill. Just as we'd been told, some seriously heavy engineering work was taking place right alongside a field full of canvas houses. We'd been warned and so had moved 100 metres away from the epicentre of the din, but some people still had their tents set up less than three metres from the drilling. Never mind the noise, the ground around them must have been physically shaking.

At first I was angry, then Esther got angry, then we were both angry for a little while until we caught each other's eye and realised that it was a complete waste of time. Instead, we both ended up laughing about it and gave each other a big hug. After a short debate about whether moving to the opposite side of the toilet block would make any difference and deciding we couldn't be bothered, we jammed earplugs as deep into our skulls as they could go without losing them forever, mimed our goodnights and closed our eyes.

Vital Statistics – Day 5
Start Point: Guggini
End Point: Zermatt
Distance Hiked: 15 km
Hiking Time: 5 hours
Ascent: 350 metres
Descent: 800 metres

Icefall

We did get some sleep that night. Not a lot, but some, mostly after the work died down at 4 a.m. although that was soon replaced by the sounds of Zermatt coming to life in high season. We were soon awake again and by quarter to seven were packing away our damp tent, nibbling at our overnight oat bran and tossing titbits of the mixture to the eager sparrows plying their trade around us.

The campsite manager couldn't have been more understanding and apologetic about the noise, waiving our camping fee without hesitation and without us even asking for him to do so. He'd complained for months, he explained, about the local council scheduling overnight track maintenance next to the site in the middle of high season, his busiest period, but they'd refused to change the schedule. Also, although he'd originally put laminated signs and free earplugs around the camping, warning people about the noise during the scheduled times so that they could go elsewhere if possible, the last two nights weren't even scheduled. The work had initially stopped a week earlier but had suddenly started up again with no warning, which is why he'd spent the previous evening at a meeting with the council and not been there when we arrived. Could we, he asked, help by sending an email to the council ourselves to complain and add weight to his argument? Naturally, we did so immediately.

In the interests of fairness, we soon received a very reasonable response from the council citing seasonal temperatures and the fact that all goods in Zermatt have to arrive by train as a reason for the overnight, summertime scheduling. They were very apologetic about it.

The campsite manager was not only a genuinely very nice guy, it turned out he was also an experienced mountaineer who gave us some helpful route advice.

Having spent our first five days following a variation on the Tour of the Matterhorn, our thinking at the time was to continue following it but with a few added detours around Zermatt first. While the Tour of the Matterhorn basically continued directly south into Italy, via a crossing of the glacial Theodul Pass, we'd decided that to dash straight out of the head of the Mattertal when we had no reason to rush, would be a missed opportunity.

Esther had spent time staring at our map to find the highest altitude hiking trails she could string together into a feasible loop and had come up with an exciting combination of 'Magical Mystery Detours'. It was an ambitious plan and it would sound complicated to describe in detail, but in essence it amounted to a large, three day loop around to the west and south of Zermatt, taking in several 3000 metre plus peaks and some high-altitude refuges before arriving at the start of the Theodul Pass crossing.

Initially, I'd resisted the idea, concerned it was a little too ambitious for two people for whom 3000 metres was still a fairly recent and unfamiliar place to be. But it was Esther's plan, she was excited and after talking to the campsite manager who reassured us it was all 'hiking' rather than climbing, I agreed to give it a try. He also told us that although wild camping was technically prohibited in the area, people he knew often did it in the quieter parts of the valley head and we would have little to worry about if we were discreet.

But we still had three more jobs to do before we could start any of that. First, we needed food for another four days of hiking. Second, we wanted to know if we could repair Esther's broken trekking pole. Finally, I needed new boots. Not only had my boots remained sodden overnight, but closer inspection with fresh eyes showed they were right on the verge of dropping to pieces. There was no way I could attempt the route we'd planned in shoes whose soles might drop off at any moment.

Esther did the food shopping while I waited with the bags, earning myself the opportunity to watch infants in lederhosen driving a herd of blackneck goats down the high street, which is not something you see every day. The goats didn't seem to mind being surrounded by camera-toting tourists, restaurants and shops. One even tried to make a dash for the butcher's store, an odd choice I thought at the time, but he was shooed away by the bloody-aproned patron. Even though it was early morning, the streets of Zermatt were already bustling with hikers and sightseers of all ages and nationalities, all eager for a dose of mountain life. Whether this particular display still counted as mountain life, I wasn't sure, but everyone looked happy with it.

Our bags were soon re-laden with the necessary kilos of pasta, oat bran, nuts and dried fruit, so it was time to start visiting outdoor stores. In terms of pole repairs, one helpful store agreed to try but soon returned to say it was a tricky break and that because our poles were 4-piece rather than the standard 3-piece, they just didn't have the parts. We thanked them for at least trying by leaving the broken pole with them on the off chance they could use the pieces to help the next visitor with a broken 4-piece.

We were glad we'd at least asked around and that the pole might have a new life, one way or another. It wasn't that the pole had been an expensive one when we'd bought it six years earlier, just that we're saddened by the throwaway culture that seems to pervade so much of the world now. I know a lot of people feel the same way. "Have a broken device? Get a new one!" seems to be the only sensible option most of the time, new items being often cheaper than a repair. Which is why, when we have something that might just be reparable, we always try to get it fixed.

In this instance, as it couldn't be fixed, I did suggest to Esther that she consider getting a more modern, lightweight replacement. But even though the pole Esther had been given was heavy and bent, she said she'd become attached to it. "It's doing the job" she told me "and it symbolises the kindness of strangers. I want to keep it for now."

Sadly, repair wasn't even close to being an option with my dilapidated boots. However, in terms of footwear, Zermatt was clearly not in short supply with dozens of stores overflowing with brand new shoes and boots suited to all possible terrain. Unfortunately, this enormous supply didn't translate into price reductions, with most stores sticking rigidly to recommended retail prices. However, some stores did have clearance racks, including one with a shelf full of half-price Kayland boots outside. They even had my size (UK 9), which is rare when it comes to end-of-line discounts. If only I'd been born with size 5 or size 14 feet, I could save a fortune on shoes.

At the time I'd never even heard of Kayland, so I didn't know whether the stated original price of 240 francs was realistic or not. I'd later find out they are indeed a well-established brand, but all I knew in the store was that they felt comfortable enough as I masterfully tackled the three-foot instore slope several times and that 120 francs was about the cheapest Gore-Tex boot I was likely to find in Zermatt.

The shop assistant was enthusiastic about them. Then again, Edward was enthusiastic about everything. He was like a bouncy puppy, nodding and moving around constantly as he quizzed us about our route, the places we'd been and the places we might go to, always with a big smile on his face and wide, excited eyes. Even after I'd bought the boots he carried on chatting like we'd known him for years and then, when we did walk away, he looked so crestfallen we wanted to go back and give him a fuss just to cheer him up. Or maybe that was just me missing our dogs.

All in all, it had already been a busy day when we started out from Zermatt at half past ten, power-marching briefly through some narrow, cobbled streets before starting up the steep switchbacks above the western edge of town. It's not that we intended to go so quickly, but after the bustle of the shops and feeling a little wired from lack of sleep, we had some nervous tension to burn off. Before we knew it, we'd ascended the 300 metres to the Alterhaupt restaurant in just half an hour. With an already hot sun beating down on us from an almost cloudless sky, the sweat was dripping from our chins as we made our way past the busy terrace to continue further uphill.

From here, the trail was much quieter and we'd burned off some steam, so we shifted down a gear to a more sensible pace. Also, my feet were already starting to hurt, which should come as no great surprise to anyone who's worn a new pair of stiff-soled boots before. Although I was enjoying the solid feeling beneath my feet compared to the softer, well-broken in lightweight pair I'd been used to, I was gradually becoming aware of a number of apparently growing razor blades that were slowly cutting my heels to pieces. The rest of the boot was totally comfortable, but when I couldn't take it any more and slipped them off, I discovered a tiny ridge of material that had formed in each heel due to a tiny movement of my foot. It can't have been more than a millimetre high, but it was enough to inflict great pain and cause serious blistering on both heels.

I knew that the material would soften eventually and that there was little I could do at the time except put on blister plasters and grit my teeth, but it still made me a little fearful by the time we reached the 2337 metre Hotel du Trift at midday. How bad was it going to get before it softened? With sore feet and a still fragile knee (although it did seem to be getting better slowly) I was going to have to watch my step.

Unlike the other Swiss Alpine Club refuges we'd visited so far, Hotel du Trift was a privately owned 'Berggasthaus' and we were swiftly greeted by the owner as we approached. He was very kind to us, immediately agreeing that we could leave our bags in his boot room while we climbed higher and also that we could camp nearby that evening (because the hotel was already fully booked). He couldn't chat for too long as he was obviously busy meeting and greeting others, but as he moved away he invited us to join the people in the hotel that evening, either to eat and drink if we wanted, or just to relax in the warm.

The immediate surroundings of the Hotel du Trift were astonishingly beautiful. Nestled just at the lip of a hanging valley, we'd been unable to see very much during our approach via a narrow gorge, but now it had opened out into a huge glacial arena enclosed by enormous peaks. Between the Zinalrothorn (4221 m) and the Obergabelhorn (4063m), which just six days earlier we'd been on the other side of, was a rocky ridge which never dipped below 3500 metres. Beneath this ridge was a steep cliff face that dropped towards a higher plateau than the one we were sat on, a plateau that we couldn't yet see although we could see the tip of the Triftgletscher emerging from it.

Our onwards route was towards the summit of the 3406 metre Mettelhorn, and it was initially steep going as we began heading up a surprisingly soft and grassy slope covered by a meandering network of criss-crossing trails. After the first hundred metres or so it levelled out onto a more gently sloping plain, where two workmen and a small digger seemed to be in the process of making a single, well-made path to funnel visitors and so reduce the clearly visible erosion.

The higher we climbed the more the view expanded until, less than half an hour after leaving the Hotel du Trift, we turned around to find the Matterhorn itself had emerged from behind the Höhbalmen shoulder directly to the south.

This was our first view of the Matterhorn from its most iconic angle, showcasing the narrow and severe Hörnli ridge on the northern-eastern face of the peak. With clouds streaming from the summit towards the various other 4000 metre plus neighbours and the countless giant glaciers which hang on their flanks, it was a magnificent, postcard-like view. And yet, we still had much further to climb.

Saying hello to a large herd of blacknose sheep grazing at the head of the grassy plain, the final 600 metres of ascent was through much rockier terrain. Above us we could see the previous day's rain had left a light covering of snow down to around 3200 – 3300 metres. Some of it was already melting, but our own destination still had a distinctive white cap that emphasised its height in the early afternoon sunshine.

Initially, the trail itself was snow-free and still well-made, but the higher we climbed the harder it became to tell what was path and what was simply rubble? A few groups of rope-carrying, helmet-wearing climbers were descending towards us, each group taking a very different route down towards the clearer sections of trail below. Choosing a group at random, we retraced the steps we had seen them take, following a handful of small cairns connected by a barely discernible groove in the stones. Although we weren't gaining altitude rapidly at this point, because we were mostly traversing sideways across a scree slope, the ground fell away so sharply to our left that any mis-steps would be potentially very dangerous. At one point we had to negotiate a thirty metre wide patch of wet snow, digging our poles hard into the soft surface and doing our best to tread in previous footprints to avoid the otherwise inevitable high-speed fall.

"We're certainly pushing our boundaries on this adventure" I smiled back at Esther.

"I just love it up here" she replied. "Look at where our feet can take us."

At 3100 metres we reached a rocky saddle separating our mostly stony, south-facing ascent from the snow-packed, glacial terrain on the other side. At this point, blue and white signposts confirmed this was very much 'Alpine' route territory, although they never say whether it's T4, T5 or T6. We had another 300 metres of ascent to reach the top of the Mettelhorn and the route now continued directly across the thick snow in front of us. Many footsteps had gone before us so it wasn't a difficult route to follow. That said, we knew that beneath the snow was a glacier which, combined with the fact that we were well above 3000 metres altitude, added a definite extra level of excitement to what we were doing. Perhaps that's why we made such a huge error of judgement just a few minutes later.

Crossing the snow had been technically very easy and hadn't felt especially unsafe considering what we were doing and where we were. The path was clearly well-trodden and the angle of the mountain wasn't very severe, so a slip at this stage was unlikely to lead to an unstoppable slide. However, as we progressed and the conical summit of the Metterlhorn emerged back into view, we realised that to reach the final rocky switchbacks we'd have to walk across a short but steep section of exposed glacial ice.

Because of the way the ground dropped away at this point, it was impossible to see just how far down the exposed section of glacier went, or what was beneath it. Would a slide down the ice stop in snow after 100 metres or did it lead to a sheer drop? We couldn't see. The contours on our map showed a drop, but not whether the exposed ice went that far down. All we knew was that we really wanted to get to the top and that we only had to cross about fifteen metres of ice to make it easily possible.

Our error of judgement was not knowing when to turn around. We didn't have crampons or micro-spikes with us and we didn't know the terrain well enough to take the risk. To be honest, I'm embarrassed to say we didn't even stop to think about it. We just ploughed on.

I went first, immediately startled by just hard it was to stay upright on the ice. I grew up playing ice hockey and am usually fairly sure-footed on slippery surfaces, but this stuff was almost impossible to stay vertical on. Unable to turn around for fear of slipping down the unseen slope that I'd stupidly put myself above, I made the snap-decision that it was safest to power forward and up, pushing back hard with my metal-tipped trekking poles as my feet skidded about beneath me. It only took me about 45 seconds to make the crossing in this way, but by the time I stepped back onto solid ground I was panting like I'd been sprinting.

Beneath me, Esther was still struggling on her first few steps with nothing but ice vanishing downhill beneath her. I did my best to speak calmly, coaching her forward one step and pole push at a time, telling her how close she was to the end, that it got less steep etc. Some of it was true, but mostly I was only hoping to give the sense that everything was under control, which wasn't really the case. It was a huge relief when she was finally able to grasp the tip of my outstretched pole and I could pull her towards the edge of the ice.

We knew immediately that we'd messed up and even though we were now within striking distance of the top, Esther made the instant decision that she wanted to go straight back down over the ice.

"I just won't enjoy being at the summit knowing I've got to go back across it. I want to relax on top, not worry" she explained.

I wasn't going to argue. I wanted exactly the same thing that Esther did, which was to get down from the mountain safely. We'd climbed to over 3000 metres and trekked across a snow-covered glacier already, a big first for us. The shock of the last few minutes had reminded us that reaching the summit didn't matter if it stressed us out.

We scanned the rocky col we were stood on, assessing the easiest point at which we might attempt going back down over the ice to where the snow began again. Eventually we settled on a point right on the edge of the col where although there was more ice to cross, we had less sideways distance to reach the snow when we did get level with it. That way, we hoped, if we did slip we'd have more chance of scrambling across to snow as we slid downhill.

Mercifully, it worked, and without any slipping. As we stomped back down the snow towards the blue and white signs at the col we were able to relax again and discuss just how foolish we'd been. "No more ice crossings without the right gear" we agreed.

Back at the blue and white signs, we were loath to give up the magnificent views we'd reached so soon. Fortunately, climbing directly up from the signs was another very steep but totally ice-free trail to the adjacent 3345 metre Platthorn, just 60 metres lower than our original target.

As the name implies, the Platthorn was every bit as 'horn-like' as the Mettelhorn had appeared and so rewarded our efforts with a view that made us want to stay there forever. I can't even begin to list the countless peaks, glaciers and valleys arrayed before us on the vast canvas of blue, white, black, grey and green that greeted us on the top. It was the entire head of the Mattertal and much more beyond. We could see everything from the vapour trails of passing aeroplanes to the wisps of smoke emerging from farmhouse chimneys. We could see the glacier we had just been slipping around on and the rockfall at the end of it. We could see the Matterhorn, of course, and Monte Rosa and pretty much every 3000 metre plus summit on our map. We could see glaciers so enormous they could bury a city and the way they would have once flowed together along the contours of the mountains they'd carved. And we could trace out much of our route so far and for the days immediately ahead. It was such an all-encompassing viewpoint, in fact, that it almost didn't look real. Everything that we knew was monumentally large looked tiny against so many other gargantuan landmarks.

Being here, so high and removed from the human busyness far below, was a gift. An opportunity to see the entire system and the way it worked together to create this amazing, wild landscape. The rain, the snow, the glaciers and the rivers, each existing in their narrow band of mountainside before transforming into the next.

Even time didn't seem real up here. We had some food, dozed in each other's arms and took way too many photographs even though none of them came close to capturing the sensations we were experiencing. My watch told us we'd been there for well over an hour, but it felt like just a few minutes.

We'd seen many amazing places over the years, and it's foolish to try and compare 'amazing' with 'more amazing', because perception changes over time. However, I feel confident when I say that nothing we had seen before could match the spectacle we'd just enjoyed in terms of sheer scale.

We descended in a somewhat ecstatic daze. Questions like "did that really just happen?" and "have we really just done that?" flew between us as we waved for a second time at the black-nose sheep and said goodbye to the view as it slowly vanished one footstep at a time.

Back at the Hotel du Trift by early evening, we collected our stuff and double-checked where we might camp for the night. We were told that the usual spot for campers was cordoned off for helicopters delivering path-maintenance supplies. We could camp there, we were told, but only if we made sure to move by 6 a.m. unless we wanted a helicopter for an alarm clock. We didn't, so instead we found a private spot on a grassy field just out of sight of the refuge itself. It did mean we lost the sun a little sooner, but we appreciated the seclusion to reflect on the magnificent day we'd enjoyed.

Esther did some stretching while I cooked up a tasty dinner of lentil pasta, tomatoes, garlic and mushrooms, along with some nice fresh salad since we'd only left civilisation that same morning. Several hundred mosquitoes arrived to keep us company as we ate, but marvellously our Incognito repellent spray actually worked. Not only were we not stung (very much), but after over 1700 metres of climbing in the heat, we smelled a hell of a lot better thanks to its fruity aroma.

As per our earlier invitation, we did meander over to the Hotel du Trift to sit on the terrace for a while and use the bathrooms, but the owner and his staff were all so busy serving dinner to the other guests that we only got to say a brief hello and thank him as he fleeted past with a tray of rolls. We bought a few postcards and some apples for the next day by way of a small financial acknowledgement of his kindness, but it was obviously not expected of us. Given that the apples we received were all the size of large grapefruits and cost only 1 franc each, I'd say we came out of the deal pretty well.

Vital Statistics – Day 6
Start Point: Zermatt
End Point: Hotel du Trift
Distance Hiked: 12 km
Hiking Time: 6 hours
Ascent: 1750 metres
Descent: 1000 metres

Schön

It was another warm start to the day as we began the 300 not-too-steep metres up onto the Höhbalmen shoulder early the next morning. I can't imagine there are many better places to appreciate the Matterhorn from than this giant grassy knoll on a fine summer's day. At 2600 metres, with just a few wispy clouds adding a little contrast behind the grey-white magnificence of the Matterhorn, we were quite literally walking towards one of the most famous mountain landscapes in the world from the most often-photographed angle, directly in line with the Hörnli ridge. We didn't have to stop, or turn around, or even crane our heads. It was just right there, directly in front of us as we walked. Just imagine how many triangular chocolate bars have been inspired by this view alone.

And it wasn't just the Matterhorn we could see either, although it was obviously the most eye-catching feature. There was also the Theodulgletscher, the enormous Gornergletscher and countless other ice flows in sight. There were the lofty summits of the Breithorn, Pollux and Monte Rosa to name just a few away to our left. And there was the broad sweep of the Mattertal beneath us. It wasn't quite as expansive a view as we'd enjoyed from the Platthorn, because the view to our right was blocked by the hillside we were walking across (the lower slopes of the Gabelhorn incidentally), but with the Matterhorn that much closer and looming directly above us, it was simply phenomenal.

The easy-to-follow trail meandered very gently southwards for over an hour, hardly ever losing sight of Europe's most iconic summit. "How many climbers are up there?" we wondered aloud. They couldn't ask for finer weather. Then again, apart from a few people yawning on the terrace at Hotel du Trift, we were yet to see a single other person today. We'd seen a few sheep and said good morning to them, but with no wind creating a near-silent hillside it was almost possible to believe we had it all to ourselves.

Eventually, the trail began to veer right to head westwards up the Zmutt valley. As we moved around the hillside and climbed slowly towards 2800 metres, a new perspective opened up to us, revealing the sometimes less-seen intricacies of the Matterhorn's flanks. Features like the Matterhorngletscher clinging precariously to the flatter, northern face, looking like it might slide away at any moment and fall into the scree-lined Zmutt valley. Or the north-western ridge which dips steeply eastwards before rising back to the summit of Dent d'Herens (4174 m).

While the majority of visitors to Zermatt, understandably, hop onto one of the various cable cars strung out to the south and east of the town, the Zmutt valley to the west can only be reached by a long walk. There are no cable cars here. Instead, this enormous valley, bounded on three sides by a continuous ridge that includes the Matterhorn, Dent d'Herens, Tête de Valpelline (3799 m), Tête Blanche (3707m) and Dent Blanche (4357 m), is an ideal place to visit for wanderers seeking some relative peace and quiet in one of Switzerland's most visited destinations.

Our reason for coming this way was the Schönbielhütte at 2694 metres, from where we hoped to continue higher towards the Schönbielhorn at 3472 metres. Enthused by yesterday's magical mystery detour, we were eager to crack on and were soon descending from our high traverse in the mid-morning heat to reach the start of a mighty moraine that would take us towards the refuge. From above, it had looked like much of the Zmutt valley was full of glacial debris, however, now that we were back down at 2200 metres and closer to the grey surface, we could see that the ice still extended far beneath the boulders.

Here and there we could make out the contours of crevasses and ice bridges so covered in dust and dirt that we had to stare hard to convince ourselves it was ice at all.

Climbing close to the apex of the moraine, several hundred metres above the surface of the ice, we reached the final steep switchbacks which carried us to the Schönbielhütte and another sun-warmed refuge terrace. The squat, grey stone building was constructed in 1955 and, with its red window shutters and Swiss flag adding a touch of colour, looked idyllic on the green hillside with the dark rock and white ice flows of the valley head beyond.

Easing ourselves onto a wooden bench for a pause, we were soon approached by a lady with a pad and pen asking what we wanted to drink. There followed a brief moment of tension when we first asked to sit a while and were told we either needed to make a purchase or move, but it was all soon sorted out.

We knew the deal of course. If you sit on the terrace you consume refuge produce. If you want to sit for free and eat your picnic, you sit on the ample grassy spaces nearby. Fair enough. Refuges need to make money to stay open, part of which they make from overnight fees but much of it they make selling food and drink, which in this case all has to be delivered by helicopter. Yes, food is expensive at many refuges, but for a good reason.

Anyway, it all got sorted swiftly and we did buy some food (carrots and apples), before leaving most of our gear in the boot room in preparation for our ascent towards the Schönbielhorn. The guardian had assured us there was a walking route to the top, even though the black dotted line on our map was missing in some places. Certainly, we were struggling to find a sign or painted marker that indicated where we actually needed to start climbing again.

In the end it was Esther who spotted a brown smudge in the green above us that "might be" a path, so we simply walked up the steep grassy slope towards it.

Thankfully, Esther was right. It was a path and it was a tough one. After about 100 vertical metres of slogging up loose dirt, we emerged onto a bare plateau to look up at what can only be described as a steep, dangerous-looking pile of stones with some sheer rock faces above it. There were some cairns though, so we began following them as the plateau began to rise gradually into the chaos of stones.

A few days earlier we'd crossed the Wasulicke and described it as the closest thing we'd ever done to climbing. The previous day we'd been slipping around on a patch of exposed glacier above 3000 metres and pushed our boundaries still further. We were about to do so again.

Following the string of tiny cairns that were barely discernible from random piles of rocks, we began to scramble our way up a scree slope so steep I almost couldn't believe we were doing it. The hillside was at least a 60-70% gradient, the ground was unbelievably loose and with almost every step a cascade of pebbles bounced away beneath us. At times we seemed to be treading on a path that other hikers had followed, a dustier groove in the disorder, but at others I had no idea what we were even doing up there. Above us, the scree funnelled towards a narrow col beneath a sheer cliff. Below us was a painful, possibly fatal, fall.

Agreeing that we'd never, ever follow such a route had it not been drawn on a map and endorsed by a refuge guardian, we pushed on anyway, mostly because going up was easier than the idea of going down. Because it was so steep we gained height quickly, quickly reaching a shelf just below the rocky col. All that was left was a few metres of a six-inch wide trail next to a 300 metre drop and we were there.

We decided we'd had enough after that. From our map, we could see that we'd reached a point beneath the Schönbielhorn at about 3200 metres. Looking higher, there was nothing at all we'd comfortably describe as 'path' and quite a lot that could be described as almost-certain-death. Not wanting to repeat the mistake of yesterday in pursuit of a 'summit', we settled down onto a large flat rock to drink in the scenery.

Just as with the Platthorn, there was too much to see to focus on any particular detail, all we could do was try to take in the whole. Scanning from left to right as we sat facing south, our eyes swept first across the mighty Hohwänggletscher dominating the nearby slopes, then the graceful curve of the green and grey Zmutt valley framing the mighty snow-capped peaks and glaciers to the east, then the southern flank of the Zmutt valley rising sharply all the way to the top of the mighty Matterhorn which then fell away as the scene continued around, sawing from peak to peak above the snow and ice to finally reach the limit of our view at Tête Blanche. Not a bad place to have lunch really.

Food was followed by yet another high-altitude doze in the now roasting afternoon sunshine. Were it not for the few clouds that had built up, occasionally blocking out the sun and allowing the breeze to cool us down, I fear we might have cooked like eggs on hot stones. I must have slept deeply since Esther has a photo of me resting on my coat, with a bandana over my face, looking a lot like a corpse with no shoes on. Apparently, I also snored, though I deny the charge.

We stayed up there for over ninety minutes. Several times after our nap we heard enormous crashes and snapped our heads around just in time to see ice spraying up beneath the tongue of the Stockjigletscher, from where a block had broken away and smashed on the rocks below. Once, after much staring, we even managed to see one fall. Whether it was the size of a car, or a hotel, we simply couldn't tell in a place of such large proportions. But it was definitely huge and made plenty of noise. We all know glaciers are dynamic, that they move and carve the earth beneath them, but to see that dynamism in real life is enchanting. And a little sad since the glaciers are now receding so fast. Who knows how long we'll get to enjoy them for?

Eventually we were prompted to leave the summit by the gathering clouds. We were over 3000 metres and with such a technical descent ahead of us, this was not the sort of place we wanted to get rained on, or worse.

Having steeled ourselves against what we knew was to come, the descent itself passed largely without incident. We slipped quite frequently when the rocks we stood on gave way, and sometimes a larger stone decided to slide onto the top of one of our feet, but our boots were up to the job. Despite the continuing razor blades in my heels I was wonderfully glad I'd had the sense to change my boots when I did. The stiffer sole was definitely making this sort of thing a lot easier for me, as was not carrying my fully laden pack.

It had only taken us an hour to ascend the 500 metres from the refuge, and it only took us 45 minutes to get back down, once again yielding up our hard-won view one footstep at a time. We'd already decided that we weren't even going to ask the guardian if we could camp close to her refuge and our decision to keep moving was further cemented when we found the terrace at Schönbielhütte crowded with climbers and trekkers, most of whom we guessed were staying the night based on the time of day and distance from Zermatt.

Pausing only momentarily to grab our gear, we trotted down the switchbacks and the moraine trail, retracing our route until we reached a nice spot alongside a river where we decided to have dinner. We didn't know where we were going to camp yet, but we did know it was half past five and we were hungry. Far better to arrive late and pitch with a full belly than to stagger on light-headed. The only downside was that we appeared to have picked an ants' nest to sit on. Who knew ants could be so invasively kinky? Dancing around with my pants around my knees trying to remove the explorers trying to go where no ant has gone before, I was lucky not to expose myself to some of the late evening trekkers still heading up towards the refuge.

Dusk was approaching by the time we started walking again. Esther was all in favour of just carrying on in the direction we planned to take the next day, until we found a spot, while I was all in favour of deviating off the route towards a spot we'd noticed earlier and which would probably allow us to stop sooner. I knew it was a detour but I was knackered and was also fighting the sleepiness of a full belly. We'd already been hiking for over 6 hours with 1300 metres of ascent. Unfortunately, it caused a little disagreement between us.

Pretty soon we were arguing about "your [Esther's] bloody detours are too ambitious and you won't give a damn inch once you've got an idea into your head!", to which Esther countered "well, if you'd just say what you wanted instead of waiting for me to make the plans all the time...."

Thankfully, it was over fairly quickly. We've met a few other hiking couples over the years and they've all said similar things about tension on the trail. As one couple put it, "if one of you doesn't demand to know 'whose bloody idea was this anyway?' on a daily basis, then you're not doing it right!"

By the time our little flare up had fizzled out, we'd passed the turn to the spot I'd wanted to camp on and were pass through a quarry at the apex of the Zmutt valley.

"Okay, I'm sorry." I offered. "How about we stop just here among the trees. We're still at 2200 metres and we'll be well hidden. It's eight o'clock. We can't keep going much longer anyway and I know you're tired too."

"I'm sorry as well. I'm ready to stop." replied Esther.

And that was that. One brief argument and one spectacular day had come to end. We pitched the tent together before lathering up with fruity mosquito repellent so we could stay out and enjoy the evening. Esther did a few stretches, as usual, her Downward Dog mimicking the sharp point of the Matterhorn which towered above our home for the night. A little later we simply sat and held hands, feeling awestruck beneath the silhouette of the Matterhorn now framed by stars.

Vital Statistics – Day 7
Start Point: Hotel du Trift
End Point: Stafel
Distance Hiked: 17 km
Hiking Time: 7 hours
Ascent: 1300 metres
Descent: 1400 metres

To Glacier Or Not To Glacier

    It rained heavily just before dawn and was still drizzling when we woke up, packing away our tent surrounded by a cold, thick mist that hid all of the magnificence we had so enjoyed for the previous two days. In the early hours of the morning, when we'd woken up to pee, the clouds had yet to blow in and we'd been captivated by the sight of lights flickering high up on the Matterhorn. The thought that those lights were being worn by human beings scaling one of the most challenging mountains in the Alps, in near pitch darkness, gave us goosebumps. Now that we'd woken up to find awful weather had arrived, we only hoped they were all still safe somewhere above us.
    Our intention had been to start the day with a brisk 350 metre climb towards the Schwarzsee, a small lake with a historic chapel immediately adjacent to one of the main cable car stations above Zermatt. From there, we'd planned another magical mystery detour towards the Hörnlihütte at 3260 metres, beautifully positioned at the foot of the precipitous and eye-catching Hörnli ridge. This is the starting point for most climbers attempting to summit the Matterhorn from the Swiss side of the mountain.
    Our ultimate goal for the day was to arrive at the edge of the Theodulgletscher, from where we hoped to make the crossing into Italy the next morning. We'd started having doubts about this part of the plan over the previous couple of days, but that was a bridge we'd have to cross later on. Currently our concern was that the Schwarzsee was basically on the way, but the Hörnlihütte definitely wasn't. The route up and down to the refuge was pretty much at a right angle to the direction we actually planned to go in.
    Which obviously begged the question, was there really any point trying to go so high in the rain with such poor visibility? After 8000 metres of climbing in 7 days,

mostly beneath a heavy pack and including several especially demanding trails, my thighs audibly creaked when I stood up after tying my bootlaces. Was an extra 700 metres uphill, in drizzle and fog, just to come down again really worth it?

True to form, we decided not to think about that either, setting off into the gloom with a plan to see what we found at the Schwarzsee. We'd occasionally been lucky enough over the years to walk above the weather, starting out beneath clouds yet ascending into a majestic world of sunshine and summits anyway. Perhaps that would be the case today? We seriously doubted it, but we could still hope for the best.

A short distance from our camping spot we passed an ugly, squat building humming loudly with the sound of turbines. At first, we assumed it was generating power from the steady stream of water bumbling along the Zmutt valley, but a nearby information board told a different story. Bizarrely, it turned out that this facility was actually pumping water *uphill*, directly through the bedrock of the mountains and all the way to another reservoir some 500 metres higher and several valleys further west. This building, in fact, was just one of five similar pumping stations. Together, they helped to funnel water from an enormous catchment area fed by some thirty-five different glaciers to a single enormous reservoir called Lac des Dix at 2400 metres altitude. From there, the water flows down through a series of four power stations to generate over 2000 Megawatts of electricity, almost double that produced by a nuclear power station and enough to supply 400,000 Swiss homes, apparently. It was an unexpectedly interesting story for an ugly concrete building buzzing in the morning mist. We always knew that the Swiss liked mountain-sized engineering, but from the schematic showing the tunnel system they'd created, this must have involved almost biblical scale earth moving.

And speaking of biblical scale earth moving, as we left the hum of the turbines behind us and began shuffling up the soggy slopes beneath the unseen Matterhorn, our otherwise monotonous trudge was broken up by a collection of faded signposts recounting some of the region's folk tales.

One sign claimed that the Matterhorn was originally formed by the footprints of a giant who had once lived on the warm, southern side of a high rocky wall. Because of the warm climate and the rich soil, life was easy on this southern side of the wall. Milk literally ran in the streams. Yet this wasn't enough for the curious giant who simply had to see what was on the other side. Unfortunately, as he tried to step over to Zermatt and investigate the northern kingdom, the wall collapsed, leaving only the Matterhorn standing tall surrounded by heaps of rubble. Even more unfortunately, his moment of carelessness meant that the previously lush southern side of the wall was no longer protected from the cold north winds, and snow now covered the ground there for half of the year.

It was an engaging tale, although the same sign also contained another possible version of events. In the second story, it was said that God himself came to Earth to review his great work. On stepping across the Theodul Pass, his Alpenstock (walking stick) became lodged in a crevasse and no matter how hard God tried it just wouldn't come out. Eventually, God pulled so hard that the stick broke and it was the remnants left behind in the Earth that became the Matterhorn.

Personally, I still think that the geologists might be on to something with their tectonic plate theory, but God's walking stick and the curious giant have an engaging imagery to them, so perhaps we shouldn't rule them out just yet.

Another sign entitled "Zermatt in times long past" also spoke of a tropical paradise and a beautiful village that once existed on the plain now covered by the ice of the Theodulgletscher. One day, the sign claimed, the eternal 'Wandering Jew' visited, but nobody would take him in so he cursed the village, ultimately leading to the village's glacial fate. Apparently, on bright moonlit nights, the souls of the lost villagers have been known to appear as white mist to lead hikers astray. A later sign also said that it was the same Wandering Jew, returning to the area 1000 years later and seeing the destruction of his curse, whose tears formed the Schwarzsee we were hiking towards. Poetic and somewhat disturbing stuff really, which says far more about attitudes and humanity than the formation of glaciers and mountain lakes.

It took us just over an hour to reach the Schwarzsee ourselves, not being led astray by any angry souls, although we probably wouldn't have seen them had they been trying. The Schwarzsee isn't that large, but we could only see a few metres across the water. We knew that the historic Maria Zum Scnee (Maria of the Snow) chapel wasn't far away, in the rain, but we still decided not to make even the world's shortest pilgrimage to reach it.

According to legend, the existence of the chapel arose from a promise made by two inhabitants of Zermatt. Hopelessly lost in thick fog on the Theodulgletscher, they threw themselves on the mercy of God, promising to build a chapel if they survived, which of course they did. After its construction in the 18th century, the chapel soon became a popular place of pilgrimage. On the patron saint's feast day on 5th August, both locals and visitors flock to Schwarzsee to celebrate mass in the open air.

Our route led us instead to the warm and hospitable Hotel Scwarzsee at 2583 metres, where we joined a small huddle of damp hikers hovering just inside the porch of the smart restaurant. Wonderfully, the staff didn't seem to mind the comings and goings of soggy walkers as they looked after the seated diners. Despite the drizzle and continued poor visibility, Esther was still keen to try for the Hörnlihütte and I wasn't totally opposed to the idea myself. I knew it made no sense in terms of seeing very much and saving our energy for the rest of our hike, but the prospect of kind of climbing a bit of the Matterhorn was still hard to pass up, even if it was 'climbing' on a hiking trail to the start of the hard stuff.

"Well, it still might be clearer higher up" Esther suggested.

"If they let us leave most of our stuff here, let's go" was my reply. "I don't want to slog all the way up there carrying everything just to stand inside a scenically-positioned cloud."

As per usual, Esther's smile soon worked its magic, with a helpful waiter called Mark showing us the way downstairs to the currently empty 'boot room'. "Just leave it here" he told us. "Nobody really comes in here so it'll be safe and dry."

We thanked him profusely, shedding our wet packs onto the tile floor and hungrily eyeing up the bunk beds at the back of the room. It didn't look like anyone was actually sleeping here at the moment, but given the weather outside there was a part of me that was tempted to slide under a big heavy blanket and just keep quiet for the rest of the day. We didn't, of course, there was still a big, damp mountain waiting for us outside. And not just any mountain, a world famous mountain that we just happened to be circumnavigating.

We set out with just the bare essentials yet again, moving fast to try and generate some body heat to drive out the pervasive chill. Happily, during our time in the windowless basement, the sky had brightened ever so slightly. We still couldn't see much immediately around us, but directly overhead there was just a hint of blue which suggested better things might be on the way after all.

Just quarter of an hour after leaving the hotel, small gaps began to appear in the ever-shifting mist, creating tantalisingly short-lived windows onto the peaks and glaciers which surrounded us. One moment we could see the Gornergletscher, then it was gone. Then we could make out the Mettelhorn across the valley to the north, then that too vanished. Incrementally, these windows became larger and more persistent. Fairly soon, as we zig-zagged and traversed, the view became more open than hidden and we could begin to see the lower portion of the Matterhorn's famous ridge extending into the summit clouds. There was even an occasional beam of sun to transform the otherwise dull colours into a more vivid snippet of scenery.

From the Schwarzsee, the climb up to the Hörnlihütte is really a climb of two parts. Up to around 2900 metres it is very much a hiking trail, albeit a somewhat exposed one with a couple of metal platforms spanning otherwise sheer drops, so it still requires a head for heights. The final 350 metres or so, in contrast, is an Alpine route. As Alpine routes go, it's an especially well maintained and safety-minded one because it's so popular, but it is still an Alpine route and so requires firm footing on the sections close to sheer drops, metal staircases and occasional rope assistance.

We maintained our fast pace all the way to the Hörnlihütte, arriving in just under an hour stripped down to just our upper base layers but still sweating hard and steaming in the cold air. After a week of hiking and pacing ourselves, it had felt good to let rip on the lower slopes and once we'd started it had been so much fun that it had been hard to stop.

Also known as 'Berghaus Matterhorn', the original Hörnlihütte was built in 1880 and had just 17 beds. Expansions and renovations over the years peaked at 170 beds in the early 1980's, however, the current hut which was completed in 2015 has a deliberately limited capacity of 130. It's the first mountain shelter in Europe to purposely limit the number of beds to try and control overcrowding on the climb above it, which is also why camping anywhere near the refuge is strictly prohibited.

The refuge also offers a decent restaurant for day visitors, so after taking a few photos of the climbers we could see abseiling on some vertical slabs of rock above us, wondering if any of them had been wearing the overnight lights we'd seen, we ducked inside for a warm cup of tea. In previous years we probably would have stayed outside in order to dodge the need to buy an overpriced brew, however, we weren't feeling in the mood to do that this time around. I mean, how often do you get to visit a hut so highly placed on such an iconic peak? We didn't want to feel rushed because we were too cold to hang around this time.

The first successful ascent of the Matterhorn was in 1865 and was marred by controversy. Of the seven climbers led by Englishman Edward Whymper, four were killed on the descent when one man slipped and dragged three of his companions with him. Whymper and the two guides who survived were later accused of cutting the rope to prevent them being dragged down as well, although they were later acquitted. As the last 'great Alpine peak' to be climbed, it is sometimes said that its first ascent marked the end of the so called 'Golden Age Of Alpinism', when gentleman climbers could still find new challenges to set themselves.

Of course, just because it had been climbed didn't make the Matterhorn safer. Over 500 people have died climbing the Matterhorn since that first ascent, which is part of the reason authorities are so keen to prevent overcrowding. A leaflet tucked inside the restaurant menu told us that around 2500 climbers a year start their Matterhorn climb from the Hörnlihütte.

Sitting in the warm fug of the glass-walled restaurant area, sipping 4 franc tea and gazing up into the clouds at the abseiling adventurers dangling from frail ropes, we could only imagine how it felt to be on such a precipitous rock face looking back down that razor-sharp ridge. "How long does it take them do you think?" we wondered aloud after spotting a notice on the wall informing guests that setting out much earlier than 4 a.m. was disruptive to others and so not allowed.

Asking at the desk, we were told that most groups led by an experienced guide took 5 or 6 hours to reach the top from the refuge, although that varied a lot depending on conditions. This information only made it even more incredible when we spotted a bland little print out of split times for a man called Andreas Steindl who, the notice suggested, had run all the way from Zermatt church to the very top of the Matterhorn *and back down again!* His total time was just under four hours! "That can't be right" I thought. How could he possibly scale almost 3000 vertical metres, 1200 of which are up the Hörnli ridge, and get back down again so quickly and survive. That's not running, that's falling. Perhaps there was some special route assistance or something?

I was so flabbergasted I had to look it up online just to check. Incredibly, it was true. This local superstar and sky-running legend had indeed managed to get all the way from the centre of Zermatt to the top of the Matterhorn in just 2:38:37, with no more assistance than some usual ropes left permanently in certain places. He'd then turned straight back around and got back to Zermatt in 1:21:15 to arrive just 8 seconds under the 4 hour barrier. Well, I say barrier, but there can't be many mortals who can get too close to that mark. Never mind 'Steindl', Steinborg seemed like a more suitable name for such an athlete!

Inspired by Andreas, I energetically and bravely relaxed in the Hörnlihütte for another two hours, sipping tea and watching as the mist gradually cleared away to reveal the full extent of the scenic extravaganza outside. Although the tops of the highest peaks remained hidden in grey clouds, the moody light cast across the scene gave a sense of power to the brooding glaciers dominating the vista. There were so many enormous ice sheets in sight that the overall effect was of a world frozen in time. How could there be life in this land bounded by ice, clouds and grey scree? Yet life there was, in abundance. From the soaring birds above us to the colourful human shapes we could see bustling over the ice and stone, not to mention the hint of green emerging out of the low clouds which still filled the bottom of the Mattertal, emphasising its graceful curve northwards.

Our eventual descent was swift and beautiful. Every corner revealed a new viewpoint into the powerful wilderness spread out around us. The Matterhorn may have towered up behind us, but in front of us was a miles-wide panorama still bounded by the clouds both above and below. The trail was still busy with people coming up, most of whom were day hikers although some carried the compact bags of climbers, with ropes and ice axes slung to the outside in anticipation of an early morning ascent themselves. Amazingly, one hardy soul had his sturdy boots slung to his bag and was ascending the Alpine route towards the Hörnlihütte completely bare-foot!

As we approached the Hotel Schwarzsee to collect our gear, the sun began to emerge more fully and illuminate larger patches of mountainside. The snippets of blue in the sky began to expand and within the space of just a few minutes the day switched from gloomy and threatening to hot and sticky. The atmosphere of the landscape was totally transformed, from powerful and dominating, emphasising our smallness against nature's magnificence, to inviting and playful. What a playground was now spread out before us.

We decided to take another short rest in the boot room and work out what to do next because, now that we were right on the edge of walking towards it, our doubts about whether crossing the Theodulgletscher was a good idea or not had grown significantly.

From a few days out, back in Zermatt, the prospect of crossing a national border on a glacier had been mostly exciting. It was going to be a big new experience for us. As you already know, we didn't have any crampons or even micro-spikes with us, however, the Zermatt campsite manager had been encouraging. "Normally you can just follow the snow plough track and it's very easy" he'd told us. "It's still a glacier though, and because it's been such a hot summer a lot of the glacier is snow-free. You should ask one of the higher refuges for a report on the snow coverage. If it's ice, then it will be much harder near the top where it isn't so flat."

Well, the thing was, we'd gotten a decent look at the glacier from the Hörnlihütte and couldn't see very much snow on it all. We'd also asked at the desk and been told it was indeed mostly ice, as far as they knew, but that we should call the refuges either side of the glacier for their information.

To cut a long story, over the next hour in the boot room we made a lot of phone calls, most of which we should have made days earlier. We spoke to refuges and mountain guide organisations, in Switzerland and Italy, and basically found out several important facts. Yes, the glacier ice was exposed all the way across. No, you can't rent spikes at the refuges. No, there are no guides available tomorrow morning. No, this sunshine won't last. It's stormy tomorrow afternoon and high winds for two days after that. The first time anyone can help you across it is in four days' time.

In summary, we needed a new direction. After our experience beneath the Mettelhorn we were feeling much more risk averse and since it was such a long crossing, we just didn't want to take the risk of heading out there in just our boots. Had we actually committed to the Tour of the

Matterhorn more specifically and made plans to have the right equipment or a guide with us in advance, we could have easily crossed, no doubt, but we hadn't.

The new plan we settled on was essentially the only one open to us if we weren't crossing the ice, namely to double back along the Mattertal. We had two page leaflet with us showing, on one side, an outline of the Tour of the Matterhorn, but on the other side it showed the adjacent Tour of Monte Rosa, the Alp's second highest mountain after Mont Blanc. We'd picked the leaflet up back in Zinal and had carried it along for ideas, just in case. Put together, the two large loops created a giant figure-of-eight on the map.

The leaflet showed us that by hiking back along the 'other' flank of the Mattertal in search of another route into Italy, we'd basically be starting a nine day loop around the Monte Rosa massif instead. Also, as both loops shared the Theodul Pass crossing, when we got around to the other side of the Theodul Pass at Breuil-Cervinia, we could just pick up the Tour of the Matterhorn again and carry on. We hadn't so much given up on a glacier crossing as gained an extra slice of adventure, or at least that's how we chose to see it.

Decision made, we stepped out of the boot room to find the restaurant eerily quiet, startling the young girl mopping the floor who stared at us with her mouth open. Ignoring her surprise, we smiled and stepped over the wet floor to use the loo before heading back upstairs towards the main doors, which were locked. Unknown to us, the restaurant had closed half an hour earlier and the staff were about to leave on the last cable car of the day. If we'd hung around ten minutes longer we'd have gotten to spend the night in the boot room after all.

A dusty, dry descent into Zermatt took us from exposed ski slopes into pine forests. A few more information boards on the way down told us the tale of the hardy stone pine trees and the nutcracker bird who, for centuries, was hunted by locals in order to try and 'protect' the forest. It wasn't until the 1950s that research revealed the birds actually helped the forest to grow by spreading the heavy pine seeds around. Sadly, it seemed a very human approach to nature and had a depressing irony to it. Assume it's a problem and kill it, just in case, only to protect and encourage the same animal years later.

Before we knew it, we were back in a roasting hot and very busy Zermatt by dinner time, sitting outside the same Coop we'd bought supplies from three days earlier. We were no longer mentally hiking the Tour of the Matterhorn, but the Tour of Monte Rosa, though again it all felt a little arbitrary what we chose to call our route.

Overall, the Tour of Monte Rosa is 162 km long and includes 13,000 metres of ascent, a similar horizontal distance to the Tour of Mont Blanc but with about a third more climbing metres, so it's definitely not an insignificant challenge. Unlike Mont Blanc and the Matterhorn, Monte Rosa isn't such a well-known summit outside of the climbing world, which is surprising considering it's the second highest peak in the Alps and the highest in Switzerland at 4634 metres. The Monte Rosa massif actually has a total of ten peaks over 4000 metres and of its four faces, three are in Italy.

As evening approached in Zermatt, it was time to find a place to sleep. We did go to the camping briefly to speak with the owner and thank him for his advice. He was pleased to see us, happy we'd had a nice time and agreed we'd made a safe decision. He was especially surprised to hear the top of Mettelhorn glacier had been snow free, which he said was especially rare.

Sadly he still couldn't guarantee a noise-free night on his site. The work, he told us, had continued during the time we'd been away and neither Esther or I could face another night of drilling, especially after the previous two blissfully quiet nights in the hills. Instead we marched quickly into the gathering twilight, already exhausted by a thousand vertical metres of climbing and a vertical mile of descending but motivated by the prospect of seclusion and calm. The worst case was that we'd stay at the camping in Täsch, but it was so late and we were so knackered by now that we were eying up every flat patch of grass we passed.

In the end, we didn't make it to Täsch, stopping instead on a quiet, flat space that couldn't be seen from the trail. It was crawling with ants and there wasn't a patch of non-spiky floor to be had anywhere, but it was enough. It had to be, because we were done! It was almost pitch dark and I don't think I could have managed another step.

Vital Statistics – Day 8
Start Point: Stafel
End Point: Outskirts of Täsch
Distance Hiked: 22 km
Hiking Time: 7 hours
Ascent: 1100 metres
Descent: 1700 metres

Suspended

 Fresh raspberries soaked in morning dew was our surprise breakfast on our ninth day of adventure. Esther stumbled into an enormous patch of ripe berries just a few metres from our tent and there were so many that we ate until we could hardly contain any more. It was another damp and chilly start to the day but only due to the steepness of the valley between Täsch and Zermatt hiding us from the morning sun. The clear blue sky above us suggested a fine morning was on the way and it was hard to imagine that a powerful afternoon storm was forecast.
 We arrived in Täsch just in time to see the campsite stirring to life as the sun hit the valley floor. We'd stocked up on food in Zermatt the previous evening, so we had nothing to do except work out the best route up the eastern side of the valley to find the Europaweg trail. All being well it would take us two full days moving north along the Europaweg to reach Grächen, at which point we'd round the end of the Mischabel Wall, leave the Mattertal and start heading south along the adjacent Saastal. After that it would take us another two days to arrive at the non-glacial Monte Moro Pass and cross the Swiss-Italian border.
 The words 'rest day' had started floating around in our heads a little at this point. Eight days in the wild, nine thousand vertical metres and six nights in the tent had taken a toll on our energy levels. We were fine when we were moving, but when we stopped our limbs seemed to quickly fill up with lead that took a long while to shake off afterwards. Then again, we still had no fixed plans to stop for a day, just the knowledge that if the chance arose we should at least consider it.
 We enjoyed our second breakfast of cantaloupe melon and a punnet of cherries, both bought in Zermatt and both things I had no intention of carting a thousand metres

uphill, sitting in the heart of Täsch while watching the world go by. As we sat we were passed by hundreds of hikers and their luggage all making their way to the ugly train station nearby. Whether they were heading up towards Zermatt or down and out of the valley, we couldn't know, but what we couldn't help but notice was the nearby bins overflowing with litter and a handful of junk food wrappers blowing along the road. It was nothing, of course, compared to the centre of a major city, but it was still upsetting to see the downside of all of those smiling faces and happy holidays. The Swiss manage it all very well, I'm sure, but it's still hard to control the waste output of 2 million visitors a year.

Wishing them all a happy day, we began our search for the Europaweg. Often referred to as "the most beautiful two-day hike in the Alps", the Europaweg is a high-altitude trail between Grächen and Zermatt that was given the name Europaweg in 1997. With a refuge called the Europahütte (2265 m) about halfway along for overnight stays, it's a popular route for those seeking a manageable dose of mountain spectacle with a lot of reward for their two days of effort.

Following high level trails on the slopes of the Mischabel wall and only coming down when almost in Zermatt, the Europaweg is usually hiked northwards so that the Matterhorn is in sight for much of the way. Although we'd chosen to cross the Wasulicke instead and then followed the valley due to rain, we could have just as well elected to use the Europaweg earlier on as part of our Matterhorn Tour. Part of the Europaweg that we were especially excited about was that it included the world's longest pedestrian suspension bridge at 494 metres long, spanning a gorge a short distance beneath the Europahütte.

Strictly speaking, we'd already missed out a bit of the Europaweg by taking the low-level route to Täsch the previous evening, but we weren't planning on doubling back to Zermatt just for the sake of it. Instead, we would simply take another trail up to the Europaweg directly from Täsch and carry on from there.

Our chosen route left Täsch on a minor road, snaking gently uphill until a small gap in the bushes marked the start of a trail. It was a narrow, dusty path through dense trees, climbing steeply all the way until we stumbled out onto a wide expanse of solid path that we guessed must be the Europaweg. Sure enough, over our shoulder was the tip of the Matterhorn poking out above the sloping sides of the Mattertal, the sharply pointed summit framed once again by a clear blue sky after yesterday's clouds.

From the moment we joined the Europaweg it was clear that the creation of a slightly more cultivated trail at such an altitude had required major investment, with corrugated metal tunnels and protected overhangs on several sections of the path. Later on, as we moved northwards, steps and hand-ropes featured on the more precipitous parts, plus a long tunnel with automatic lighting that had been carved through the mountain side.

Not that the trail was overly-sanitised or 'easy', far from it. There were still plenty of sheer drops close to the path and short but steep inclines as the route weaved along the mountain's contours. But with the volume of traffic expected to pass this way, it was clear that significant work had gone in to making a route that was both relatively safe and resilient against many hundreds of thousands of footsteps. We certainly had plenty of people to say hello to on this fine bright sunny morning. A father-son pair in particular, Digby and Saam, were on their final day of their own anti-clockwise nine day Tour of Monte Rosa. As an avid trail-runner himself, Digby had actually completed the Ultra Trail du Mont Blanc and would soon be volunteering at the 2019 'Ultra Tour Monte Rosa'.

"You mean they run around this one as well?" I asked in disbelief. "It's a lot more climbing than the Mont Blanc loop!"

Digby and Saam were a lot of fun to talk to and it was inspiring to see a father-son duo making memories in this incredible place. They also told us to watch out for a path closure ahead. A section of trail beyond the Europahütte had been cordoned off due to a path collapse and they'd had to come all the way down to the valley floor between Herbriggen and Randa. With tired legs, a big down-and-up wasn't something we were too pleased about, but like most things it was something we'd worry about later. For now, not only was the Matterhorn clearly in sight, towering above the southern horizon, but the view across to the western side of the Mattertal was equally stunning.

You might think that after almost a week in and around the Mattertal (since crossing the Augstbordpass on our third day), we'd have grown familiar with this one valley. But the truth was that every step we took offered us a slightly different perspective. During our traverse of the western flank heading towards Zermatt, we'd marvelled across at the Mischabel Wall but not been able to see fully what was directly above us. Now we got the chance to switch the views, staring up at the giant triangle of the Weisshorn (4506 metres), the fifth highest peak in the Alps and considered by many to be the most beautiful due to its symmetrical pyramid shape and pure white slopes (incidentally, the Matterhorn is the sixth highest peak, just 28 metres lower, though both of these rankings depend on how you classify peaks – a technical world I have no intention of dipping into. That said, some might argue they're the eleventh and twelfth highest respectively).

With more than 3000 vertical metres visible from the valley floor up to the summit of the Weisshorn, yet again we could see every facet of Alpine wilderness arrayed in front of us. From the human concrete and tarmac fading into dense pine forests, then up through the thinning trees onto the pale green pastures, then further still into the grey scree beneath ice falls, vertical cliffs and, eventually, brilliant white snow beneath fluffy clouds and blue sky. It's not something you really can get tired of.

With just one long pause along the way, it took us four hours to get from Täsch to the 'Charles Kuonen Hängenbrücke am Europaweg', to give it its full name. Built in 2017, this 494-metre-long monument of high tensile cable and mesh walkway hangs at 2080 metres altitude, with a drop of almost 100 vertical metres down into the gorge it spans. It looks like more though, especially when you're on it and because of the way the bottom of gorge slopes away so steeply downhill.

On the one hand, this is no 'Indiana Jones and the Temple of Doom' style flimsy rope bridge. It's a solid steel construction that's obviously been built with many tens of thousands of visitors in mind. Although a sign at the end of the bridge advises a maximum capacity, there's nobody around counting and I'm sure there's a significant buffer built in. On the other hand, when you step out onto it, it's surprising just how bouncy it is. With the combined motion of a couple of hundred feet all walking out of step with each other, the overall effect is of trying to walk around in a mildly turbulent and see-through airplane. It's also surprisingly narrow, just 65 centimetres wide, with a mesh walkway that is easy to look down through and high sides of criss-crossed wire that came up to our shoulders. Those sides angle outwards slightly, but with our large packs on we still had to ease gently past some of the bigger adults coming the other way. It was also hard work. The bridge dips significantly towards the middle, making the second half of the crossing noticeably uphill.

For people who don't like heights I can see it being a challenge. Thankfully, for us, it was mostly just a really exciting piece of engineering and a nice change from dust and stones. We even saw some dogs going across quite happily, although special mention to the guy we saw carrying the enormous Labrador retriever over his shoulder.

We paused for lunch on the northern end of the bridge, scanning the sky for signs of the forecast storm and chatting to a nearby Dutch family. The father, Girard, was a particle physicist by day and an international adventure racer at the weekends, so had a lot of fun stories to share.

Unfortunately, the weather warning signs were only getting more obvious and nobody wanted to linger for too long. The Matterhorn and other peaks at the valley head had now disappeared behind almost black clouds and there was a strongly gusting wind moving the hot, humid air that surrounded us. Even since we'd first crossed the bridge there were noticeably less people around and we began to feel like we should probably get going again as well.

Having been warned of the path closure and bearing in mind the impending weather, rather than head uphill for another 200 metres to the Europahütte, we decided to go straight down to Randa from the bridge and look for somewhere in the valley to stay. It was a 600 metre descent, still very busy with day trippers heading down, but it took us less than half an hour thanks to the motivation of the ever-darkening sky and our determination to start marching along the valley.

We did get slightly delayed on the outskirts of Randa, when Esther waved innocently at an elderly couple on a balcony and we ended up being invited in. It was completely impractical in terms of our own plans for the day, but they seemed so happy to be chatting that it was hard to say no when they came downstairs and started beckoning us inside. They didn't speak English, but thankfully Esther's German had come back quickly during the past 4 days. Over the next half an hour we managed to communicate fairly well, mostly about mountain weather, the many 4000 metre summits they'd climbed together over the years, the best iPad apps for tracking storms and that the Weisshornhütte (which we hadn't visited) was the "beste hütte im Schweiss". Although it raised our chances of being caught in the storm, for us it was lovely to see an older couple that'd spent a lifetime adventuring together.

Speaking of storms, the drizzle began just as we approached Herbriggen following a sore-footed dash along the same riverside path we'd walked four days earlier. Reaching a bridge where the walking route would have us crossing away from the main road and back into the forest, without speaking to each other and with no forward planning whatsoever, we silently veered the other way and approached the road instead. Later on, we'd both claim we were following the other, but eventually agreed it was a moment of inspiration that happened to hit us both at the same instant.

Now, we'd never hitchhiked before. Not once. Not even as students. It was always something that we'd been told was dangerous and frowned upon. Yet as we entered Herbriggen we began discussing the possibility for the first time in our lives. Later in the summer we'd speak to an elderly French lady who'd tell us that hitchhiking had been much more conventional when she was younger, when not everyone owned a car and public transport wasn't quite as extensive. It wasn't a 'thing' that some people did, but simply how people without other means got around. She lamented that societal fear now makes it seem like such a high risk activity, as though every car driver is an axe murderer just waiting for their chance.

That said, at least in France we'd become aware of organised schemes for car-sharing, or 'covoiturage', and websites such as BlaBlaCar which allow people undertaking long journeys to advertise for passengers to share the cost with, using an application-style process and a driver/passenger review system to build trust.

Which is not to say that common sense doesn't still come into it, but we'd been hiking for six hours so far today and "not walking any more" was a thought very much at the forefront of our minds. At the same time, with the current light drizzle, a much heavier storm obviously imminent and a day of rain forecast for tomorrow, the words 'rest day' were also growing increasingly loud inside our rain-spattered heads. What had started out as a gentle suggestion while feeling fresh that morning had rapidly morphed into a firm objective under the insistent nagging of our throbbing feet. "We need to get somewhere where we can get a room and take a day off" we agreed.

Spotting a car reversing out of a space on the outskirts of Herbriggen, an impulse inside me rose up and I started urgently prompting Esther to run and stop him. "Ask if he might take us a little further along the valley" I called after her, convinced that her smiling face would be far more effective than my own. "or even Saas-Fee" I added, the most obvious large place to take a rest day.

Less than ten seconds later, we had a ride. Our first ever attempt at hitchhiking (if stopping someone in a car park counts?) had just turned out perfectly with Johan, a Belgian national turned Swiss Mountain guide, driving us happily along the valley. He told us that he'd spent the morning taking a client to the summit of Pollux (4092 metres), setting off at 4 a.m., and had just woken up from a much-needed doze before driving home. He then went on to tell us how he's always loved the mountains, visiting as often as he could until one day he decided to just go for it, becoming certified as a mountain guide and moving to Switzerland to try and make a living from his passion (on account of Belgium being partly famous for its total lack of mountains).

Johan was an incredibly inspiring man and we soon began quizzing him about glacier crossings, how to gain confidence and how hard the summits really were to climb etc.

"With a guide the first few times and a little training, if you're fit you can do a lot up there" he told us. "For example, apart from a short climb at the top, Pollux was mostly a long walk across snow today. So if you get confident at snow and ice walking and learn some safety techniques, you could go higher as well."

It was an exciting image and instantly had us both daydreaming of maybe summiting some of those white peaks ourselves one day. Johan spoke so calmly and encouragingly that I'm sure one day we'll try. We also asked him about the Theodulgletscher crossing we'd turned away from, and the Arolla glacier crossing that the Tour of the Matterhorn required to come back from Italy into Switzerland. "Give me a call and we'll arrange something" he told us, passing us his card.

We came to a stop after just twenty minutes and already I felt reluctant to climb out of the softness of the car seat. "This is a good hitching point" Johan told us as he pulled into a bus stop on the edge of Stalden, right at the point where the road splits towards either Zermatt or Saas-Fee. "I've used it myself before. Good luck."

Enthused by our 100% success rate so far, I confidently encouraged Esther to stand by the roadside with a barely legible 'Saas-Fee' sign hastily scribbled using the blunt pencil we had with us. A few people visibly slowed down, although they all mostly pointed up towards Zermatt before taking the turning we didn't want. As motorhomers ourselves, we were optimistic that one of the many passing motorhomes would stop for us, but it wasn't to be this time around. We could understand why. Motorhomes are big but they're cumbersome to drive and not all have extra passenger seats in them.

Since this was our first proper hitching experience, I didn't really know what to expect in terms of success rates, so I wasn't sure if we were doing something wrong when we were still stood by the roadside after half an hour. We weren't stranded because there was a bus stop, although when the next bus arrived and we asked the driver the cost to Saas-Fee, we decided to give hitching at least another hour of effort. Thirty francs each, about £23, for a half hour bus ride felt steep even by Swiss standards.

    Thankfully, just ten more minutes later a car finally pulled over, a Belgian plated estate car with a single lady driver, two small children in the back seat and a mountain of suitcases. Smiling and telling us she was also going to Saas-Fee, Anneke jumped out and rearranged her entire car's worth of luggage simply to fit us and our rucksacks in with them all. Not only that, but it also turned out that she was right at the end of an eventful ten hour drive from Lake Como as part of a whistle-stop week long holiday through Italy and Switzerland. She really didn't have to stop for us, but she did, even after all of those empty SUV-style cars had waved and shrugged as they passed us by. We were bowled over that this obviously tired single mother, with a car full of stuff and two kids, had been the one to pull over and offer us a ride at the end of the day.

    We reached Saas-Fee thirty minutes later, a place we had visited just once before. We couldn't remember very much about it, apart from the fact that we'd caught a cable car/funicular railway combination to a ski station at 3500 metres where we'd been able to wander around a cave system carved inside a glacier complete with fluorescent snowmen and slides. It had been really quite awesome. Maybe we'd get to do that again, we wondered, on our now-almost-certain rest day.

    Like Zermatt, Saas-Fee is a car-free zone, with an enormous multistorey car parking complex on the edge of the village, which is where we said goodbye to Anneke and her kids. A brief scan of Booking.com gave us the names of the least expensive hotels that had rooms available online so we set off to find two of them and ask what the best price they could offer us as walk-ins was. With 20 millimetres of rain now forecast for the next day, my heart was now totally set on a two night booking and a day off despite the minimum 100 francs per night price tag. We'd been hoping for less, but this was Saas-Fee in August. We had to be realistic.

We checked into the Hotel Europa in the end, taking a basic room in their three star annexe with breakfast included, for 110 francs per night. The room was clean, compact and had a shower, but what had really made our minds up was that the Hotel Europa had a spa, with a sauna, steam room and jacuzzi. Now that sounded like the kind of rest day we wanted to have.

As the overnight rain continued to fall outside we both took a long, hot and hugely overdue shower, watching the grime swirling around the plughole and revelling in the warmth and security of knowing that we didn't have a cold evening waiting for us on the other side of the screen, just a soft, warm bed. I also couldn't help noticing, as I caught a sideways glimpse of myself in the bathroom mirror, the first mirror we'd seen in a while, that my body had changed. I'm never going to have the six-pack of a male model. At best, my scars leave me with a two-and-a-half pack in a good light, but the curviest, softest parts of my belly had definitely shrunk. I could almost see muscles. "Esther" I called out excitedly, "I got buff!"

Bodies washed, we unpacked our whiffy camping gear into the wardrobe, handwashed our filthy clothes in the bathroom sink and settled on the bed in just our backup pants. We floated the idea of finding a movie on the TV, but settled in the end for giving each other a much-needed shoulder and back massage while listening to the BBC proms in the background. Mozart's Requiem was a little dark given the circumstances, but it was easy to lose ourselves in the familiar music.

We'd ended up nowhere near where we expected to end up, and in completely different circumstances, but as the sky darkened further and lightning began to flash across the sky, we knew we'd made the right choice. We were also here largely thanks to the kindness of strangers and the peculiar quirks of circumstance that bought those strangers across our paths at just the right moments. As we settled back into our big, plush pillows and turned off the light, we offered up a little thank you to whoever it was that had been watching over us today.

Vital Statistics – Day 9
Start Point: Outskirts of Täsch
End Point: Saas-Fee
Distance Hiked: 13 km
Hiking Time: 6 hours
Ascent: 790 metres
Descent: 900 metres

Nude

After a week of air mattresses and fiddling with zips in the dark whenever we needed to pee, I was surprised that sleep was so hard to come by when confronted with a soft, wide mattress and a fluffy duvet. Perhaps it was the heat in the room which was much warmer than we'd grown accustomed to, even with the window wide open. Whatever it was, by two in the morning we were both wide awake and restless. Instead of lying silently side by side, in the dark and frustrated, we spent the time together choosing photos from our camera and backing up our favourites via the hotel's WiFi connection. It was slightly disappointing to be awake, having envisaged a long, unbroken, deep slumber. But it was still a nice moment and an opportunity to reflect on the many and varied events of the previous nine days.

We did manage to drift off again, eventually, waking up a second time to find a grim daylight seeping through the window and the sound of heavy rain hitting the glass. We rose slowly, still yawning and crunching our eyes against the downpour as we made our way across to the main hotel for our breakfast. We arrived to find ourselves confronted by a colourful and aromatic display of culinary extravagance. After largely rationing our supplies up until this point, apart from a couple of Coop feasts, we'd resolved to remain both sensible and healthy at breakfast. In the end, however, our stomachs overruled our heads on this one.

In case you haven't guessed by now, Esther and I choose to eat a mostly plant-based, whole food diet. It was a change we'd initially made many years earlier, for personal health reasons, although over time the ethical and environmental side of cutting out animal-products had become an increasing part of our commitment long term. By the way, we're aware that our continued use of goose down sleeping bags and jackets clashes with our views on this. All I can say is that we bought the jackets before we made the change and that our attitudes regarding using manufactured items for as long they last, instead of replacing them prematurely, has caused us a lot of soul searching on the issue. In the end, we decided that selling or simply discarding them wasn't the way to go either. When they do eventually wear out, however, we'll be replacing them with synthetic alternatives which are just as good.

Naturally, when we first started to change the way we ate we'd gone through the usual excitement and evangelism that comes with any new lifestyle that gives such rapid and powerful results. Weight loss, an increase in energy, greater clarity of thought. All the things that usually get talked about alongside a mostly plant-based diet had been our experience, so we endeavoured to maintain a high nutrient density in our diets no matter what the circumstances.

When we hiked our *Turn Left At Mont Blanc* adventure, we went to some quite extraordinary lengths to keep our fresh fruit and vegetable intake as high as possible. I can still remember the face of a hotel chef after we asked him to blend up a mixture of green vegetables for us, producing an undeniably healthy but equally undeniably brown sludge that was carried back to us at arm's length.

Three years later and nothing had changed in terms of our food preferences and beliefs about giving our bodies lots of greens, beans, seeds, nuts and other vegetables to maximise our vitality. Nor had anything changed regarding our personal commitment not to consume animal products. If anything that was stronger based on our experiences and continued research and evidence backing up the health and environmental benefits of doing so. The only thing that had evolved slightly was our willingness to be pragmatic about it in terms of keeping our pack weights down. Carrying cucumbers and watermelons over high passes can be done.

We knew because we'd done it right around Mont Blanc and beyond, but on this adventure we didn't want to add too much pack weight for the sake of fresh tomatoes and jars of sauerkraut.

In practice, as you've maybe also picked up on, this focus on pack weight did mean our food choices on the hills were a little repetitive, which is true whether you eat plant-based or not. For us, overnight oat bran, dried fruit, nuts and lentil pasta with tomato puree were wonderful and sustaining foods, but after nine days the sudden availability of fluffy fresh bread, homemade jam, sweetened muesli and limitless fresh fruit salad went a little to our heads.

Puffing and sweating back up the stairs to our room in the simple annexe building, we decided we probably wouldn't need to eat again for the rest of the day and stretched out on the bed in a post-breakfast food coma which lasted until early afternoon.

We knew that a small part of our room charge had been to cover the local tourist tax, because we'd been given a pass which gave us access to most of the cable cars around Saas-Fee and several local bus routes. Despite the continued heavy showers and occasional sound of thunder, Esther was still determined to make use of hers (for the sake of it) while I was happy to continue feeling bloated in Saas-Fee. We still decided to take a short walk across town together though, holding hands and browsing in shop windows as we meandered through the almost deserted streets during a rare break in the rain.

Saas-Fee, at 1800 metres, is very much the main village in the Saastal. Surrounded by thirteen different 4000 metre summits, it is known primarily as a ski resort with the glaciers on the side of the Dom (4545 metres, the third highest mountain in the Alps) and Allalinhorn (4027 metres, the so called 'easiest 4000' to climb) providing year-round winter sport opportunities. There are over twenty different ski lifts in the area plus the funicular railway up to 3500 metres that we remembered taking on our previous visit, giving access to over 100 km of ski runs and 350 km of hiking trails. Also, thanks to Wikipedia I can tell you it's where Wham's music video for 'Last Christmas' was filmed in 1984.

Sadly, due to the weather we couldn't see a single mountain peak or Christmas jumper as we strolled around. After quarter of an hour the rain started again, so I headed back to our room while Esther continued towards the main lift station on the other side of town. Half an hour later, she was back and knocking on the door. Evidently, the people who run the cable cars are smart enough to know when not to bother switching them on.

The spa we'd been so excited about was due to be switched on at three in the afternoon, and almost to the minute we donned our smartest pants and headed down to check it out. It was a surprisingly cavernous space underneath the main hotel, with a central jacuzzi and two separate sauna / steam room areas, one on either side. Plunging straight into the jacuzzi, we switched on the bubbles and began to feel the ingrained aches of nine days fizzing out of us. Having arrived so promptly, it was almost totally empty with only one other couple and a single lady to be seen moving between the various areas. With such a large area space overall, we could imagine that in the dead of a winter's night in the middle of ski season, this could become very crowded and we were grateful we had so much peace around us.

After the bubbles we tried the sauna and steam rooms, finding only one of the two sides was switched on. We steamed first then ducked into the sauna next door where I could just make out a single figure in the distant gloom. It was only when she stood up to leave that I realised she was completely starkers. I hardly knew where to look. Actually, correct that. I did know where to look but decided it might get me told off if I did, so I looked at my feet instead.

Nude saunas in Germany are very much the thing, I've heard, and we were very much in German speaking Switzerland so perhaps this was just the way things were here in Saas-Fee? Did that mean we had to get our bits out as well? Were we committing a major spa faux-pas by covering up?

We weren't sure, although the lady in the buff didn't seem phased by the fact that we had our underwear on, so we carried on as usual for another couple of rounds, alternating our spells in the heat and bubbles with a wonderful relax in one of the beds provided in a dedicated quiet area upstairs. It was only on our third visit back to the sauna that we noticed the small lettering on the door separating the sauna / steam area from the rest of the spa. It said "Nackter Bereich", the nudie-area. But they'd only switched this one side on. Now, I don't expect my love-spuds are ever going to win any awards for aesthetic beauty, but I've always been quite attached to them and I've shared a lot of changing rooms in my time. When in Rome and all that.

"I'm up for it if you are" I said to Esther.

"I don't mind" said Esther.

So we whipped off our undies, hung them on an empty peg and strolled into the sauna in the raw. Fortunately, or unfortunately depending on your perspective, the naked lady was no longer there, replaced by a lone naked man from the couple we'd seen earlier on. Tentatively easing our bare bottoms on to the scorching wood, we soaked up the heat and sweated away quite happily and wondered what all the fuss was about. Perhaps it would be more awkward if it was crammed bum-cheek-to-bum-cheek with strangers, but with ample space around us, apart from the plank marks burned across our buttocks it was a total non-event. I'm sure if I ever find myself marooned at the Playboy mansion, I'd give it another try.

Eventually, after an hour and a half in the spa, I'd had enough. Esther stayed a little longer while I went back up to the room for some unsatisfying channel-hopping and to let the wrinkles ease out of my well-soaked and definitely clean skin. We don't have a television in our motorhome so we hardly ever see anything current on TV. Pretty much every hit series and 'binge-worthy' talking point, from Peaky Blinders to Downton Abbey, is a total mystery to us. Yet every time I get the chance for a quick channel hop I come away thinking I'm not really missing out. I like a good movie now and then, but multi-season series seem to be much more fashionable in recent years, with Amazon Prime and Netflix gradually taking over the cinematic world.

Esther got back around seven, so we took another stroll through town to enjoy the fresh evening air. It was still drizzling slightly but after the heat of the spa it was nice to feel the coolness on our faces before heading back to repack our bags and think about our route for the next day.

Vital Statistics – Day 10
Start Point: Saas-Fee
End Point: Still Saas-Fee
Distance Hiked: Nope
Hiking Time: Also nope
Ascent: Staircase up (slowly)
Descent: Staircase down (also slowly)

Lost In Fog

We enjoyed another decadent breakfast experience before checking out of the Hotel Europa. The forecast we'd seen had predicted a sunny start to the day but although the rain had stopped, a persistent and thick covering of dark grey clouds suggested it could go either way at any moment.

Our plan for the day was to resume our hike around the Monte Rosa massif, adding in a slight detour to include a nearby 3000 metre col that we'd noticed on our map. According to signs in the centre of the village, the most direct route to the border crossing on the Monte Moro Pass would involve about six hours of hiking from Saas-Fee and, in theory, the addition of the interestingly named Jatzilicku (3081 metres) for no other reason than it was so high would increase that by some margin. However, by making use of the Saas-Pass that had come with our hotel stay, it was possible for us to catch a bus and a couple of chairlifts across the valley, right up to 2300 metres and so saving several hours and almost 700 metres of climbing at no extra cost!

We caught the bus just before ten and a little over an hour later were stepping off of our second chairlift alongside Bergrestaurant Heidbodme. With each stage of our journey over from Saas-Fee I'd been aware of a gnawing reluctance in my gut at the thought of getting going again. From Zinal it had simply been exciting, but after nine days on tour followed by a day of near total relaxation, there was a definite residual heaviness in my legs and a deep attachment to the seat I was sitting in. In much the same way that a bed is never comfier than just before you get out of it, the closer we crept back towards wilderness and independence, the more I could feel myself savouring the comforts of civilisation, the same comforts that had looked so decadent and unnecessary from the mountain tops just a few days earlier. Even riding up in the exposed chairlift, each of us sat next to our packs in a different seat and waving across the void in between, I was willing the enormous, whirring cable to slow down just a little and prolong the moment before hiking began again.

It wasn't that I didn't want to hike. I still had the adventurous urge to see just beyond the next mountain or bend in the river, but it was being tempered by my very human attachment to soft, cuddly pillows and on-tap hot water. Also, it hadn't exactly escaped my notice that our packs were re-laden with several days of supplies and our water was topped to the brim, bringing them straight back up to 'full-food' weight.

On the plus side, after nine days of walking with a heavy bandage chafing at my skin, today was the first day I was going to risk walking without additional knee support. I was grateful that whatever I'd been doing seemed to have worked and I definitely wasn't sad to see the back of the now-off-white bandage either. The rest day had even let some of the rubbing sores heal slightly and the thought of the extra freedom to move and not want to scratch all the time was marvellous.

We set off into a forecast-defying dense mist, with the deep bowl of the Furggtälli valley just visible on our right beneath the mirk and a winding, muddy trail stretching into the gloom ahead of us. Our immediate destination was the Antronapass at 2838 metres, at the head of the Furggtälli and right on the boundary between Switzerland and Italy. We could guess, from the shape of what little land we could see and the length of the valley below us that it was likely to be a long slow climb to the Antronapass, and so it proved to be.

While online pictures and descriptions marvel at the magnificent panoramic views available from Bergrestaurant Heidbodme and the valley we were climbing, waxing lyrical about the majestic massif of Monte Rosa, our own personal experience was mostly limited to damp grass and muddy footprints. Even the pyramid-like Stellihorn (3436 metres) which we knew to be towering over the opposite side of the valley was completely invisible to us as we marched ever onwards.

It took a good two and a half hours of plodding, mostly along flat or very gently angled paths, before we began to make our way across bare rocks and the final remnants of snow clinging on at the valley head. With little light breaking through, it was a bitingly cold day with an unwelcome wind blustering from behind us that cast an uninviting mood over the mountainside as we passed through it. It was much more like a cold November day in the Lake District than an Alpine summer, except without the reassuring promise of a comfortable and warm pub just a short descent away.

We paused for lunch at the top of the Antronapass, sheltering from the now icy wind within a small stone shelter. We did consider firing up our stove to make a warm drink, but it was too cold to sit still for very long and we knew the best way to keep warm was to keep moving upwards.

We were now in a world of bare rock, straddling a national border with thin clouds all around us and occasional thicker patches fleeting quickly just above our heads. On the Italian side, at least, there were occasional breaks in the mist which showed us crest after crest of high ridgelines folding away into the distance and a large lake, which we guessed might be Lake Orta, but they were short-lived treats in an otherwise grey world. Mostly the bleakness of the scene made the notion of even having countries and national borders up here in the wilderness seem ridiculous. Certainly, administrative boundaries are necessary to manage resources and people within varying regions, but the more we'd travelled over the years, the less

I could understand the national fervour and attachment people feel to the place they happened to be born. As I said before, we're all trapped on the same lump of rock and so all, ultimately, have the same interests.

Drawing our jackets tight around us, we set off upwards across a wind-whipped ridgeline. Alternating between an easy to follow track in the stones and more challenging tumbles of boulders, the red-and-white markers led us south along the national boundary as the visibility continued to alternate between poor and non-existent. At times, we could at least see the ground falling away either side of us, but sometimes we could hardly see each other. The trail was also steep, although rarely very technically difficult until right at the top. Here, a series of narrow ledges over vertical drops were supplemented with ropes to provide a little extra security. On the one hand, it was not a very nice day to be hiking so high and the fact we hadn't seen much of the spectacular views we might have seen was disappointing. Yet on the other hand, it was really quite sensational to be in this barren, rocky playground, perched so high on bare stones with clouds racing around us.

Rounding a final bend in a ledge, we arrived unceremoniously at the 3081 metre Jatzilicku, though we didn't linger for more than a minute because of the cold. The descent that followed into the much broader Oftental valley was via easy to follow paths that gradually weaved their way back towards the Mattmark reservoir and the main Tour of Monte Rosa. Windows in the clouds continued to reward us from time to time with views of what may have been the summit of Monte Rosa itself, although it was hard to be certain exactly which summit had popped out to say hello for a moment. A couple of passing ibex were the first other living beings we'd seen since stepping off the chairlift. Returning to such an isolated state again had added further to the sense of wilderness, even though we knew we were just hours from the industrial scale business of tourism in the region.

Ninety minutes later and we were traversing through a final boulder field towards the head of the Saastal, just 400 metres beneath the Monte Moro Pass. However, it was also half past five and we'd been out in the cold for almost seven hours now, with little food and moving for most of that time to keep warm. We were also at 2500 metres altitude and while there were plenty of green spaces nearby to pitch our tent on, if we attempted the pass this evening then there was no such guarantee we'd find a good place higher up. From what little we could see, only a short distance above us the terrain was mostly solid rock.

We decided to stop for the day, finding a little shelter from the wind behind a truck-sized boulder and doing our best to prepare dinner. Wearing all the clothes we had, we weren't yet straying away from our trusted lentil pasta and tomato puree feast, and it almost stayed warm while we ate it too. Then we snuggled up in the lee of the boulder, spread a sleeping bag over our legs and waited for it to feel late enough to put up a tent. Perhaps others would have just put the tent up straight away? I mean, we'd only seen one couple come down from the Monte Moro Pass in all the time we'd been cooking and eating. Yet we didn't. It wasn't how we liked to do things, especially so close to a busy route.

Half an hour later I began shivering uncontrollably. Sitting still in temperatures that can't have been much above zero had allowed my core temperature to fall too far.

"I-i-i th-think I n-n-need to p-p-put up th-the t-t-tent n-now" I stuttered. Principles be damned, I needed shelter soon otherwise I was going to get hypothermia. Alternating between unrolling canvas, threading poles with shaking hands, pegging out and simultaneously doing star jumps and sprinting on the spot, we just about managed to get our sleeping quarters ready for the night. I ran a few laps of the boulder and dived inside, sliding deep into my sleeping bag fully dressed and waiting for the warmth of my exercises to infuse the fluff around me.

The wind continued to howl outside and whip at our tent material as the sky darkened and we attempted a short game of cards, to occupy our minds from the cold, but with such a challenging night in prospect ahead of us, I mostly just wanted to try and get to sleep before it got too uncomfortable. Not that we were unhappy, just tired and ready for the sun to come back the next morning. It had been an exciting challenge to hike the trail we had in such conditions, but we both hoped the sunshine would be back by morning.

Vital Statistics – Day 11
Start Point: Saas-Fee
End Point: Tälliboden
Distance Hiked: 12 km
Hiking Time: 7 hours
Ascent: 880 metres
Descent: 700 metres

Benvenuto in Italia

With ice on our tent and the silhouette of an enormous Ibex on the rocks above us, the day began in fine Alpine style when we poked our noses out into the crisp morning air . It had indeed been a very cold and windy night, and remained a very cold and windy morning, so we did our best to pack our things away inside the tent before fully emerging into the daylight. Probably we would have lingered in the tent for longer, but even though it wasn't even seven o'clock yet we could already hear the unmistakable tick-click-tick of trekking poles on the trail a couple of hundred metres away from our tent.

Despite the cold, the sky was clear and blue when we first emerged. Looking back north along the Saastal, we were treated to a hint of the view that had been hidden from us the previous day. Green and grey crags swept up the valley sides towards lofty, darker ridges topped with overhanging snow pockets, while the tongue of the Scwarzberggletscher was just visible on a nearby slope. Unfortunately, we were on the wrong side of the valley to get any of the direct morning sun, which was teasing us from about 400 metres away.

"Let's just carry our stuff over to the sun for breakfast" I suggested. "I'll even carry the tent over so that it thaws and dries while we eat". Yet no sooner had we carried our tent and bags across the rough hillside towards that tantalising patch of warmth, than a band of freezing fog materialised and blocked the sun immediately. We'd had less than 60 seconds of warmth and were now sat eating our cold overnight oat bran with fingers that could hardly hold our sporks.

By now there was a sparse but steady stream of hikers heading up towards the Monte Moro Pass, so we joined them on the obviously man-made but still challenging ascent towards a distant statue on the slopes above us. We soon rose above the fog again and the extent of our view back along the Saastal grew as we climbed, stretching far beyond the Mattmark reservoir and even the Saastal itself towards the hard to discern but still enormous mass of the Bernese Alps.

Given how early it was and how high we were, it was odd to find so many people coming down the path towards us, some of them carrying mountain bikes. About halfway up, a father with two children in tow stopped us with the exclamation "Rab coats, too easy. You must be British". His name was Mark, a very friendly guy who told us he was working daddy-day care from a nearby house while his wife was away working in Vienna. Wanting to give the kids an adventure, they'd hiked up and over the pass the previous day, stayed in a hotel in Macugnaga (our destination) and were now on their way home again. We got the impression that Mark was excited to be speaking his native tongue with adults, possibly for the first time in a while, and were it not for the still biting cold we got the feeling he might even have come with us back to Italy.

A short stretch of snow marked the final approach to the golden Maria at the top of the pass, crowded all around with people flowing up from the Italian cable car station perhaps fifty metres below the top. So that explained the volume of traffic coming the other way.

We'd later learn (from an information board in Macugnaga) that this was the "Madonna delle Nevi", the Madonna of the snow, and had been guarding this border crossing since she was inaugurated in 1966. We'd done it. We were in Italy at 2853 metres. And right there, across a huge expanse of Alpine air, was the Alp's second highest mountain, Monte Rosa with its tallest spire, the Dufourspitze, towering above an east-facing expanse of rock, snow and ice.

The descent towards the cable car station was over large slabs of sharply-angled, smooth rock, so metal steps with handy rope lines had been hammered into the stone for the many visitors to the Madonna. Looking down, it was like a constant precession moving slowly uphill, passing from step to step and swelling the already large numbers clustered around the statue. "Have we arrived on a holy pilgrimage day?" we wondered. If so, many of them were showing extreme devotion by standing around in shorts and t-shirts in what can't have been more than a few degrees minus windchill. More likely, it was toasty warm deep in the valley and they'd not thought to bring any extra clothes. We knew, because we'd done it ourselves.

More than a decade earlier, we'd Interrailed in Scandinavia with a couple of friends. On a fine August morning we'd decided to go walking and so hopped on a bus up into the hills. Wearing just shorts and light jackets over t-shirts, we'd sweated our way to the bus station but arrived on a Norwegian fell to find little more than a freezing cloud covering a scrubby landscape. The bus driver smirked at us as we stepped off the bus, so myself and our friend Phil instantly decided we weren't going to give him the satisfaction of getting back inside the comfy warm tube of salvation he was driving. Passing our jackets to Esther and Phil's partner, Sarah, we stood about shivering in shorts and t-shirts while he watched us in silence, with the door open, waiting for us to change our minds. He drove off ten minutes later, which is when we began the cold and painful business of walking back down the road, the same way we'd just come up. What can I say? There's nothing like a twenty year old ego for making totally logical and safe decisions! I like to think my older, almost-forty year old self wouldn't have even got off the bus. Then again, I'm not sure?

Jogging around the traffic moving towards the Madonna, we soon reached and passed the cable car station, setting a brisk pace again to keep warm. The terrain around us was all cold stone and sharp rocks, so with the nasty wind that continued to push us around this wasn't exactly a place to find comfort or rest, at least outside anyway. There was a refuge nearby, but we were keen to crack on because we knew we had a very long descent ahead of us.

Macugnaga (which is pronounced something like Mackoo-nyarga, as we discovered after many blank stares), was more than 1500 vertical metres below us, metres which felt both steep and relentless as we moved through the high-level scree fields and down towards slightly greener pastures. At some point, the clouds began to break so that by the time our aching knees carried us into forested slopes above Macugnaga we were sweating hard beneath a roasting sun.

As we'd lost height the summit of Monte Rosa seemed to have grown even more imposing while the Valle Anzasca, in which Macugnaga sits, had opened up to reveal a semi-circle of towering grey cliff faces arrayed around its head. Dark green pine forests lined the hillside all around us while the still bright green pastures we could see across the valley gave a lush, vibrant feeling to the day. It seemed we had woken up in winter but had walked our way right back into high summer.

Macugnaga seemed a pleasant town, still very much in the full swing of visitor season as we approached. Passing a 13th century church on the outskirts, we meandered into the main square in search of a grocery store to get something fresh to eat for lunch. We still had plenty of dry food, but with the sun beating down hard and a pharmacy sign declaring that it was 27°C, the idea of hot pasta or more stodgy oat bran was much less appetising than the idea of a juicy nectarine and some watermelon, which is ultimately what we bought.

It was now early afternoon, so we found a shaded spot just off the main square to eat our fruit and watch the world go by. After a while, Esther lay down in the shade of a police station office and fell fast asleep, while I visited the tourist office to see if they had any helpful information regarding our onward route.

Our Tour of Monte Rosa leaflet and map showed us that for the next few days we'd basically be climbing in and out of a series of deep valleys, with long climbs and equally long descents either side of the high passes. Our intention, therefore, was to try and camp in the high altitude sections. However, before we did so I wanted to try and verify what the situation was regarding wild camping in the region. Like Switzerland, Italy formally declares that wild camping is not permitted. However, while that is an excellent idea in, for example, the city of Rome, the question was whether it was fully applicable here? I'd once read that bivouacking was tolerated above 2500 metres in Italy and I wanted to find out if that was true.

The tourist office staff were overwhelmingly friendly, providing me with a more detailed map of the immediate area and reassuring me that for a single night up in the mountains there was unlikely to be any problem sleeping in a tent. As long as we were respectful of buildings and pastureland, nobody would mind. However, they also told me that there was no need to camp above Macugnaga since there happened to an almost brand new bivacco with space for 11 people directly on our route.

We'd heard about bivaccos a couple of times before, hearing them described as small unmanned refuges available for use on a first-come-first-serve basis. A small number, we'd been told, are the size of the manned mountain refuges, but most are much, much smaller, often with space for only single figures. Many of these smaller ones were paid for by endowments made by families many years ago, while others, such as this new one above Macugnaga, was funded by the council. There's no real standard for bivaccos, just that they tend to be in wild places and are intended to provide shelter for people passing through.

Well, it was certainly an enticing prospect, especially after the bitterly cold night we'd just experienced. All we had to do, according to the tourist-office was hike another 800 metres uphill to Bivacco Lanti.

We set out at four o'clock, hoping the heat of the day would have faded slightly. It hadn't, but if we didn't get going soon we'd have no chance of reaching the bivacco before dark. The signposted Tour of Monte Rosa trail out of Macugnaga was closed due to a bridge collapse, so we started out of town along the main road for twenty minutes before picking our way through a small cluster of houses in search of the 'TMR' trail markers.

The route was fairly flat at first, heading past a bustling café and a lakeside picnic area still full of happy families waving ice creams and playing badminton in the afternoon heat. A wide and well-made track came next, climbing gently into an area of loosely forested hillside as we began making our way up the Valle Quarazza towards tomorrow's pass, the Colle del Turlo (2738 metres). As we progressed the sights and sounds of happy holiday makers faded away and we soon became lost once again in the calm of nature, interrupted only occasionally by the decaying remains of the now-abandoned industrial gold mining activities in the area.

According to the information board, evidence of mining activity in the region could be traced back to Celtic and Roman times, however, it wasn't until the 1900's that the process became large scale. It continued until the 1950s, when falling demand for the local gold-bearing ore made it uneconomical to carry on. That's when the villages, cable ways and processing plants constructed over the previous decades were all left to fall back into nature, leaving an eerie quiet where once there was a hive of activity. In the 1980s, parts of the site were sealed in a concrete 'sarcophagus' due to the high levels of arsenic in the ore in addition to the cyanide and mercury that had been used in processing.

Fairly soon we began to emerge into more open spaces. We hadn't climbed far yet, only to about 1600 metres, but we could clearly see the rounded valley head immediately in front of us, including the notch that we guessed we were ultimately heading towards. It was a landscape very different to the ones we'd been surrounded by for the past week and a half, with far more trees, bushes and long grasses that were more reminiscent of the opening scenes of Jurassic Park than the sometimes forbiddingly bare scree and rock falls we'd seen so much of. Everywhere we looked around the valley head were waterfalls of all shapes and sizes, gushing down onto the plateau we had reached before flowing together down the valley.

A series of steep switchbacks through dense undergrowth carried us up the eastern edge of the valley as evening began to close in and biting insects appeared to keep us company as we sweated in the now humid heat. The path remained well made, primarily with large rounded stones set into the earth to create a roughly cobbled trail that was rarely steep, which was nice since we could feel ourselves starting to flag at the end of a long day.

We had a quick boost when we bumped into Wim and Wouter, a pair of young Belgian men also hiking the Tour of Monte Rosa (in the other direction) and trying to do the whole thing in 6 days.

"Fuuuuck. We are so fucking tired…." they began, doing the casual swearing thing we've heard a lot from young people who speak excellent English but as a second or third language, so seem to have no fear dropping the F-bomb into polite chit-chat.

"Oh man. It's like so fucking hard." said Wim.

"Fuuuuck. Yes" agreed Wouter. And so it continued. They were fun fucking guys, telling us how they'd ploughed straight fucking out onto the Theodulgletscher on their first fucking day, without any fucking spikes at all.

"Fuck. We were just fucking slipping everywhere. There were these big fucking crevasses that we thought we'd fall down. It was fucking hard. It was fucking awesome."

Eventually the fucking mosquitoes motivated us all to say good fucking luck and we continued into the softening evening light, watching the shadow silhouettes of the mountains gliding up the hillside around us.

A final almost flat traverse carried us the rest of the way to Bivacco Lanti at 2150 metres. What we found was an angular, red-coloured metal shed about six metres long, three metres wide and four metres tall. Through the large window at one end we could see a couple of faces already inside and there were three more hikers arriving at precisely the same time as us. It was seven o'clock, the perfect time to meet the people we'd be sleeping with that evening.

David and Tomasz were in their early twenties and were spending four nights at this bivacco while they did some walking in the nearby area. They'd been here once before and stayed in the old, now disused bivacco next door, a tiny stone hut with only two decrepit bunks in it.

"It was so fucking cold" they told us, continuing the swearing game.

David was an architecture graduate while Tomasz had studied Greek and Latin and now wanted to re-train as a butcher. "I just love meat" he told us later, "and I want to work with my hands."

"I'm a vegetarian" I told him in response, maintaining a completely straight face.

"Really?" he asked.

"Sì" I said, using one of my three Italian words.

"Oh, well I respect that and, erm, well people have to make their own decisions, and…erm….err…."

At that point I started laughing. I really am a vegetarian, but I was only winding him up and he immediately saw the funny side. They were such great guys and we spent much of the evening with them, talking about life, politics in Italy and the UK, buildings, design and their hopes for the future. They were so full of dreams and ambitions and were also clearly excellent friends. I could tell from the way they constantly insulted each other, even using English for their insults so we could understand them.

"You will never have sex with a girl. Not with that crazy guy beard." said Tomasz.

"At least I am man enough to grow a crazy guy beard" responded David. "You are like three foot high. A midget man."

And so the evening passed. Our other three companions were two men and a lady, also Italian, who had lived together at university. They were now spread around Europe for work and had come back together to spend five days trekking in the region, moving from bivacco to bivacco. We didn't speak so much to them but they were just as friendly when we did.

The inside of the bivacco was wonderful, with a dining space at one end and nine bunks at the other, three on either side and three at the end. There were also two extra bunks high above the dining table (so high I had no clue how I'd get into one), and all of the bunks had clean blankets and a pillow each. The whole interior was finished in bare, clean pine and because it was so new you could still smell the wood when you went in. With only seven of us staying the night, there was ample room to spread out our possessions, get changed and move past each other without feeling awkward.

We'd only stayed inside of a single mountain refuge in the past, Rifugio Bonatti in the Italian stretch of the Tour of Mont Blanc. Back then we'd actually argued about whether it was necessary and had felt panicked at the thought of sleeping so close to total strangers, a relic of our health conditions and some bad experiences in our childhood. Yet this time, there was no angst at all, just a happy camaraderie. Possibly this was due to a change in our own attitude, though there was no denying that an intimate little bivacco was a very different experience to a giant bed factory.

Everyone cooked dinner outside, where the air temperature had dropped swiftly now that the sun had set behind the mountains. Esther and I retreated inside to eat, with Esther livening up the evening by spilling boiling pasta on her trousers and staining them a lovely turmeric yellow for the rest of our trip. But the rest of the evening was simply joyfully companionable as we smiled, played cards, laughed and swapped jokes alongside tips for places to stay and nearby routes. It remained warm in the bivacco and the conversation flowed freely in all directions around the table as the sky turned from blue to black outside and the stars emerged.

It all drew to a close at the sensibly early time of ten o'clock, when the trio announced that they were off to bed. They didn't mind if we left the light on and carried on chatting they told us, but we didn't feel the need to and neither did David and Tomasz. By half past ten we were seven 'almost-strangers' happily, safely and comfortably snoozing alongside one another at over 2000 metres in a brand new garden shed.

Vital Statistics – Day 12
Start Point: Tälliboden
End Point: Bivacco Lanti
Distance Hiked: 14 km
Hiking Time: 7 hours
Ascent: 1320 metres
Descent: 1660 metres

How Much Higher?

After an unbroken eight hours of sleep in the comfortable, warm and pleasingly quiet bivacco, we were awake bright and early the next day and eager to make a start on what promised to be another chunky day of hiking. With several hundred metres left to climb to the Colle del Turlo (2738 m), we'd then be descending another vertical mile into Alagna (A-lan-ya) before climbing back up again in search of a place to camp. After the 1500 metre descent into Macugnaga, we knew it was going to be a challenging day physically, so it was ever so slightly frustrating that as half past seven approached, everyone else in the bivacco was still sound asleep. Our packs and our kit were piled loosely alongside everybody else's gear under the bunks and we didn't want to disturb the sleepers, but then again we didn't want to hang about too much long either.

"They must have bladders made of iron" we joked, looking across from the dining table at the stacks of motionless sleeping bags.

"We must be getting old, that's all. Everyone knows you wake up earlier as you get older. And pee more."

Eventually we decided to bite the bullet and just get our stuff, dragging our packs outside to restow our loose kit before slipping the suggested five euros each into the donation box. It would have been a shame to go without saying goodbye, so we were pleased that our bedfellows did emerge just as we were shouldering our packs. It was a happy farewell, with handshakes, hugs and swapped email addresses.

"Good luck with the butchery" I called back to Tomasz as we disappeared round a bend to the sound of him laughing.

"Did you see any one of them wander away to pee?" I said to Esther, smiling. "No, neither did I. Honestly. Iron bladders, I'm telling you we're getting old!"

The route upwards was wide and gradual, following paths more reminiscent of roman roads than hiking tracks. In many places the sides were built up with dry-stone walls and had large flat slabs laid across the top to make a solid foundation that didn't have to dip with the contours of the earth. We thought it must be some sort of recent construction, but would later read that Vittoria Emmanuelle II, King of Italy from 1861 – 1878, had various hunting tracks like this built in certain regions to allow his donkey train to follow with his possessions.

While it was an impressive feat of engineering, we found it hard on our feet to be plodding so monotonously on stone slabs. Towards the very top, as the terrain surrounding the track grew increasingly rocky, it was very much like following a roughly cobbled road. In part, it did detract a little from the sense of wilderness, although it did give us a taste of what it might have been like to travel around the Roman Empire.

It had been a sunny start to the morning, with a lovely mountain sunrise over the eastern ridge of the Valle Quarazza, but a thin cloud had materialised on the Colle del Turlo as we'd approached and remained there as we passed through, masking whatever scenery lay ahead of us until a few hundred metres into our descent.

What we saw as we stepped out beneath the mist was that we were high in a wide hanging valley, terminating in a small mountain lake surrounded by boulders of all shapes and sizes. Beyond the lip of the hanging valley the ground fell away sharply into greener hillsides that transitioned into pine forests very much like the valley around Macugnaga had done. To our right was the Monte Rosa south wall, a feast of snowy summits and glaciers, while to our left we were looking along the contours of the thickly tree-lined Valle della Sesia.

It was another long slog downhill, a very long slog, and one that was further extended by the fact that the town of Alagna was several kilometres further along the valley. Passing several goat farms, it took us two solid hours of knee-busting effort to descend down to the sprawling Rifugio Pastore and the nearby botanic garden at 1575 metres, but from there it was another hour of almost solely tarmac marching to reach Alagna itself. With the effect of the hard donkey tracks and tarmac put together, our feet were complaining louder than ever before as we limped into Alagna at half past twelve. Despite only being lunchtime, we already had almost five hours of walking clocked up for the day.

Alagna is very much a mountain sports town and has been a UNESCO World Heritage site since 2013. According to the lady in the tourist office, Alagna is credited with a crucial role in the development of mountaineering, with the first attempts on Monte Rosa all starting from Alagna. It continues to be a popular climbing base today and the highest building in Europe, the Margherita hut at 4559 metres, is usually reached from here. The pictures on the wall showing the hut certainly looked impressive and there's even a mountain running race up to it! I could almost see the twinkle of a magical mystery detour forming in Esther's head (even though this one was definitely beyond us), so I changed the subject quickly.

Mountains and climbing exploits aside, Alagna itself seemed a nice enough place, with a fine church at the head of the main street surrounded by four-storey buildings styled as 19th century mountain lodgings. Wondering why it was quite so busy, we did a quick check on Esther's phone to discover it was in fact a national holiday, one of thirteen in Italy each year. This one was 'Ferragosto', the day that Roman Catholics celebrate the Assumption of the Virgin

Mary into Heaven, although it's a day that was celebrated long before it took on a religious association. In practical terms, it's a great opportunity for Italians to have a long summer weekend away, which is why the holiday destination of Alagna was completely heaving with people. Quite a shock to the system after our quiet night in a secluded bivacco.

We began to seek out fresh food, exploring the back streets and coming across an elderly lady and a gentleman in a wheelchair staring up a short, but steep, cobbled hill. Despite speaking no Italian, I began making pushing motions in the air and pointing to my chest to communicate that I could help, if they wanted me to. They did, and as I pushed firmly uphill I found the lady's hand resting on my own as she insisted on helping too. Halfway up, the gentleman started going "wheee" and several people coming the other way were laughing. It was a lovely moment and we felt lucky to have arrived when we did. There were no words needed, just a delicate moment of friendly connection.

Shortly afterwards we found our way to a market that was just packing away and acquired some marked-down fresh figs and a cantaloupe melon, which we ate for lunch along with a bread roll and a tin of mixed beans we found in a small supermarket. It was a filling although not especially exciting lunch. Unfortunately, while the two small grocery shops we'd found were well stocked with crisps and chocolate, they didn't have much in the way of our preferred alternatives. This was a bit of a snag for us since we knew that it would be at least three days until we'd reach another decent sized village and we needed some more long term supplies.

Of course, in Italy there's always pasta, so after acquiring a huge bag of fusilli, some very expensive raisins and the only bag of oats in the entire village, we decided we could probably make it work.

We rested for a good couple of hours in the end, mostly tucked away behind a little stall in the centre of town. At one point I wandered off to find a toilet and by the time I came back I discovered Esther fast asleep on the floor, her head propped up on her pack and an elderly couple looking like they were about to see if she was still alive. I almost didn't want to wake her, but we now had a decision to make.

It was mid-afternoon and we'd already spent the best part of five hours walking. We also knew that there was a campsite on the outskirts of Alagna. Stopping for the day, therefore, was an option. Alternatively, we could continue following the 'TMR' signs, climb up into the hills and find a place to wild camp in more secluded circumstances.

We left Alagna at four o'clock, power-marching up an initially very steep and dusty ascent towards the hamlet of Otro, a climb which saw us gain over 500 metres altitude in just 45 minutes. There must have been something in those beans! Our hope was that we wouldn't have to climb too much further before we found a suitable place to stop for the day. However, as we emerged onto the more open hillside, we found ourselves surrounded by houses and farms which prevented us from even thinking about pitching up for the night just yet.

A gradual traverse up the green Valle d'Otro followed, clouds coming and going on the craggy ridge ahead of us as we continually scanned our environment for a place we might sleep. A derelict barn maybe, or simply a copse of trees? But there was nothing suitable.

Two hours after leaving Alagna we were still walking, forcing our way up a narrow and slippery dirt trail hemmed in on all sides by dense bushes and pink flowers. It looked hardly used with plants even growing thickly on the track itself.

"Can this really be the TMR?" we asked each other. Or had we taken a wrong turn? If so, with seven hours of walking in our legs and twilight fast approaching, this was hardly the ideal time. Up, up and up it continued, snaking around and apparently heading towards a dip in the craggy ridge which we hoped was the 2432 metre Passo Foric, the next high milestone on our route.

"Surely we won't have to climb the whole way up there to find a place to camp?" we questioned.

Not that it wasn't beautiful. Even beneath a cloudy sky the pink flowers surrounding us created an attractive frame for the panorama of crags and ridges we were enjoying across the valley, while beneath us the farmhouses and herds of goats we'd passed earlier in the climb were shrinking into toy-like houses.

Eventually we came to the end of the slippery track, emerging onto a slightly flatter but very lumpy area covered in deep grass that made it difficult to leave the path to check for possible tent pitches. It looked okay, but the grass hid a veritable minefield of tufts and holes that could have easily snapped an ankle, which I very nearly did in pursuit of some fresh water.

We found a spot in the end, just a hundred metres or so beneath the top of the climb. It wasn't completely flat, but our batteries certainly were and we simply needed to stop. We'd just climbed 1200 metres out of Alagna with almost 'full-food' on board in just two and a half hours, after already ascending several hundred metres in the morning and descending a vertical mile. Now that was a big day and a big physical achievement for us, but we still had a tent to put up, dinner to make and a sunset to enjoy.

We may have emptied the tank to make it here but it wasn't without reward. From our little shoulder of east-facing earth at almost 2500 metres, we watched the clouds drifting across the horizon shift through a palette of colours as the sun fell away behind us. It was a wild place, just as we'd sought, and it was an undeniably peaceful one.

Vital Statistics – Day 13
Start Point: Bivacco Lanti
End Point: Passo Foric
Distance Hiked: 15 km
Hiking Time: 7 hours
Ascent: 1800 metres
Descent: 1550 metres

Ski Slopes

Another day, another descent. Our Tour of Monte Rosa was certainly shaping up to be a hell of a physical challenge. Somewhat surprisingly, since we were a solid two and a half hours of hiking above Alagna, we were woken before seven o'clock by the sound of hikers shuffling past outside.

"Blimey, how early must they have set off!" we whispered to each other as we enjoyed our still standard morning cuddle moment, "what adventures do you think we'll have today?"

After our late evening power march we weren't in a spectacular hurry to get going, even with the occasional handful of hikers going by, so we took it very slow and steady as we packed up our sleeping gear and waited inside for the morning sun to reach our tent. As we'd slept on an east facing slope, we expected the sun would reach us fairly early, which it did, sending its warming rays through the thin fabric of our tent just before eight.

We lingered around our camping spot for another hour, partly to allow the sun to dry the dampness out of the tent but mostly because we were simply tired. Since leaving Saas-Fee three days ago we'd been freezing cold, roasting hot and had notched up about 4000 vertical metres, three quarters of them in the past forty eight hours. We could feel it in our legs and while we were definitely in much better shape than we had been two weeks earlier, the exertions were noticeably taking their toll. And besides, with a clear blue sky revealing the full extent of the grassy slopes and distant ridges surrounding our lofty position, it was a lovely place to enjoy breakfast. Life was, quite literally, buzzing, fluttering and crawling all around us.

It was an effect we'd been enjoying ever since we'd first set off, that every time the sun came out the mountainside under our feet sprang to life. Grasshoppers just seemed to emerge from nowhere. So many times, over the previous fortnight, we'd been walking along trails chock full of criss-crossing critters all launching into random 'flight' at the sense of our shadows. I guess when your main predators are birds it doesn't matter which way you launch yourself, it's the speed of the take-off that matters.

We did eventually start walking after nine, taking quarter of an hour to slowly shuffle up the final chunk of slope to the Passo Foric at 2432 metres. Once again, we were rewarded with sight of Monte Rosa's south wall, its white frosting framed by bright blue and standing tall above the crags at the head of the Valle della Sesia.

There was a tiny bit of descending next, taking us onto the southern flank of a small valley immediately to the west of Alagna. This was a valley we could have ascended directly out of Alagna the previous evening but had chosen not to, partly because the signposted TMR route went over the Passo Foric but mostly because of the ski-lifts which plied their trade on this particular hillside. Not that they were overwhelmingly obtrusive, but given a choice between undeveloped slopes and ski-lifts, we'll take undeveloped almost every time.

We'd only just left the Passo Foric when we bumped into Ava and Briana, almost literally, as we edged around each other on the steep grassy bank. Talking at a thousand words a minute, often at the same time, these two effervescent Irish ladies told us of their own TMR adventure so far and of the many other varied and fascinating places they'd walked. Sometimes it was hard to follow the thread as they talked over each other but, almost like magic, the net effect was that the fullness of the story just seemed to absorb into our brains. They were "grand", to use their term for anything and everything amazing. A lust for life just radiated out of their bodies and we were very grateful to have met them, even if only for a quarter of an hour chat. They uplifted our energy levels on an otherwise slightly lethargic morning. For them, they told us we'd inspired them by not having killed each other yet. They said they couldn't imagine trying anything like this with their husbands, so we were obviously doing something right.

Fairly soon we were climbing again, this time up some loose stony switchbacks towards our next lofty destination on the Colle d'Olen at 2881 metres, and we were almost there this time when a cloud formed on the top of it. That made it four days in a row that the col we were aiming for had clouded up just as we approached it: Jatzilicku, Monte Moro, Colle del Turlo and now this one!

It seemed the deity in charge of benign but irritating clouds was following us around. I can only assume it was Zeus's fault in his day job as King of the Gods and ruler of clouds, thunder, rain and lightning. What a git! Then again, he'd been quite kind at other times and had so far scheduled heavy rain only when we were inside, so he's still on my Christmas card list.

There were a handful of people both above and below us, but not very many. In fact, incredibly well camouflaged among the boulders and scree a few hundred metres to our left, we could make out almost as many ibex as we could people. There seemed to be an entire family, or perhaps herd is the better term, slowly picking their way through the rubble with large, stocky males and more slightly built females shepherding tiny kids. It was a delightful and heart-warming sight and we stood for many long minutes just to watch them behaving so calmly and naturally.

We reached the Colle d'Olen after two hours of hiking, although we'd definitely not been hurrying this time around. Because of the angle of the col itself, we could no longer see the Monte Rosa massif though we could still see the foothills rolling away in the west as a series of huge grey folds heading towards the distant but still prominent white lump of Mont Blanc on the horizon.

We paused close to the top for a little snack and then paused again when we reached a plateau of crags about halfway down. We'd come down about 400 metres so far, so we 'only' had another 600 metres to descend into the valley bottom at Stafal although once again it was through a landscape modified by ski runs and cable cars. While the hard and bare rubble surfaces of the ski runs made it easy to find the way, it was hard going on already tired knees. Plus, we just didn't want to rush any more. We knew we'd been pushing hard since Saas-Fee and we also knew we didn't really have to, at least not today.

There are few pleasures more satisfying than dozing in the early afternoon sun, snuggled up with a loved one in a wind-sheltered grassy groove and gazing up at one of Europe's highest mountains. And so that's exactly what we did, falling almost instantly asleep in our secluded and warm little spot a hundred metres or so from the main trail. The ground around us was a sea of green peppered with light grey boulders, hiding us almost totally from the rest of the world. Not that anyone was likely to be looking for us up here in the beautiful vastness of the hillside. I mean, I'm not even sure anybody knew which country we were in, never mind which slope. In that moment at least, we were one hundred percent off the grid. Marvellous.

When we did get going again, about an hour later, it was just a short distance down to the cable car station at Gabiet, an explosion of human-focused hustle and bustle since it was lunchtime on the long holiday weekend, and from there down to Stafel via a gorge beneath the cable car line.

By the way, I realise now that I might have given the impression in the past few pages that I'm somehow anti-cable car, but that isn't the case. I know some travel writers and hikers describe them in terms such as "scars on the landscape" etc., but my personal view is that something which enables people who, for whatever reason, aren't able to walk up to these beautiful places to still see and appreciate them is a good thing. Yes, I agree that some places overdevelop and build too many. And yes, I agree that some of the earth-moving done to craft specific gradients on ski slopes is hellishly ugly when the snow melts and the quarry-like bleakness is displayed. But that doesn't mean I want to condemn all cable cars and ski-lifts. Like most things in life, there are no absolutes. It's about compromise, which unfortunately sometimes seems to be a dirty word in a media-driven modern society that thrives on polarising language.

Anyway, back to the hillside and by mid-afternoon we'd arrived in the thronging little hamlet of Stafal at 1800 metres, a place which is mostly made up of car parking spaces close to a cable car station and a very small handful of shops and restaurants. Pausing briefly to buy a little fresh fruit in the tiny 'alimentari', we then found a bench to do our daily weighing up of options.

Our little schematic leaflet showed that we had two route possibilities directly ahead of us. Either we could go up and over the Passo di Rothorn at 2689 metres, or we go a little further north over the Colle di Bettaforca at 2672 metres. Both routes started out following the same gravel road up to the cable car station at Sant'Anna, but from there the path diverged.

We'd been able to have a good look at both options during our descent from Colle d'Olen and had seen that the Passo di Rothorn option was greener, quieter and much less developed, while the Bettaforca option basically continued to follow a gravel road beneath a chairlift all the way to the top. A no-brainer for us you might think. However, while the Passo di Rothorn option was definitely more like our usual choice, Esther had spotted a possibly amazing magical mystery detour if we took the Bettaforca route. Weather permitting, from the Colle di Bettaforca it was possible to hike all the way up to a refuge at 3600 metres, the Rifugio Quintana Sella, right in the shadow of some the highest peaks on the Monte Rosa massif.

Which is basically why we found ourselves spending yet another early evening marching quickly up a long and tiring hill for two hours, except this time we had the added monotony that we were following a wide gravel road with occasional 4x4 vehicles driving down it. For the first hour we could still see the Monte Rosa massif, just about, with an excellent view of the Glacier del Lys carving its way along the valley above Stafal. But for the second hour even that distraction was taken away from us by the fact that the road we were following tracked down the opposite side of what was possibly an ancient moraine, but was now being used for chairlift pylons. It was the closest thing to a gym workout we'd experience during our entire adventure, counting off one pylon after another as the relentless slope with a non-existent view seemed to go on forever.

We made it in the end, after what seemed like a lot longer than two hours, reaching the almost 2700 metre Colle di Bettaforca just after six o'clock. The chairlift had just stopped running for the day and the small wooden restaurant at the top had also closed, so it seemed that we had the entire stony saddle to ourselves. Well, not counting ibex anyway. Unfortunately, there weren't any genuinely flat surfaces to pitch our tent on at the col, unless we put it directly in front of the restaurant, and we didn't feel that would be fair without asking for permission. Instead, we eventually settled on a slightly angled pitch just to the side of the col itself, out of sight of the restaurant and the chairlift station, just in case anyone arrived super early the next morning and took exception to us being up here for the night.

At least the ibex didn't seem to mind. They were everywhere around us. There must have been at least forty of them, many of them huge males with testicles as big as my face and massive horns (on the top of their heads, just to be clear). Quite a lot were clustered outside of the restaurant and didn't seem the least bit nervous of me when I strolled past in my search of a fresh water source.

By the time the tent was up, guyed down with rocks, and we'd refilled our dehydrated bodies with water, the sun was beginning to set. And what a sunset it was. We had a fantastic location to appreciate it from, with an unimpeded view west across the foothills of the Monte Rosa massif and with just enough cloud cover to scatter and reflect the shifting light.

As the sky began to change, the valley beneath us filled with a layer of cloud leaving us in a world of only summit silhouettes and rainbow colours. Wrapped in our fluffy jackets and joined by a small party of ibex who'd assembled about fifty metres away from our tent, it was as though they had also come to watch the fading light show with us and say farewell to another fantastic, though demanding, day.

Vital Statistics – Day 14
Start Point: Passo Foric
End Point: Colle Bettaforca
Distance Hiked: 15 km
Hiking Time: 7 hours
Ascent: 1500 metres
Descent: 1230 metres

The Dude

"Cooooool!" boomed the beanie-hat man with the grey goatee beard, walking towards us with his arms spread wide and grinning like the proverbial Cheshire Cat. "Good to see you. Welcome. Come in. Be comfortable."

We'd risen with the dawn, unsure of what time the restaurant and adjacent chairlift station might spring to life on this summer Saturday morning. We'd even taken the rare step of setting an alarm just to make sure, its relentless chirrups coinciding with the sound of two engines driving by our tent in quick succession.

It wasn't a cold morning but it wasn't exactly warm either as we made our aching way up the short but steep, rubble-constructed slope between our overnight spot and the restaurant and chairlift station. The valleys on either side of the Colle di Bettaforca were filled with white mist, while the sky above us was a soft morning pink. It was daylight, just about, but a dark ridge in the east was still managing to hide the sun.

Passing a cluster of lingering and undoubtedly male ibex, we parked ourselves on a bench just beyond the restaurant where a quad bike, it's engine still audibly cooling in the crisp air, had been parked. We guessed this was one of the engines we'd heard and that the barrel-chested man in a tight t-shirt carrying a stack of chairs, the one with the orange beanie hat and grey goatee beard, had been the guy riding it.

Considering we were a couple of bleary-eyed and slightly smelly hikers huddled against the wall of his restaurant, it was almost overwhelming that he greeted us so fondly, as though we were long lost friends. We accepted his larger than life invitation immediately, stepping out of the morning chill into an aromatic wall of coffee and toast that made our mouths water, and we don't even drink coffee. It was a homely restaurant, the walls decorated with skis, snowboards and magnificent images of people doing amazingly dangerous things on snowy mountains. A television on the wall completed the theme, blasting out Eurosport X-Treme (or something like it) at full volume.

"Awesome" boomed one presenter.

"Gnarly" agreed another, as they watched someone learn the apparent art of 'drifting' a car. I'd never have guessed that skidding cars could be a competitive sport, but it really is. They even have a world championships.

Anyway, we weren't going to complain as the beanie-hat man approached us with a big smile and asked what we'd like in English. Obviously, we didn't look very Italian.

"You wanna drink? Wanna food? We're having a party here today. I'm cooking my famous polenta outside. We'll have live music. It's going to be great."

His enthusiasm was infectious and after bringing us over some scalding hot cups of tea, we asked if we could possibly buy some fruit. We'd seen a stack of oranges behind the bar and wondered if we could buy a couple for breakfast.

"They're really for cocktails. But who cares? I can get my mother to bring some more when she comes later. They're yours."

Danielo, for that was his name, continued bustling around the restaurant, stopping every now and then to ask if we needed anything else. He was so overwhelmingly friendly, immediately rearranging a pile of stuff at the back of the room when we asked if we might leave some things while we visited the Rifugio Quintana Sella.

"Cool. Nice rifugio. Very beautiful. You're gonna love it" he said, his wide smile never leaving his tanned face and kind eyes. This was his restaurant he told us, which was "awesome" because in winter he could work the morning shift and then go snowboarding. He was probably in his mid-fifties but clearly had the energy of a teenager, possibly three teenagers, dancing around the room as he moved. It was impossible not to feel happy in his presence. Whatever he was on, if you could bottle it then you'd make a fortune.

Day bag ready, we asked him what he'd like for the tea and the fruit, but we had to push him to accept anything at all, eventually convincing him to take just five euros from us which he put in the tip jar.

"Just make sure you find me when you come back" he told us. "It will be busy here, but I'll look after you. Have a great time and be safe up there."

The route we'd be taking followed a ridge that climbed north from the Colle di Bettaforca towards the Monte Rosa massif, and since it began at 2700 metres it was rocky and demanding from the outset. We began by winding up beneath overhanging crags before emerging onto more exposed slopes that overlooked the mist-filled Stafal valley. Frequently, we'd spot an ibex or three perched on a distant outcrop, framed by the low hanging clouds below them to create a postcard photographers dream composition. And all we'd had done to deserve it was to get a reasonably early start.

We'd left Danielo's just after eight, only moments after the chairlift came to life, so there were hardly any other hikers in sight as we crunched our way over the stones. Looking up, it was hard to believe that a trail could even exist through such a pandemonium of loose-looking rubble and crags balanced on such a precipitous slope, but sure enough we could see colourful rucksacks shuffling through it somehow.

Unlike Switzerland, in this part of Italy the trail markers were basically all yellow, often with an associated number painted inside a yellow circle or simply sprayed onto a rock next to a yellow line. Local tourist maps depict where each of these numbered sections leads to, so you can decide if you want to follow '1', '6' or '13' etc. The numbers repeat in different valleys, of course, but in theory they're far enough apart not to cause confusion on a day hike.

Today, for example, we were following trail '9' towards the refuge, which told us nothing at all about the difficulty of what was soon to come. Italian signposts do often have a difficulty rating on them, but since almost everything above 2000 metres seems to be 'difficolta EE', it covers a very wide range of challenges. Then again, so does T2 and T3 in Switzerland, so no system is perfect.

Now that we were over 3000 metres altitude and plugging our way up a steep ridge, the landscape around us was once again on such a huge scale that it was hard to take it all in. The air was crystal clear and the morning clouds had dissipated allowing us to see for hundreds of kilometres. The higher we went, the more exposed and 'gnarly' the climb became. It was still a trail because the yellow '9' signs were frequent and there was usually a visible groove among the dust and boulders to emphasise it was a well-trodden route, but it was also steepening and would fairly soon cross a boundary between hiking and scrambling.

It was the final approach to the refuge that was the most exposed and dangerous. The ridge we'd been climbing had been fairly broad, up to now, but for the final few hundred metres of ascent it narrowed dramatically into a knife-like crest cutting through this world of ice and stone. Ropes and metal hand grips had been strung across the route in most places, but with a bare stone path that was literally just a metre wide at times, with a long and vertical drop either side of it, it was like nothing we'd ever hiked before. Years earlier we'd actively avoided ridge walks like Sharp Edge and Striding Edge in the Lake District, unwilling to put ourselves in a sheer drop situation. But this was a whole other level. The rock beneath our feet was rust-coloured and lined with deep grooves and cracks. At one point the ridge had even collapsed completely, replaced with a short wooden platform spanning the gap that put me mind of flimsy ladders strung across glacial crevasses.

 Later on in the day we'd see some (obviously sensible) people ascending it wearing via-ferrata harnesses and helmets, clipping themselves to the safety rope as they inched slowly forward. But we didn't have any of that. We just kept moving, drawn ever onwards by the magnetic pull of the enormous summits ahead of us and the buzz of the moment. Our two frail little bodies, swaying in the breeze at over 3500 metres while traversing a string of stone spires surrounded by monumental ice flows and rock falls. It made us feel so vulnerable but also powerfully alive.

 It only took us two hours of adrenalin-fuelled, happiness-driven hiking to reach Rifugio Quintana Sella at 3620 metres altitude, a whole hour quicker than the signposts suggested. Not because we were especially fit or fast, though we'd certainly improved, but simply because it had been so wonderful that we'd felt like we were floating up the mountain. All of the tiredness had evaporated from our bodies, replaced with a bounce and zest for life that must have been what Danielo drank for breakfast as well.

 At the top we found a simple, large wooden hut constructed on a flat and lifeless plateau, the walls covered in solar panels and flanked by a couple of outbuildings which turned out to be toilets. A nearby cairn decked out with colourful prayer flags added some rainbow splashes to an otherwise pale-toned scene, with light grey and rust coloured stone leading out onto a vast glacial surface which rose gradually towards the summits behind. And what summits! It was as though we could see them all, in every direction. With such clear air, we'd never experienced a view anything like as all-encompassing as this one. It was even grander than we'd marvelled at atop the Platthorn. We don't know how we kept managing it, but the boundaries of our adventure just kept growing.

Directly above us on the Monte Rosa massif was the undulating white chain of the Breithorn, Pollux and Castor, while to the west we could see the Alpine giants of the Matterhorn, the Grand Combin *and* Mont Blanc as clear as though they were just a stone's throw away. In the south and east, looking away from the massif, was an ocean of cloud-filled valleys where endless and nameless ridges vied to strike out above the whiteness and underline the monumental scale of the scene. To the south-east we could see even more far-distant summits, this time of mountains we knew belonged to the Vanoise and Ecrins National Parks in France. With its distinctive shape, the Barre des Ecrins (4102 m), Europe's southernmost 4000-metre peak, was obviously identifiable despite being more than 200 kilometres away, but the view even extended to mountains much further beyond that. All of which doesn't even start to capture the flowing, carving, sweeping grace and power of the glaciers upon the slopes directly beyond the refuge, with various lines of roped-up human dots shuffling across them.

Despite these being some of Europe's highest mountains, our position at 3600 metres made them only a relatively short climb away, almost like climbing a Lake District fell were it not for the glacier in between. Like approaching a temptress offering the promise of unknown rewards, we soon found ourselves daydreaming once again of advancing our own experience so that we might also step out on to the snow-covered ice with confidence one day.

Settling down a little way from the refuge, which was increasingly busy with day-trippers like us in addition to climbers still wearing their crampons and flushed with a morning summit or two, we did what we'd been doing throughout our adventure and drifted away into a sun-soaked post-ascent doze. After about an hour or so of uninterrupted bliss and snoring, we stirred ourselves back to life. Esther then went to explore the inside of the refuge, returning quarter of an hour later with what appeared to be two house bricks.

"Well, I noticed they had vegan options on the menu and thought, why not? I just never expected them to be this big." she said as she juggled two paper plates and a cup of tea towards me.

The bricks turned out to be roasted courgette and garlic houmous sandwiches, with garlic being very much the defining feature. They were very tasty, don't get me wrong, and the wholemeal bread was cut in encyclopaedia-sized wedges so it was also very filling, but the garlic oil was just oozing out of every pore and wrinkle, dripping onto the plate, the floor and, largely, my lap. They were so large that Esther donated almost half of hers to me, and by the time I'd finished I smelled like I'd been swimming in marinated garlic.

Quietly belching garlic burps and trying to diminish the incriminating greasy stains in my crotch, we began to explore the rocky shelf a little more and take in the view from different angles. This was not a view you could ever tire of. A strong wind had built up from the east while we'd been relaxing, but we hadn't noticed because we'd been lying down. Now we felt its full force as we tottered over the uneven ground towards the eastern fringe of the plateau.

We spent three hours up there in total, only leaving when prudence and the reality that we potentially had 2000 metres of descending waiting for us dictated that we make a start. Of course, we could have planned to spend another night by the chairlift station, or even asked Danielo if we could crash on his restaurant floor, but there was still a part of us (specifically of me), that wanted to make a little more progress. It wasn't especially logical, but I could still feel an urge to move forward somehow.

We left the top at half past one and were back at Danielo's less than an hour later. There'd been a bit of a traffic jam along the most vertical sections of ridge due to a series of slow-moving groups, and when we'd finally been able to edge safely around them, I'd started hopping and jogging merrily downhill, letting gravity have its way with me a little. Just behind, Esther assured me it was actually helping her to keep moving quickly and so focus on her footing instead of the drops either side of the path. It was also easier on her knees. It had been fun, jumping and dodging from stone to stone, skidding slightly around the hairpin turns and feeling my feet dancing quickly beneath me. I've always loved running downhill. It's like skating down a mountain, and it felt freeing not to have the burden of a full pack.

Danielo's was crowded with smiling people when we returned, with the main man himself at the centre of it all and stirring up a big pan of his 'famous polenta'. He still made time to greet us like old friends though, swamping us both in a huge bear hug and laughing loudly enough to drown out the rest of the crowd. He let us go, eventually, inviting us to join the fun, party and help ourselves.

We sat to get our breath back, tapping our feet and swaying to the upbeat brass band music that had just struck up inside. Moments later, other visitors began to sing, belting out lyrics that were totally unintelligible to us but were clearly a popular folk song. Everyone was happy. Everyone was relaxed. Almost everyone was singing. But as tempting as it was to spend the whole afternoon in booze and polenta sozzled reverie, we decided we didn't want to stay too long. It was still another 1000 metres down into St Jacques (1689 m), a place we had imagined passing before finding a place to camp for the night. Either we went for it now, or we stayed another night on the spartan col with the angled slope and big-balled ibex.

Another couple of bear hugs later and with an invitation to come and stay at Danielo's house whenever we wanted, we were off again. The way down from Colle di

Bettaforca was beneath another chairlift, although this one wasn't switched on. It was another beautiful valley but I suppose we'd been rather spoiled for views so far in the day and we were a little oblivious as we resumed our semi-jogging pace downhill. Our main focus was finding some fresh drinking water, especially as the temperature rose back towards 30°C as we lost height. It had been comfortably warm at over 3000 metres, so you can imagine what it was like as the afternoon sun reached its most powerful much further down in the valley.

By the time we reached the Rifugio Ferraro at 2072 metres, it felt like our skin was cooking. We drank greedily from the refuge fountain and parked our exhausted, sun-baked bodies on a wobbly bench hidden in the shade of a storehouse wall. The vigour of our visit to Rifugio Quintana Sella had ebbed away unnervingly fast in the scorching heat, replaced by the heavy-limbed reality of four days of long ups and downs. On the plus side, however, because we'd made such an early start there was at least plenty of daylight left to permit us to take another hour resting in the welcome shade. As usual, we bought some apples from the refuge and delighted in their cool juiciness as we let our bare feet relax in the hot breeze.

It was five o'clock when we started out again, happily discovering that the TMR markers actually avoided the final 300 metres of descent into St Jacques. Instead, they cut straight over from the refuge to the mouth of the valley that would lead us up and over to Breuil-Cervinia, the place we would rejoin the Tour of the Matterhorn. That, however, was for tomorrow. Our aim now was simply to find a place to camp as soon as we could.

It was fairly easy walking from the refuge, undulating through trees that provided some blessed shade on trails with just a few other hikers on. One particular hiker was an Italian man with two dogs and, we noticed, only one arm. He spoke a little English and we asked him if he also wild camped. He said he did, but the language barrier stopped us getting any more tips on whether he knew a good place nearby.

"That was amazing. Walking on his own, with one arm and two dogs like that." Esther said, which turned out to be quite prophetic given what Esther would do later in the summer. But I'll say more about that at the end of the book. Seeing him had certainly planted the seed of an idea.

The camping spot we found was a flat patch of grass next to a fast-paced river at about 2200 metres altitude. It was right beside the trail, so we decided we couldn't put the tent up right away and would have to wait until dusk. Until then, Esther passed the time stretching while I stripped off for a wash in the river, rinsing my clothes and then sitting in the sun to dry. When the sun dipped too low and left us sat in the shade, Esther then decided to have a wash as well.

"You'll freeze" I said. "Why didn't you do it while it was sunny?"

But obviously Esther is simply a lot tougher than I am, splashing about in the nude in the racing, icy stream with no apparent discomfort. If I tried that, I'm fairly sure important parts of me would snap off. We warmed up with a special meal. Actually, that's not true at all, it was lentil pasta and tomato puree again, but it's amazing how good any warm food tastes when you're sat on a damp rock. We then leaned against each other and reflected on our dreamlike day as we waited for twilight to arrive.

The patch of grass we'd picked was nestled in a little gulley, surrounded by trees and with a fifteen-metre-high rock face nearby on both sides, so it was a lot like having our own private oasis for the night. In all the time we were waiting we saw just one pair of hikers pass by, so as the last dregs of sunset drained from the sky we popped up our tent and prepared our sleeping gear. But we still weren't quite ready to say goodbye to such a fantastic day.

For the previous fortnight Esther had been shepherding a couple of herbal tea bags around with us, though we'd never actually bothered making them because we were always too cold or tired (or both) at the end of the day. This evening, however, felt like the right time. We may have been knackered and chilly, but with our own little temporary garden around us we decided that a hot cup of tea would be just perfect. We were right.

Passing the steaming saucepan between us, clasping it tight against our chests and gazing up at the pale stars hovering just on the edge of sight, the sound of the river gurgling in the air, in that moment we didn't want to be anywhere else ever again.

Vital Statistics – Day 15
Start Point: Colle Bettaforca
End Point: Pian de Cére
Distance Hiked: 14 km
Hiking Time: 6 hours
Ascent: 1160 metres
Descent: 1700 metres

Sick

Just before going to bed, I'd spent a chilly half an hour outside using my irrigation kit, so when I'd climbed back into the tent feeling slightly shaky and chilled inside, I'd assumed I was simply cold. Yet when I was still awake an hour later, an uncomfortable headache building at the back of my skull and still feeling cold, I began to worry it was something more. Unfortunately, I was right.

A few hours after dark and I was alternating between shivering cold and sweating discomfort. I knew that I was having a fever of some kind, though I optimistically hoped it was some sort of short-term thing. If I could only get to sleep, I tried to convince myself, then perhaps it might be gone by morning?

I also decided there was no point worrying Esther by waking her up in search of sympathy. I'd never suggest that 'man flu' isn't a real thing, many of my friends catch it from time to time, but I've been doing my best over the years to buck the trend and suffer in silence. When I'm poorly, trying to get me to admit just how ill I feel is a little like trying to get a politician to give a straight answer. Obviously, this doesn't always work out for the best. My 'no time for anaesthetic' moment in accident and emergency at the start of this book is a prime example of suffering in silence leading only to greater suffering.

However, this time around, I just didn't see any practical benefit from waking Esther. We were in a tent on some damp grass in the middle of nowhere. There was no hot bath available or a warm cup of lemon and honey waiting for me in the kitchen. I lay as still and as quietly as I could in the dark, trying to focus on my breathing to take my mind off the feeling that a small, sadistic elf was hitting the back of my head with a sharp hammer and growing ice cubes in my belly.

At some points I did drift away into dreamland, immediately falling into the nightmarish world of George Orwell's 1984. I have no idea why, since I hadn't read the book for years, but every time I managed to sleep I found myself living the life of Winston Smith, stuck at a desk, scrubbing out the facts of the past and rewriting it in 'Newspeak', trying to 'Doublethink' myself into accepting that contradictory versions of events were equally true. It was like a crazy, psychedelic, repetitive nightmare. It was also incredibly unpleasant. Worse still, every time I was jolted out of the abyss by fear or the physical pain in my head, I'd check my watch to find I'd only been asleep for about six and a half minutes. It had felt like six hours in a mental prison. And so the night dragged on.

Because we were right next to the trail again, we'd set another early alarm. I decided not to say anything about my bad night when it first went off. It was only once I was sat heating up our overnight oat bran in an attempt to drive out the chilly dampness of the morning by the river, where everything was dripping with condensation, that I mentioned my sleepless night to Esther. Naturally, I downplayed it a little.

"I think I might need another rest day when we get to Breuil-Cervinia" I said, trying my best to understate how rough I was still feeling. My headache was less bad now that I was upright, but I still felt worryingly disorientated and wobbly on my feet as I moved around packing up the tent.

In theory, we had another rather challenging day planned. We'd start with a long, mostly gradual 800 metre ascent towards the Col Nord des Cimes Blanches (2982 m) above Breuil-Cervinia. After that, Esther had expressed a preference to still climb up to the edge of the glacial Theodul Pass and the Rifugio del Teodulo (3295 m), not because it was on our route but simply to have a look at the glacier. To get there we'd have to descend a little, traverse across the head of a valley and then tackle a steep 500 metre climb. After that, all being well, we hoped to find somewhere in the valley head above Breuil-Cervinia to sleep for the night. It was only our sixth day out of Saas-Fee and so it felt a little soon to be thinking about a second rest day or hotel stay, even if our legs would have quite liked one. In the previous five days we'd ascended almost 7000 metres. Whether our plan was still suitable would remain to be seen. Back in the moment alongside the river, it was coming up to eight o'clock and it was time to make a start.

We followed a slowly rising path through the trees, heading along the valley until it opened into a broad field filled with cows. Making our way through the herd, we began climbing the left hand side of the valley via a gentle slope which took us up onto an even more expansive plateau vanishing into the distance to the north.

This was scenery on an epic scale, not in the same way as our view from Rifugio Quintana Sella where we'd seen so many different things from one place, but because of the height and intricacy of the long vertical cliff face now towering above us. The ground around us was vivid and green, alive with grasshoppers energised by the morning sun, but the cliff was made up of countless grey layers stretching up over a kilometre towards the Mont Roisetta pinnacle (3334 metres). It was a marvellous contrast and one which made us feel miniscule in this long, wide and untamed place.

The path remained easy to follow, a pale brown line cutting through the green, which was good because I could feel myself growing increasingly shaky. I'd enjoyed a little spurt of energy just after starting out, adrenalin-fuelled probably, but that had faded as we'd climbed up from the cow pastures below. The longer we walked, the harder it was becoming to keep moving forward.

A sign told us that we were just one and a half hours from our target on the Col Nord des Cimes Blanches, so I noted the time on my watch, added ninety minutes and promised myself it would all be over by then. Except, it wasn't, because for the first time in a fortnight we were now moving much more slowly than the signs.

In my mind, the valley just went on and on, always green, usually easy and invariably beautiful, but I just wished it would end. After about forty-five minutes I needed to stop and rest, propping myself against a boulder while Esther gave her dad a call to wish him Happy Birthday. Phone signal had been intermittent and weak for the past few days and while we almost always treasure the peace and quiet of the wilderness, happy to be out of contact most of the time, there are occasions when it can feel sad not to be able to reach loved ones. So it was a big relief that a single-bar of signal had floated our way and managed to stay with us for almost a quarter of an hour.

Steeling myself for another round of trudging, we moved on, saying hello to a smattering of hiking parties coming towards us from the valley head. By the time a series of hard, steep climbs carried us up above two sparkling turquoise lakes shimmering in the sun, I knew we were nearly there but it still felt so far.

When we did make it to the top, arriving at a shade below 3000 metres after more than three and a half hours, the most I could manage was to lie down and fall instantly to sleep. It had been years since I could remember being ill with anything more than an occasional tickly throat. Why did this have to happen now? I could only hope that a headache and a touch of dizziness was as bad as it was going to get.

I was hardly noticing the scenery at this point, so I'm somewhat dependent on the photos Esther took when I say that we had returned, yet again, to the world of rock and ice. The Matterhorn was back as well, large, clear and dominating the skyline across the quarry-like valley to the north, while behind us to the south, beyond those shimmering turquoise lakes, the land rolled away in series of craggy waves, pale in the now midday sun.

Were it not so hot I might have slept all day, but instead I woke up after an unconscious hour feeling like a boiled egg. Dithering and still unwilling to put into words how rough I was feeling, words that might have included 'drill bit in my head' and 'hamster party in my stomach', I was grateful to Esther who had far more sense and could make an accurate enough assessment on her own. Ignoring my half-hearted and pathetic pretence that "I'll be fine, we can make it…", she took the reins and arranged for a hotel room for the next two nights in Breuil-Cervinia. Tired of my "maybe I can still camp" and "it's only one more night, I'll feel better soon", she simply fired up the phone and made good things happen.

"Feel better now?" she asked. "We know we have a comfortable place to sleep for the next two nights. We're going to have a rest day while you get better. Don't argue. It's got a spa *and* they let me have it for a discount – 65 euros a night including breakfast. Everything's going to be okay."

"Well then I still want to try and get up to the Theodul Pass first" I insisted.

Ten minutes later, trudging across a hot and dusty track that led us down into that quarry-like valley, I realised that another 500 metres of ascent was definitely beyond me. We could see the Rifugio del Teodulo, a tiny white building on a shoulder at the lip of a huge grey bowl, but the more I looked the less enticing it even seemed. Yes, the Matterhorn and the ridgeline extending from it was spectacular, a near vertical wall of rock and snow a couple of thousand metres tall, still with a few small glaciers left on it which was rare on this south-facing side. But that was on our left. To our right, in the direction of the Theodul Pass was nothing but a desolate sea of grey. I've already called it quarry-like, but we could even see a couple of earth-moving trucks below us shaping the slopes, so it basically *was* a quarry. I'm sure it's stunning in winter beneath a blanket of white, but in the heat of the sun it felt like a lifeless stone desert.

"I can't do it" I said. "I just can't make it up there."

"I already know that" said Esther, "I was just waiting for you to realise it. Look, there's a cable car going up to that even higher point, the Testa Grigia at almost 3500 metres. Let's see if we can get up there for a look around, and then we'll cable car all the way down to Breuil-Cervinia and get tucked up in the room. How about that?" Isn't it wonderful when we have loved ones who know us better than we know ourselves.

We made our way down into the greyness, arriving at the cable car station next to Lago Cime Bianche at 2808 metres. It wasn't a difficult descent, following wide and gradual roads created by the trucks shifting the hard ground from place to place. We discovered it was twenty five euros for us both to take the easy way up and back down to this point, so we decided to treat ourselves and splash out. It was with a very deep sense of relief that I stepped into the large gondola that ran every thirty minutes, knowing now that the hiking was over for the next two days and that I could hopefully get rid of this throbbing head, dizziness and the slight tickling in the back of my throat that I was just becoming aware of.

The Testa Grigia, or Plateau Monte Rosa, turned out to be a bit of a disappointment. It was a stunning outlook, there was no doubt about that, providing a fantastic view in almost every direction, which is what you'd expect at 3500 metres in the vicinity of the Matterhorn and Monte Rosa. Straddling the border between Switzerland and Italy once again, we were basically looking at the valleys on either side of the Matterhorn. To the north, we could see much of the route we'd hiked a week earlier, on both sides of the Mattertal and around its head. To the south-west, we could see the incredible Matterhorn ridgeline and a series of still unknown valleys beyond it that we'd be walking through soon. To the north-west was the Matterhorn itself, while to the south-east we were looking up into the glacial snowfields which provide year-round skiing in this famous region. And immediately below us, on both sides, were huge glaciers, especially the Theodulgletscher which stretched away down into the Mattertal.

    Famous peaks, valleys and glaciers and all those good things were all around us, above and below. But while it was visually stunning, the disappointment came from how dirty it all seemed at the station itself. Again, I'm sure that snow smartens it up wonderfully, but in mid-August all of the cabling, piping and debris from the industrial business of tourism was on display. Large patches of glacier close to the buildings were a dirty, slushy brown, while embedded in the ice beneath several of the ski-lift pylons were what looked like rusty old air conditioning units. A collection of JCB's were parked beneath the gondola station, with what looked like old parts piled up nearby. Against such a magnificent, jaw-dropping panorama of nature's splendour, stretching for many hundreds of kilometres, it was a contrast that made such an unattractive human footprint very off-putting. In fact, I actually felt a little guilty for being part of it.

    Still, we'd be hypocrites to complain too loudly and I'm sure it's all done with a respectful and sustainable touch in mind, or at least I hope it is. I'm also conscious that we were fortunate enough to have just spent over a fortnight living in the mountains, mostly in remote, difficult-to-access places. Having a critical mind was almost inevitable in a busy place like this, while the hundreds of other faces around us seemed joyful and satisfied with this rare opportunity to be so high.

    I was feeling too poorly to move around very much so Esther went for a stroll on her own, making a descent onto the bare ice of the nearby Theodulgletscher and walking a short distance up the snowy hill close to the ski lift pylons. It didn't seem as though the lifts were running, although there were plenty of people milling about with snowboards and helmets so I supposed they'd only just closed for the day.

Coming back to show me her photographs of the alarmingly deep cracks in the ice, we then moved slowly and together past the gondola station to discover a sealed up customs station, a squat and bland box overlooking the pass. I almost couldn't believe it. With the free flow of goods throughout Europe today, the idea that people used to sit up here in a small building surrounded by a world of snow in order to monitor and tax goods crossing the border was incredible. I mean, what a job!

There was also a little museum tucked away to the side of the customs post. Now this really was fascinating, charting the history of Alpinism, tourism and the construction of the cableways in the area. I was especially interested by the displays of old parts and the motors that used to drive the original gondolas so high, not to mention the images of the people that put them together. That also looked like a hard job! Anyone that could have wielded some of those spanners in the snow, one of them as long as me, must have been tough.

After the museum, we then spent a happy twenty minutes just sitting in the sun and looking down along the Theodulgletscher. Could we have walked across it all alone after all? Even without spikes? Looking from this angle and bearing in mind the experiences we'd enjoyed since, especially the precipitous climb to Rifugio Quintana Sella, we agreed we probably could have done. We could see a couple of other people walking along the route beneath the ski-lift pylons and although there were a few cracks nearby, it didn't look anything like the 'fucking' sheer-drop, death-defying crossing that Wouter and Wim had described to us. It actually looked quite gentle from above. We'd still have preferred to have some micro-spikes on though. Then again, if we had crossed it we wouldn't have had all those other adventures, so there were no regrets. Just a new perspective for future possibilities.

We caught the gondola down just before four, our minds now focused on getting down to Breuil-Cervinia asap to get clean and put me in bed. Then we hit a snag. There were two more stages of cable-car descent to reach Breuil-Cervinia, both in small and continuously running sky bubbles, and while the ticket to Breuil-Cervinia was only 15 euros each we didn't have any more cash left and they couldn't take card payments at this higher station. The only blessing we did have was that it seemed almost everyone working on the lifts spoke French, so we could at least make ourselves understood.

After some deliberation and an initial refusal, which was perhaps then tempered by my visible deflation at the thought of having to walk 900 metres downhill after all, the sympathetic attendant waved us over the barrier with the insistence that we pay the full fare at the intermediate stop, where there was a cash mashine. Yet when we tried to explain that we needed to pay the full fare from 2900 metres, the second attendant just smiled and told us it was his "present to us", and only charged us 6 euros for the final stage. It wasn't a kindness we had sought or expected, or even really needed since we would have happily paid what was due, but it was the gesture that meant more than anything. It left us feeling looked after and welcome, like someone was watching over us again.

Breuil-Cervinia in late afternoon in mid-August was unsurprisingly heaving. It is basically the Italian version of Zermatt after all and so after a short stop in the very busy supermarket, we were relieved to arrive at the relative tranquility of the Hotel Grivola where we enjoyed a delightful check-in experience.

The lady looking after us was Maria, the same lady Esther had arranged things with over the phone, and despite our bedraggled appearance and probable smell, she treated us like arriving royalty. The hotel was plush and well appointed in an obvious Alpine theme, with unique art on the walls to add some colour. We later learned, from a magazine tactically left in our room, that the artworks were all pieces from a local artist who had achieved some fame. We never asked, but we guessed he maybe owned the hotel due to the fact there must have been hundreds of his pieces around and a little gallery where you could buy them.

The room we were given was spacious, immaculately clean and comfortable, with a chocolate colour scheme that I found cosy (although Esther thought it a little dark). The bed was comfortable, there was a sofa in the room and best of all, we had a huge bathroom with an actual deep bath tub. Well, that was my evening sorted then.

We tried a little food but I had almost no appetite. Despite not eating since breakfast, I found that not only my throat but also my mouth had become incredibly sore throughout the day, so I began to run myself a bath with a plan to just get into bed as soon as I could. Esther went down to the spa, finding a small but smart space with a sauna and steam room that could be used by just a few people at a time, plus some refreshments available to the side. It was here that she met Laurent and Mathilde, a Parisian couple who were buzzing with excitement after just climbing their very first 4000 metre peak with the help of a guide, the Gran Paradiso (4061 metres) which wasn't actually that far away.

Esther enjoyed a very nice hour and half with Laurent and Mathilde in the spa, learning not only of the climb but also of their work as a teacher and NGO worker respectively, before coming back up to check on me. I'd had a bit of romantic notion while Esther was gone and had staggered out of my sick bed to find a thank you card in a newsagent's shop, which I'd left on her pillow. But the effort of doing so had totally finished me off. By the time Esther came back up I was drifting into a painkiller-assisted, feverish daze. Simply for personal preference, we rarely use painkillers for mild headaches and such, but this was no mild headache. Thankfully, not having taken a single paracetomol for several years they at least seemed to be having a powerful effect and were helping me get some much needed respite.

    Leaving me in peace, Esther said a quiet goodnight and went to do some yoga in the cavernous bathroom until about half past ten, also apparently calling her parents one more time to have a longer chat, but I knew very little about any of that since I was blessedly away with the fairies.

Vital Statistics – Day 16
Start Point: Pian de Cére
End Point: Breuil-Cervinia
Distance Hiked: 8 km
Hiking Time: 4 hours
Ascent: 880 metres
Descent: 150 metres

Sicker

If I'd hoped my headache and dizziness was a swiftly passing issue then I was to be sorely disappointed, with sore being the appropriate word. I passed another even more feverish night, alternating between sweating so hard I looked like I'd just finished a 10 km hard run on a treadmill and shaking like I was lost in a blizzard wearing nothing but a condom, a really thin one. My dreams, when they came, were less nightmarish than my 1984-themed horrors of the previous night, but they were freakishly vivid and nonsensical. By the time morning arrived I'd folded and refolded my soggy duvet countless times and gone through half a dozen towels laid beneath my body.

I was fully aware of what was going on around me when I was awake, but the headache was unrelenting and it was very difficult to swallow. Sure enough, the glands on my neck had grown into billiard balls overnight.

"Oh shit. I really am ill after all" I thought. "What adventures shall we have today?" I croaked at Esther, who smiled gently back at me.

"Peaceful ones" she said in response. Esther, who'd done some more early morning yoga in the bathroom so as not to disturb me, went down to breakfast first and I joined her half an hour later to find her happily, and a little guiltily, finishing off what may well have been a second slice of cake. Yet even the prospect of fresh-baked cake wasn't enough to stir an appetite within me and after struggling down a meagre bowl of fresh fruit salad I retreated back to my pit.

Esther stayed with me for the rest of the morning, sending a few emails to let family know we were alive and listening to gentle music next to me. I slipped in and out of sleep, hoping that each time I woke up I'd feel an improvement, but those hopes proved premature.

Esther, in contrast, was still full of energy and keen to go for a walk up the hills nearby. Unlike the desolate upper slopes, the hillsides immediately around Breuil-Cervinia were green and vibrant and Esther wanted to explore. Her hopes were dashed, however, when it started to rain heavily just as she was leaving the hotel. Still, she did bump into Laurent and Mathilde again, playing a game in the lobby, and then did *even more* yoga in the sheltered doorway of a closed shop. At this rate she was going to be like an elastic band by the time I recovered.

Esther's ability to just get on and do what she wants to do, with no regard for who's watching and what they might think, has always inspired me and this is most true when it comes to her yoga practice. In hundreds of apparently inappropriate car parks and public places throughout Europe, she's unfurled her yoga mat and just got on with it. Sometimes strangers even join in. On one motorhome aire in Spain she even ended up running a few classes for some fellow motorhomers who wanted to give it a try.

By the time the weather cleared she was too tired to go walking, so just stayed out in the fresh air until it was spa opening time, returning to the room for a quick cuddle with the patient and to check how I was doing. The answer was not good. I was still just as feverish; my throat had closed up and my mouth was also a lot more sore. A quick look in the bathroom mirror showed that it had filled up with ulcers. Pulling my lips down and tilting my head, I could count at least 40 discrete white patches, most of them small but with a few biggies near the back. It was almost a case of two ulcers per tooth, one on each side. I'd never seen anything like it. No wonder I could hardly chew.

We had a brief chat about whether hiking the next day was feasible, yet despite all the evidence to the contrary I still acted like an idiot and made noises suggesting I might be okay. It was Esther, once again, who had to rein me in and inject some reality into the situation. In her opinion we would definitely need at least one more night, but she still pandered to my reluctance to accept how poorly I was by only making a provisional booking.

Maria, on reception, was understanding and helpful, telling Esther she could hold our room until 7.30 a.m. the next morning when it would go online as 'available', unless we decided otherwise. It was obvious in hindsight that we were going stay, but I suppose at the time I just liked to continue the illusion I might suddenly get better.

Esther did her best for me, finding a bar that sold freshly made vegetable juices and returning with a pint of carrot and orange to get at least some vitamins into me. I drank it as best I could, swallowing, grimacing against the sting of my ulcerated gums, then swallowing again, knowing the flood of vitamin C should do me some good. I also tried gargling with salt water to cleanse my mouth a little, but mostly I just kept taking paracetamol every four hours and lying down.

The second night passed in much the same way as the first, in a sweaty, shivering, delirious confusion and at seven in the morning Esther confirmed we would be staying another night. I didn't even bother going to breakfast this time, leaving Esther to say goodbye to her friends Laurent and Mathilde alone. They were heading back to Paris and enjoyed another lively conversation with Esther about politics, human rights and wealth inequality, and how all of the problems being seen in Europe related to migrants were part of those same underlying issues. From Esther's descriptions, I wish I'd met them myself, but I never even saw them.

Esther did bring me up a hearty bowl of fresh fruit salad and a cup of tea, but after gumming at a few pieces of kiwi fruit I gave up because it was too painful. Instead we passed some time picking photos from our camera together to back up and watching the heavy rain hammering at the windows. After yesterday's afternoon showers and today's heavy rainfall, the only silver lining from my illness was that I'd picked good days to be holed up in a comfy hotel room (Thanks again Zeus!)

Still, the rain wasn't enough to deter Esther from another attempt at a hike. After a trip to a pharmacy to explain about my mouth ulcers, she returned with a spray I was supposed to use whenever it hurt (or before food) and another pint of orange and carrot juice. She then left me with her smartphone so that I could watch YouTube to pass the time and set off at twelve fully decked out in her waterproofs. Personally, I could understand her need to be out in the fresh air and I also knew she was partly doing it to give me the space I needed to recover in silence.

We both knew, from my historic hospital stays, that I'm a terrible patient in more ways than one, especially bedside chit-chat. I try my best, but as I've said before I mostly just like to pull a blanket over my head and be left alone. I knew that Esther was working hard to respect that and I was deeply grateful for it.

Picking up signs for the Rifugio Orionde (2808 m), she powered up into the mist with the goal of opening her lungs and having a little workout without the weight of a bag on her back. By the time she reached the refuge the sky had even cleared slightly, so she continued, following the trail ever higher in search of a chapel that was signposted. That was the moment that the bad weather returned.

I'd been dozing when the thunder started, waking up to find heavy rain blowing through the open window of our room. For Esther, at almost 3000 metres by now, she'd run back to the Refuge Orionde down a slippy path and dived inside to shelter, giving me a quick call using my own ancient handset to reassure me she was alive and well.

It was well after five when she got back, damp, flushed and smiling. She'd waited for a break in the storm and run. By now I was actually starting to feel slightly less feverish, my sore throat felt less constricted and my headache not so severe, although I couldn't be certain how much of that improvement was down to the painkillers I was still popping every four hours.

"Maybe we can get going tomorrow" I said again optimistically. The only thing that wasn't getting any better was my mouth ulcers, which put me right off any thoughts of eating actual food. The spray Esther had fetched gave relief for about 8 seconds, but the pain immediately came back. So Esther fetched me another pint of juice before heading down to the spa for a little while.

It wasn't just giving me space, but at this stage we were also being as careful as we could not to have too much contact and risk me making Esther unwell. It would have been a huge disappointment for my health to start returning only for Esther to fall sick immediately afterwards. We'd even stopped sharing a toothbrush! Not that I could do more than wave the new ultra-soft brush that Esther had bought for me in the direction of my face before it made my ulcers sting. Why were they so bad? Was I really that run down? Apparently so, but I just couldn't believe they'd appeared so quickly. Perhaps, I hoped, they'd vanish just as fast?

Another bath, a few more attempts at some fruit and I was ready for a third night in my sick bed. I just hoped it wouldn't be as psychedelic or frightening as the previous three and that I'd wake up feeling like I might try a little walking.

Vital Statistics – Days 17 & 18
Start Point: Breuil-Cervinia
End Point: Breuil-Cervinia
Distance Hiked: Breakfast and back / trips to the bathroom
Hiking Time: No
Ascent: In an elevator
Descent: In an elevator

Risking It

Thankfully, I did have a more settled night. I still woke up in a sweat a couple of times, but not nearly as severe as they had been, much more of a 'hot day' type of sweat than an 'Olympic marathon finisher' type. I also had only the slightest ghost of a headache by the morning despite not having taken any paracetamol overnight. My glands were still swollen, though not as much as they had been, so although my mouth ulcers were just as severe as the previous day, I could at least swallow more easily provided I didn't need to chew. Apparently, I was on the mend.

Arguably the sensible thing to do, since we were under no time pressure, would have been to carry on resting for another day or two to really see off the virus, or whatever it was that I'd had, before resuming our hike. However, we decided to get going and see what happened to me.

A small part of the reason we were keen to start hiking again so soon was the weather. The medium to long-term weather forecast for the Breuil-Cervinia area had a lot of rain in it, with today being the only day of complete sunshine. While we fully accepted forecasts are fallible, sometimes dramatically so, it still felt like it would be a good idea to make use of this sunny day to start moving west towards areas that had less rain on their forecasts.

More importantly, there was no guarantee that two or even three more days in a hotel would actually see me back to full strength. It might take a week, or longer, after such an intense fever. But if that was the case then we shouldn't be taking it a day at a time at all, we should simply take all the money a week-long hotel stay would cost us and use it to get back to our motorhome in

Switzerland. That way it wouldn't matter how long it took me to recover.

If, on the other hand, I was genuinely on the mend and going to see improvement with each passing day, whether I walked or not, why not try walking slowly? If I was wrong and I got seriously ill again, we'd find a way back to the motorhome. But if I did keep feeling better, then we could simply keep our adventure going. Maybe the fresh air would even do me some good.

Basically, walking might make me more ill again, but it might not. Unless we tried, we'd never know. That was the justification I came up with at the time, looking back now, it isn't completely daft. I mean, I'd set out with a sore knee and that gamble had paid off. Yes, there was also a part of me that wanted to finish the loop and walk back to the motorhome, whichever route we took. But we didn't talk about that. I wanted to trust my body, against the advice of various family members who had emailed suggesting we stay put I have to say.

The main challenge would be feeding me. I still couldn't face more than a token bit of breakfast because of my mouth ulcers and it was clear I'd already lost a fair bit of weight during the past 72 hours. I don't think I'd been this skinny since I was fourteen years old. All of the ribs on my chest and back were prominent and if I hadn't taken the chance for a shave, I might have looked like a convict emerging from a month in solitary confinement.

Which is why we went so slowly getting ready in the morning, Esther taking a solo trip to the supermarket for supplies and then peacefully packing our things away together in the comfort of our room. Because of my weakened state, Esther insisted on taking a few items she wouldn't normally carry and I wasn't going to argue. With the humility that my enfeebled state was giving me, I wasn't even trying to puff out my chest and start loading my usual burden. I needed Esther's help and she was happy to give it. We'd move as fast as we could and if that meant just a couple of hours a day, so be it.

I left my softly-furnished sanctuary just after eleven o'clock. The cleaner in the hallway seemed surprised to see me emerge. We'd kept the do not disturb sign on the door throughout our stay and Esther had been telling me that the cleaner kept stopping her to check if we needed anything, new bedding or towels etc. With Esther's constant response that "no, you needn't go in the room, we have everything we need", I'd begun to imagine she thought Esther was actually hiding a body.

We made a quick stop at the pharmacy to ask if there was anything else they could offer me for my mouth ulcers, coming away with a small bottle of medicated mouthwash that I was told to use three times a day. If they hadn't cleared up in four or five days, the pharmacist told me, I should go to a doctor and ask for antibiotics. Esther said she got the impression that he gave me the mouthwash more to reassure me than anything else, seeing how scared and nervous I was, and perhaps that was true. Maybe I didn't really need the mouthwash and it was more a placebo than anything else. If so, it worked in the sense I felt much less uncertain as I took my first rinse and then left Breuil-Cervinia.

We were once again following the Tour of the Matterhorn westwards. Our intention for the day was to cross the 2445 metre Fenêtre de Tsignanaz, descend a little and then begin the climb towards the 3065 metre Col di Valcornera. However, in the interest of "taking it easy", we intended to stop before getting to that lofty col. If we were lucky, we might get to bunk in the Bivacco Manenti at 2804 metres, but we'd looked online and it was only a two-berth shelter so we knew we couldn't pin our hopes on it. Quite how we'd convinced ourselves that 1000 metres of ascent was "taking it easy" I'm not sure. I suppose it was less than some of our recent 'big days'.

It was a fine summer's day with just a few white clouds floating around the summit of the Matterhorn and that high ridge above Breuil-Cervinia that we'd so admired. As we left town, we noticed a poster on a bus shelter advertising a speaking event, where one of the speakers was apparently the Breuil-Cervinia – Matterhorn record holder. His name was Kilian Jornet, a Catalan runner, and his time was only 2 hours and 52 minutes for the round trip! That's for a height different of almost 2500 metres!

The riverside path out of town was a perfect warm up for me after so long lying down. I was noticeably a little wobbly on my legs to start with. Not dizzy, as such, just less certain in my footing.

The climbing began at about half past twelve and it took us about two hours of slow ascent to reach the saddle of the Fenêtre de Tsignanaz. It had been a pleasant enough route, mostly through trees with a final more open approach to the col itself. It had also stayed warm, despite the gathering clouds, and there had been marvellous views to enjoy each time we looked back towards Breuil-Cervinia with the Matterhorn rising into the whiteness above it. Similarly, we'd also been enjoying the flanks of the Monte Rosa massif away to our left, the top of which was also hidden by clouds. Having both of the monuments we were circling so prominent gave us an opportunity to appreciate just how far we'd come in the past two and a half weeks.

I was starting to feel light-headed by the top of fenêtre. Guessing this was probably due to lack of food, we took the chance on the warm, flat saddle to cook up a few hundred grams of plain pasta for me. Chewing, even of soggy pasta, was still not something I could contemplate. Even the softest morsel touching any of my gums was like having a sewing needles shoved between my teeth. Instead, I settled on swallowing the pasta one piece at a time like they were pills, popping each twirl on my tongue individually, tilting my head back slightly and gulping them down in a fast almost gannet-like motion. In this way I was able to get through a saucepan full of pasta in about an hour. Esther, who'd enjoyed three mornings of hotel breakfasts, insisted she still wasn't even close to hungry.

After I'd eaten, we lingered for another half an hour on the fenêtre, appreciating the company of some nearby marmots and a few thousand grasshoppers. Looking west, we could see the Lac de Tsignanaz some 300 metres directly beneath us with bare grey mountains above it, while away to our right was the pyramidal shape of the excitingly named Mont Dragon (3353 m), equally bare and imposing against the sky.

When we did get started again it was with a gentle and grassy descent of just a hundred and fifty metres down towards a small alpage. Nestled in this petite and isolated glacial valley, with the Lac de Tsignanaz sparkling in the sun to our left, bounded by the cirque of rock we'd been looking up at, it was a wonderfully idyllic place and made all the more so by the fact it was totally cut off from roads. The only way to see this beautiful place is to walk over and have a look (or bring a serious off road vehicle).

As we crossed the pastureland above the alpage we paused to stroke some inquisitive, curly-furred calves who were sunning themselves on the grass. They can't have been more than a couple of weeks old and they allowed me to slowly approach and rub their snouts. Perhaps I was having dog-withdrawal again, but I would have happily stayed fussing those babies for the rest of the day.

The 700 metre climb towards Col di Valcornera also began across gently grassy slopes but these soon faded into more rocky paths, though still bounded by plenty of long grass punctuated with boulders. Crossing the slope at the head of the valley, we continued to be treated to excellent views over the Lac de Tsignanaz and its surrounding fells, but it was the inevitable effort required by higher slopes that was dominating my attention. The energy boost I'd enjoyed after my pasta pills was already starting to wane and I wasn't sure how much further I really had left in me. That's when we started to sing.

In addition to our morning ritual and the 'Timber' song in our tent, there was another particular song we'd sung almost daily since leaving Zinal. We sang it because it was fun, because the lyrics just fitted with hiking and because we sometimes just liked to sing, but this was the moment when the words really captured my experience the most. "One Foot In Front Of The Other" by Walk the Moon, which is even catchier than their better known hit song "Shut Up and Dance With Me", is like audio rocket fuel for tired legs. Admittedly, they sing it a little better than we do, but we only had a handful of distant cows for an audience so it didn't really matter how loudly or badly we sang. It was our enthusiasm that counted.

It took us an occasionally musical hour and a half from the grassy Alpage to complete the 500 metres required to arrive at Bivacco Manenti. Disappointingly, having started to allow myself to entertain hopes of actually getting to sleep in the bivacco instead of our tent, we arrived to find four people already lolling around outside of the tiny red-painted storm shelter.

It turned out they were a Dutch family on holiday, a father, two of his adult children and one of their friends, and they were all planning to try and sleep in the bivacco that night. To put that in perspective, the bivacco was about the size of a small garden shed but only half as tall. Inside were just two bunks, one on either side of the narrow gangway, and the roof was curved like a bomb shelter. You could probably describe it more as an overly large dog kennel. How four tall Dutch folk intended to fit comfortably inside it we didn't know, but I didn't really care. I was mostly just miffed they'd beaten us to it, especially when they told us they'd only just arrived.

Steeling myself to wild camp, the annoyingly friendly Dutch people (who I couldn't dislike, even though part of me wanted to) pointed to a spot nearby where they'd noticed evidence of previous camping, a flat grassy area partly enclosed by a low stone wall. Whether campers actually build these walls themselves for shelter, or whether they're a relic from ancient farming activities, I have no idea. I know that the last thing I'd want to be doing at the end of a long day of hiking is moving hefty rocks around to build a little wall around my tent. But, if someone else has already done the work, then it's okay with me.

One of the 'kids' from next door wandered over to chat with Esther while I was having a much-needed lie down inside my sleeping bag in the tent. I hadn't had the energy to try and eat any more and just wanted to go to sleep. Our visitor was probably about twenty years old. She explained how they were spending a week touring between different bivaccos, which seemed marvellous to us because a few weeks earlier we didn't even know bivaccos existed. They carried their own food but no tent, so if a bivacco was full then they just had to keep moving, which was why they had such motivation to make this tiny shelter work for them somehow. The dad was planning to sleep on one bunk, the kids were going to top and tail on the other and their friend would curl up on the floor on some climbing rope they'd spread out for him. How lovely!

Personally, I thought it sounded awful and instantly felt much more appreciative of the warm, lightweight air mattress that I could always call my own. We'd pitched our tent relatively early in the day (for us) since there was hardly anyone around and it was already quite cold. Grey clouds had been gathering all afternoon, so with rain always a possibility we'd decided that resting after my illness was much more important than potentially upsetting some late evening walkers above 2800 metres.

In practice, the only people likely to be higher than us at this time of day would probably be staying at the refuge which we could just make out on a lip of rock above us. It seemed we were just on the cusp of the transition between almost grassy hillside with boulders in it, to bare rock, with scree slopes and fields of house-sized rubble covering the slopes around us. It was a pretty world to return to after several days in an urban environment and a very quiet one, with just a few ibex trotting around to stir up any noise at all. Every now and then we'd hear a mournful call, which we guessed was a young ibex calling for its mother, but we couldn't see a baby anywhere.

We watched the herd we could see for a little while, moving slowly around in the stony wastes, before slipping into our sleeping bags quite early ourselves and enjoying a long hug, mostly to keep warm. Every now and then we'd hear a small rock slide outside and knew it was our goat-like neighbours making their way to wherever it was they wanted to spend the night.

Vital Statistics – Day 19
Start Point: Breuil-Cervinia
End Point: Bivacco Manenti
Distance Hiked: 10 km
Hiking Time: 4 hours
Ascent: 1050 metres
Descent: 260 metres

Woozy

Another mountain morning dawned with a bright sunrise, briefly illuminating the loveliness of the lower slopes of Mont Dragon before a thick mist descended quickly to cover it all up again. Through the fog we could just about make our Dutch neighbours preparing to depart, moving slowly and stiffly and all wrapped up in several layers of coats and hats. From drifted snippets of their conversation, which Esther could follow as a fluent Dutch speaker herself, she translated one particular expression for me. "Well, at least we survived it."

None of us seemed in a huge rush to get going. Breakfast was overnight oat bran (what else) and I managed to gulp down a few small mouthfuls, placing the lumps on the tip of my tongue then using my improving 'gannet technique' to swallow it without it touching the inside of my mouth. The medicated mouthwash I was using numbed my mouth slightly for five minutes or so afterwards, but I was yet to see any sustained reduction in the ulcer pain I was having. Thankfully, apart from when I tried to eat or drink, the background pain remained mild and my sore throat and headache were basically gone. Hopefully, our return to outdoor living wasn't going to cause a relapse after all.

The Dutch family left at nine and we started moving a few minutes later, making a very minor detour to have a better look inside the bivacco they'd inhabited.

"How the hell did four of them manage to sleep in this?" we wondered aloud. It would have been lovely and cosy for a couple, but four adults! They must have felt like uncomfortable, cold sardines.

Our climb into the world of stone and cloud was gradual at first but soon began to steepen. Surrounded by persistent and thick damp mist, we didn't even pause to look in the Rifugio Perucci (or make our standard request for fresh fruit) when we passed it after quarter of an hour. Instead, we simply tried to keep warm by continuing to follow the yellow painted arrows towards our invisible goal. Above the refuge the trail began winding through a swathe of glacial debris, although there were no longer any remnants of the ice itself. It was mostly easy to follow, with a few forks in the dusty groove which had us pausing due to the minimal visibility, but in the end all of the options seemed to come back together again. A final traverse across a rope-assisted rock face and we were there, the Col de Valcornera at 3065 metres. Less than three weeks earlier we'd marvelled at our first col because it was 'close' to 3000 metres. Now it felt like a much more familiar altitude to be visiting, a fact we were excited to acknowledge as we hugged at the top.

The col itself was a sharp, narrow saddle in a rust-tinted mountainside that had taken us just under an hour to reach. A string of colourful prayer flags tied to a wooden cross were flapping powerfully in the gusting wind, which had recently begun to build, so we sheltered on the less windy side so that I could eat a small handful of raisins.

The descent from the col required us to negotiate another maze of shifting tracks through an unnervingly steep scree slope. For switchback after switchback we sent stones bouncing down the hill beneath us, creating endless mini-landslides with our feet, constantly half-buried in dust and pebbles. Even compared to the previous few weeks, this was a particularly precarious path that required firm footing, a clear head and strong arms as we relied heavily on our trekking poles to prevent us from tripping.

Eventually, after a couple of hundred vertical metres, the ground began to level out gradually and the stones grew larger. We were still picking our way through rubble, but at least it wasn't quite as steep or prone to giving way beneath us. A long snow patch also gave us some respite, allowing us to enjoy semi-skiing through the slush without worrying about the precise placement of our feet for a few moments. But then it was back into the rubble.

After about an hour we reached the lip of the hanging valley we'd been making our way down and were able to get a better view of the larger 'parent' valley we were about to descend. We'd reached the level where hardy patches of scrubby grass were just about getting a foothold among the stones, so we were looking up into ice and crags and down into an increasingly green bowl that flattened towards a distant lake. That was the way we were going. In the far distance, above and beyond the lake surface, we could see other similar small valleys also carving down towards the water, flowing into one another like sand dunes in the desert.

We said good morning, or buongiorno, to a few other hikers coming up the hill as we continued to snake downwards. The sky was still overcast but the mist had vanished so we could at least see most of the landscape, including the small glaciers smeared across the rocks above us. For the most part the path was gentle and wide as we began making our way north towards the lake, culminating in a small forest that covered the ground above the shore.

Three hours after leaving the col and 1000 metres lower down, it was time for a more substantial rest and food stop. Our lunch spot was directly alongside a gushing river feeding into the very tip of the long lake we'd seen from above, the Lac des Places de Moulin. Now that the sun had come out it was suddenly very hot, so we hung our sodden tent out to dry over the little bridge we'd just crossed and settled down to our food. I cooked two batches of pasta that lunchtime, one for me and one that we shared, before we took our customary afternoon nap. I was out like a light instantly and when I did wake up, an hour later, it felt like no time had passed at all. It was as though I'd blinked and my watch had skipped an hour.

From the tip of the Lac des Places de Moulin, the Tour of the Matterhorn route marked on our map suggested that we should start climbing north-west along the Comba d'Oren valley, heading towards the 3069 metre Col Collon on the Swiss-Italian border. From the Col Collon, the route would then descend northwards and back into the Swiss side of the Alps via a crossing of the Haute Glacier d'Arolla. But we ruled that out straight away. It would mean taking on an unknown glacier crossing, still without any spikes for our shoes, right at a time when I was definitely not at my best. It was a non-starter.

But which route should we choose instead? We'd have to keep traversing west on the Italian side of the border, obviously, and then find another crossing that didn't involve a glacier. But where? And how much further west did we really want to go?

It was really a question of how much longer we wanted our tour to go on for? Tomorrow would be the end of our third week and in theory we still had several more weeks before we had to collect our dogs from friends and family. Did we want to start heading back towards the motorhome soon and try another tour elsewhere, or just keep going west until we reached Mont Blanc? Then we could either come back along the Haute Route or even start going south along the GR5 through France. Or how about catching a bus down into the Aosta valley and up the other side towards the Gran Paradiso peak and its National Park. We knew there was a tour around that as well. Or how about….the list went on.

We had more ideas than we knew what to do with, as usual, but the crux of the question was still how much longer did we want to keep going for? Esther, I knew, would keep going until winter arrived and snow forced her indoors. She just loved being outside and would never actually 'want' the tour to end. In many ways I felt the same, but while the open-ended nature of our adventure had been exhilarating three weeks earlier, in my weakened state it was causing me stress. Putting a plan in place that took us home in a reasonable time frame, something that I could commit to, was what I needed in that moment. And so, with the information we had at hand, this is what we came up with.

We knew that a little further west of us was the Grand Combin, the eighth highest mountain in the Alps at 4314 metres, which sits atop another huge and glaciated massif. We also knew that there was such a thing as a Tour des Combins, a seven to nine day loop around this great big lump which, a little like Mont Blanc, stands to the side of the main Alpine chain.

If you like, you could imagine the tours of Mont Blanc, Grand Combin, Matterhorn and Monte Rosa as large loops placed side by side as you move from west to east. Apart from the Theodul Pass, which is shared by the Matterhorn and Monte Rosa tours, the loops don't quite touch. But on a geological scale, they really aren't very far apart. There's even a route that goes around them all.

Among our little collection of leaflets from Zinal was another single sheet of paper with an overview map of the Tour des Combins. Looking at the map, I knew I didn't want to go all the way around the loop. It would mean another fortnight of hiking, at least, and that felt too much to commit to right now. We could, however, go just a little further west and find a crossing which joined the eastern fringe of the Tour des Combins, follow it for a day or so, and then pick up Haute Route back to Zinal. We reckoned that even if we still included an occasional detour, that would take us a more manageable eight or nine days to get home.

So, that was the plan. If it sounds complicated, then the details really don't matter. The point is, we were going back to our motorhome and expected it to take just over a week to get there. We still weren't certain of some details, because our own map didn't go quite far enough west to cover all of the route we had in mind. But we reckoned something would come up to fill in the gaps.

It did, only ten minutes later. Passing by the compact Rifugio Prax Raye, we ducked inside to buy some fruit. On the wall was a large map which went just far enough west to bring all of the disconnected strands of our plan together. Our next main landmark, it turned out, was the Col de Crête Séche (2889 m). That was where we would cross back into Switzerland.

We photographed what we needed to and began walking due west along the water. We could have stayed at that refuge for the night. It was already late afternoon and we could see another couple putting up their tent in the garden, but I was still feeling okay after lunch and wanted to keep going. Mostly this decision was weather-focused. Bearing in mind that we'd seen a rubbish weather forecast for the region, and that it was currently sunny, it seemed a shame to waste good hours of dry weather sitting in a refuge garden with a sore mouth.

The lakeside walk was delightful. Flat, wide and easy, it tracked the water's edge along the entire 4 km reservoir. The surface of the lake was a vivid turquoise, which gave an attractive contrast with the deep green of the pine trees on the far bank and the white glaciers at the northern end, while the abundant purple Alpine fireweed along the path added a brighter spark of colour to the overall scene. A handful of families were walking back towards the dam at the western end, the same direction as us, and we did briefly consider trying to hitch a lift along the road which we'd soon be joining, but in the end our nerve failed us and we just carried on marching.

We had about 9 km along the road to walk, which we expected would take us about 2 hours of solid effort.

Steeling ourselves for the soreness of tarmac marching, we got going. From time to time we spotted a possible camping spot hidden in trees by the roadside, but hiding by the road wasn't what we wanted to do. We wanted to get back into the high wilderness, if we could, and camp more openly and peacefully.

The march ended sooner than we'd hoped, thanks to a minor road that wasn't on the map we'd photographed but was signposted for the place we needed to reach. Shortly after turning, we passed a bed & breakfast and stepped inside to ask how much rooms cost, but they were already full. It was probably for the best since the garden was full of shouting children tearing around like sugar-crazed garden gnomes looking for their fishing rods. They did, however, sell us some home-made fruit juices and several tubes of smoothie which we reckoned would be a better way for me to sneak some energy past my sore gums.

It worked. It stung to chug half a litre of blueberry juice, but almost immediately I could feel my own sugar buzz rising up. By the time we left the tarmac behind and started climbing a dirt track twenty minutes later, I felt like a garden gnome myself, one who'd found not only a fishing rod but a big comfy toadstool to sit on.

The place we decided to camp was just a few hundred metres beyond the tarmac, a little patch of grass alongside an overgrown gravel road which may or may not have seen a car in the past twelve months. It probably had, but by now it was half past seven and we simply needed to stop. We'd done 7 hours of walking on very little food intake and I was physically finished for the day. It wasn't the best spot but it was quiet for the time being, the weather was warm and it was just about flat enough. The bed and breakfast had actually suggested camping somewhere along this track, so we even (sort of) had permission to do so.

A very slow and determined portion of watery oat bran and a tiny pot of nut butter that Esther had found somewhere became my dinner. Usually we just eat nuts, a small pot of creamy nut butter was a treat for me. Crikey it was nice, even though it coated my ulcers like battery acid. And that's basically the last thing I remember about that day, tucking myself into bed not long afterwards while Esther stretched and waited for the stars to come out alone outside. She might have called me to ask if I wanted to see how beautiful they were, but by then I was back in the Land of Nod dreaming of biting into a crisp, juicy apple. I can't say the whole "taking it easy" thing was going so well, but we were definitely still having a marvellous adventure.

Vital Statistics – Day 20
Start Point: Bivacco Manenti
End Point: Chez Chenoux
Distance Hiked: 19 km
Hiking Time: 7 hours
Ascent: 320 metres
Descent: 1380 metres

Thieving Marmot Bastard

"Where is it then?" I asked. "You said it was on this side of the tent, but it isn't".

"It is, because I definitely put it there" replied Esther. "I mixed it up last night and tucked it next to your pack. Let me see."

It was just after eight on a warm, dry morning and we were trying to track down our breakfast. Esther insisted she'd made overnight oat bran after I'd gone to bed and left it by the tent, but our trusty, slightly battered and well-travelled yoghurt pot was now nowhere to be seen.

"Something must have nicked it then" I concluded.

"Like what? It's porridge."

"Marmots like porridge. They're famous for it" I replied. "I bet there's a marmot out there right now enjoying our breakfast as we speak."

"But I used up the last of our raisins so it was more sugary for you, to get some energy in" Esther said anxiously, worrying about trying to keep me fed.

"Then it's a very excited marmot that's had our breakfast. If we spot a marmot running crazy circles later on then we'll know it was him."

"You're an idiot, do you know that" smiled Esther.

"Who's more of an idiot though? The person that acts like an idiot or the person who chooses to live with them?"

"Probably the latter" said Esther, with a sigh of resignation and a smile.

We replaced our stolen breakfast with another portion of watery oats, which I supplemented with one more pot of some stinging nut butter. The pain was definitely reducing though. I had no mirror to check, but I felt like some of the smallest ulcers had already vanished from between my front teeth, leaving only the really big ones beneath my tongue, around my molars and in the roof of my mouth. How people with chronic dental problems or with no teeth at all cope, I have no idea.

The ever-developing ballad of the sugar-crazed, thieving marmot bastard (and his ibex henchmen) was a nice bit of light relief to lift the fatigue of the moment. Today was the day we intended to climb back into Switzerland via the Col de Crête Séche, 1150 metres of ascent in Italy followed by a blue-and-white Alpine route on the Swiss side, according to our photographed map. In other words, we expected it to be a challenge.

We were moving by nine, our first target the Rifugio Crête Séche at 2383 metres. It was a green and tree-lined ascent with abundant wild blueberry bushes lining the edges of the path. Frequently I'd be plodding along and find myself suddenly alone, Esther having stopped to pick some blueberries and getting addicted to the process. We've known for years that Esther has an addictive personality. When we were first getting to know each other, I introduced Esther to the push-penny machines in British seaside amusement arcades, the ones with sliding shelves that you drop pennies and two-pence pieces into in an effort to win 12 pence back. I knew then that she should never be allowed to bet on horses. Eight quid that visit cost me, all lost in two pence pieces. Esther's also the only person I've ever heard of who demanded to the see the manager when it became clear that the claw was deliberately letting go of the teddy bears she was trying to win. And don't get me started on the reason we ended up with two toasters in a week when she first discovered eBay ("but I was the highest bidder, I won!").

In all seriousness, joking aside, Esther does not and has never had any sort of gambling problem. She's actually one of the most personally frugal but outwardly generous people I've ever met. She just finds it hard to stop picking tasty wild blueberries (and she really did win two toasters).

An information panel by the trail, during one of our rare inter-blueberry moments, told us a little about the Alpine mammals we might expect to see in the area, including ibex, chamois, golden eagles, ptarmigan, bearded vultures, mountain hares, deer and marmots. Happily, we realised we'd seen all of these treasures over the years but there were two more on the list that we'd never seen, the ermine and Tengmalm's owl. The mountains are such a rich habitat for so many beautiful creatures that it was a reminder what a gift it was for us to be able to spend so much time living among them.

We reached the refuge just before eleven, moving slowly due to a combination of blueberry pauses and my continued lethargy. On a serious note, since leaving Breuil-Cervinia, in addition to the physical challenge of hiking on minimal food there was also a mood-related factor to bear in mind. Because I was largely relying on fast energy, sugary snacks to give me boosts as we went along, it hadn't escaped our notice that between snacks I could become incredibly grouchy and short-tempered. We knew it was only the reality of my body struggling for energy, but it was something we both tried to be aware of when I grew snappish and rude (because Esther was picking blueberries again, dammit!)

I tried to remember to apologise and Esther did her best not to take offence, but it would be unfair to think that my problems were solely physical. The impact from my illness was also creating emotional and relationship challenges as well, though I like to think we managed to stay fairly calm in the face of my erratic moods.

As usual, there was a large map pinned to the wall inside the refuge. Interestingly, the route we were taking back into Switzerland over the Col de Crête Séche was marked on this map as the Matterhorn tour.

"Maybe the Italians promote a different route?" we mused. "Or perhaps they just changed it to make it shorter but more technical?"

Either way, itineraries are only guides and there's no rule that says you can't create your own. The refuge guardians were very friendly and sold us a litre of tropical fruit juice for me to get some sugar back into my body. Again, I wouldn't normally drink such a radioactive-looking concoction, but this time I downed it in almost one go. I half expected I'd turn bright orange, like the Tango Man in the 1992 UK advert for the soft drink (go on, look it up on YouTube. You know you want to).

Fifteen minutes later, I was buzzing. I hadn't felt so full of energy in days. I was like a whole army of garden gnomes ready to march on Switzerland.

Hoping to make the most of my sugar high, we started the remaining 500 odd metres of climbing with a fresh surge of pace. About 100 more metres of grassy ascent above the refuge took us past another bivacco, Bivacco Spataro, which looked like a metal shed. We guessed it must have room for about 6 people inside, though we didn't stop to look.

By now we had a fine view in both directions along the green Valpelline valley, but just above the bivacco that all changed. Perched as it is, on a smooth crag indicative that a huge glacier once sat there, the bivacco marked our entry into an enormous, flat-bottomed glacial bowl. Gone were the trees and grasses, replaced with a barren scene of ancient glacial devastation.

It was almost a kilometre of nearly flat walking along the bottom of that valley, threading our way through increasingly large boulders and hopping across small rivulets of water, before the gradient reared up once again. It was another grey landscape. All around us were loose lumps of stone, packed together with dust and balanced precariously as though moving a single pebble could set off a landslide.

We did our best to stick to the trail, sweating uphill in shuffling steps that left holes in the dust. Behind us the view grew wider and wider, the smooth sides of the hanging valley we'd just passed through creating an elegant frame for the hills beyond.

Somewhere along the way my fruit-juice fizz ran out. I guess this is what marathon runners mean when they talk about hitting the wall. One moment I was moving upwards and smiling, taking the shifting earth in my stride. The next, I was trying my best on wobbly knees as the horizon seemed to be shaking above me. I wanted to curl up and sleep again, except it was too cold and too uncomfortable, so I tried to focus my uncertain vision on one step at a time.

We made it to the top, just about. Passing by several late season snow patches, we eventually stepped out onto a saddle of stone surrounded by a dark and grey backdrop. Even the sky had turned grey as we'd climbed, with a chilly breeze wafting over the col around us. The valley we had climbed was grey and so was the one directly in front of us, the only difference being that the north-facing valley ahead still had a large section of glacier in it. On either side of us the ridgeline extended away for some distance before rising up into higher peaks, mostly devoid of snow and generally speaking (you guessed it) grey.

We paused for a short stop and I forced down some semi-nibbled raisins. It was while doing so that we first spotted a blur of brown fur whip past us.

"Er-be-nee" I grunted, choking on a raisin and pointing. "Ermine". Sure enough that's what it was. An ermine, sometimes also called a stoat or short-tailed weasel, (which is an actual name and not just a great insult). A tiny twenty centimetre streak of incessantly moving brown, darting impossibly fast between, over and under rocks so that we were perhaps treated to a maximum of one or two seconds glance each time. He (or she) was beautiful, his long thin body flexing like a snake as his tiny paws flung him from place to place.

It took us a while to work out the way into Switzerland. Every direct route seemed to take us straight to a sheer drop onto the glacier. A blue-and-white signpost did point in that general direction, but we couldn't see any more markers. Had the path fallen away? Collapsed? Was it actually still possible to get down?

It was only when we turned our attention further afield that we spotted a faded splash of blue and white paint to the side of the col. Because of the sheer valley head, it turned out that the only way to get down was to climb further still, following the ridge that extended sideways to reach a place where we could begin a more realistic descent. Traversing smooth, bare rock, it took about ten minutes of gentle climbing before we spotted a steeply angled track descending into a scree-field on our left.

It was a technical descent, but after three weeks of practice we were getting used to that by now. With the Glacier de Crête Séche always in sight, we carefully negotiated our way down the trail, occasionally assisted by metal chains hammered into exposed patches of bedrock. Even when we reached the flattened bottom of the hanging valley, we found that we still couldn't relax because of the jumble of rubble that the path went through. Every single step required us to concentrate on our footing, leaving us almost oblivious to the scenery around us.

Fairly soon we decided we needed to rest. It was overcast and not very warm, but by mid-afternoon it was time for an attempt at lunch, sunshine or not. I broke out the cooking gear and prepared some more of my best friend (soggy lentil pasta) while we sat back to take in the wilderness. Sat in a hanging valley at about 2300 metres, we were looking almost directly north towards a huge and triangular shoulder of rock which rose up to the Pic d'Otemma (3403 m). Either side of the shoulder the valley split away, to the right rising slowly up the long Glacier d'Otemma, while to the right the valley dipped and vanished out of sight. That was the way we were going, into the unknown in search of the Tour des Combins. Apart from some tufty grass immediately around us, almost everything we could see was still grey, white and bare, a far-reaching wilderness of stone and ice which made us feel very much surrounded by nature's power.

After a lovely snuggled up doze on the bumpy floor, we started moving again by four o'clock, our intention being to find a place to pitch our tent as soon as we could. The grey clouds were noticeably darker than they'd been when we'd sat down and we were pretty convinced it was going to rain soon. Reaching the point at which the two valleys split, we made a steep descent down to the river gushing out of the Glacier d'Otemma to discover a small concrete dam and some industrial equipment tucked into a man-made cave. The water was raging over the dam, boiling up like an inverted waterfall, and we guessed it was generating a decent amount of power somewhere, but it was the cave that most interested us. Could we perhaps just pitch the tent in there?

After some serious contemplation, we decided against it. The cave wasn't very deep and the last thing we wanted was to get fined for trespassing on private property. There was probably a camera somewhere, so we carried on hiking just as the drizzle began to arrive, spitting lightly in intermittent bursts that were blown sideways by the gusting wind.

As we followed the dirt road away from the dam, the vast bulk of the Grand Combin massif drifted into view. The top was shrouded in dense cloud but the visible contours of the various merging valleys around it was still a beautiful sight to see, a taster of what we might enjoy tomorrow.

In theory we were less than half an hour's walking from a refuge, the Cabane de Chanrion at 2455 metres, but we were hoping to stop even sooner than that. Directly ahead of us was the green and lumpy slope up towards the cabane which looked like an ideal place to conceal a small tent in one of the many grassy recesses.

That we even bothered to check out the handful of nearby buildings first was little more than wishful thinking at the time. Ever since we'd discovered that wondrous empty cabin on our fourth day, and now after experiencing bivaccos, we were always on the lookout for unmanned storm shelters that we might reasonably bunk down in.

The first couple we tried actually looked like they might have been refuges once upon a time, with long tables and bunk beds visible inside, but they were totally locked down. There was one more building we could see, a bland concrete box a few hundred metres across the grass, slightly above us, and at first I was too tired to even carry my pack over to it. Esther went on her own, but when she came back to say it was unlocked, had space for beds in but was "weird", we decided we needed to take a look together.

What we'd stumbled upon, from the outside, looked like a cow shed. It was long and thin, with clean concrete walls, a pristine pine door and a solid metal roof. Inside, it was a mystery. One wall was panelled with wood but the others were bare, dirty concrete. There was random furniture scattered around, including an electric oven that was upside down. There were kitchen units with doors hanging off and, the most pleasant part of all, there was a moderate amount of dried cow shit on the floor. So far, not so good. There were also random metal hooks driven into the walls and various industrial sized tools, like a pick-axe about as long as me.

Yet among all of this mess and strangeness was a collection of wooden bunks built against the far wall in standard dormitory style, with some mouldering foam pads underneath to suggest it was, or at least had been, a shelter. There was also a separate area by the entrance, boxed in, containing a still-working, flushing ceramic toilet.

All signs suggested it was an abandoned shelter now used for random storage. Yet the weirdest and most unsettling items were a bag of mouldy carrots (dated just two weeks earlier) and a plastic bowl containing a spoon and some not-yet-mouldy sweetcorn on a table in a corner.

Was someone actively living here? Right now? Browsing a little deeper, we discovered a patch of graffiti on the wood panelling close to the bunks. It was a series of dates denoting several days every August for the past 10 years. At the top of the list was the name 'Piotrek' and next to the dates was a cartoon man, wearing a farmer's hat with a piece of straw sticking out of his mouth, huge sideburns and his eyes looking in opposite directions.

"Well, I hope he isn't living here" I said.

The most likely explanation, we hoped, was that this Piotrek chap came here for a few days every August, and that this time he'd just decided to leave without his carrots, spoon and sweetcorn. There was a chance he might show up later, we supposed, but we were so tired by now and it was raining hard outside, so we decided to risk it. We didn't feel like walking further and putting up a tent outside now that we were here felt like a lot of work.

There was already one clean foam mattress on the wooden bunks, which I planned to sleep on, while Esther would use her air bed. I cooked up some nice, soft stewed apples with a little oat bran for dinner, followed by some saucepans of tea as we waited for darkness to fall.

The rain eased off just after dark, so we stood in the now clear air for a while to reflect on just what a varied adventure we were stumbling through. Of all the places we'd stayed, this was the strangest by far. Yet Piotrek's hut, as we were calling it, had all the comfort we needed and more.

However, just to be sure, we decided to bolt the door overnight and balanced the key on the door frame. That way, if anyone did start rattling to get in, we'd at least have some warning.

Vital Statistics – Day 21
Start Point: Chez Chenoux
End Point: Piotrek's Hut
Distance Hiked: 12 kilometres
Hiking Time: 6 hours
Ascent: 1210 metres
Descent: 560 metres

Hot and Bothered

The key hit the floor at 2 a.m., landing with a clang that jerked us instantly awake and upright. Outside, thunder and lightning were ripping across the sky, creating deep rumbles that we could hear reverberating between the mountains. When the lightning flashed, we could see rain beating against the window and running down in thick streams. This was not the time we wanted to be greeting Piotrek, or anyone else wandering around in a storm come to that. Fumbling for my head torch, I shone the beam at the door and waited. Fifteen seconds went by, and then thirty. It was just the wind after all, though it had been an abrupt way to be woken up in the middle of the night.

Although it was an eerie place, most of our nerves were really just due to the worry we might be doing something a bit naughty by taking shelter in this strange, abandoned bunk house. The mind has a tendency to play tricks in the dark, but the reality is that the mountains above two thousand metres really are incredibly safe (in terms of crime at least). I mean, honestly, who's going to be wandering around out there in the dark on the off chance they'll find someone to be mean to? It's hard to say it, but if someone really wants to cause harm to another human, busy cities are much easier places to do so. I suppose the fear is primal. The fear of not knowing, of feeling exposed. It's probably even something to do with sabre-tooth tigers.

For us, as we lay back again and listened to the storm raging outside, we were mostly just incredibly grateful for the solid concrete walls and metal roof. Another storm, another night in a building. It was as though we were weather Jedi!

When we woke up again at seven, the sun had returned. Taking a couple of the old deck chairs lying around the place outside, we parked ourselves in the first rays of warmth arriving on the hillside and nibbled at last night's leftovers.

In the clear morning sunshine, the very tip of the Grand Combin massif could just be seen emerging from behind a nearby ridge. It became increasingly visible as we began the short, easy climb towards Cabane de Chanrion, taking a dirt road that zig-zagged the short distance north. By the time we stopped for a brief pause on the terrace of the cabane itself, we could see much more of the broad expanse of the massif across the valley to the west.

Unfortunately, following the usual pattern, by now a cloud had expanded over the highest cluster of summits though it didn't prevent us enjoying fine views of the glaciated slopes and cliff faces across the valley. Standing out especially was the tongue of the Glacier du Mont Durand, flowing down from Mont Avril and Tête Blanche, while the stone-covered Glacier de la Tsessette was nestled at the foot of the vertical eastern face of the massif. We were now officially on the Tour des Combins.

From the Cabane de Chanrion we had two options, a high route and a low route. Both would take us along the five kilometre length of Lac de Mauvoisin, a reservoir created by the 250 metre high barrage above the village of Mauvoisin, the eleventh highest dam in the world. Signposts suggested both routes would take almost the same amount of time, with the high route being slightly less distance but requiring a little climbing in order to pass over the 2635 metre Col de Tsofeiret.

We decided on the high route (what else), setting off across the slopes on the eastern side of the Mauvoisin valley. The path was easy, following a well-trodden brown track through grassy hillside. After just a short while we passed across the mouth of another long glacial valley, home to the Glacier du Brenas, though the remaining tongue of ice was some distance away from us.

Marmots were frequent sights, dashing from burrow to burrow and chirruping their warnings as we approached. So far we were yet to see any other human beings apart from the guardians at the cabane which, along with the unmoving air and warm sun, made for an especially peaceful mood on this happy August morning.

Our photographed map reached only as far as the barrage, so we had no idea exactly how far north we'd then need to go to find the Haute Route, but we were sure something would come up once again. Until then we just had to meander through this pleasant Alpine landscape, with the bulk of the Grand Combin massif to our left and a tangle of intricate hills and ridges on our right. Not a bad place to let life unfold around us.

We soon crossed the Col de Tsofeiret, enjoying a delightful view over the small Lac de Tsofeiret as our reward. Situated just below us, with bright blue waters surrounded by lush grass and a herd of cows drifting slowly across the northern end, it was a classic Alpine scene.

The route stayed relatively level after that, trending downwards only very slowly and easily, although it felt like a long, long way to the barrage. Several small groups of hikers passed us on their way up the gradual incline, but it was mostly just the two of us meandering far above the chalky blue waters of the long thin reservoir.

With a short stop for a snack and a doze, it would be over two hours before we started down the steep descent to the water's edge. Once there, we were excited to find that the final approach to the barrage included several tunnels cut deep into the mountain, some of them with massive openings behind waterfalls plunging into the reservoir. To be stood just a few metres behind a thundering deluge of white water, the ground shaking beneath our feet and the thick spray breezing across our faces like a revitalising mist was an exhilarating experience. Not to mention a welcome one in the rapidly growing heat of the early afternoon.

By the time we crossed the barrage itself at half past one, we'd been on the go for about five hours. We'd been taking it very easy, but we were definitely in the mood for a more substantial rest and some food. A series of thirty large photographs were spaced along the 520 metre long barrage. A notice at either end told us this was an annual art installation, "a must-see event for contemporary art-lovers and Alpine hikers", apparently. This year's guest artist, Batia Suter, had aimed, so we were told, to create visual poems by fading several photographs into one. Some of them, I have to say, were very engaging and it definitely brightened our stroll across the concrete walkway, a concrete walkway that just happened to have an Alpine reservoir on one side and a 250 metre drop on the other!

Which is, of course, why it's such a useful concrete walkway (and not just because we needed to cross it). Sitting, as it does, on top of a system that generates around 400,000 kW of electricity via 4 separate turbine stations downstream, this particular heap of tactically-placed concrete makes a sizeable contribution to Switzerland's electricity needs.

A short and hot section of tarmac walking took us down to a small restaurant and car park at about 1900 metres altitude, a base for many day hikers it seemed from the number of cars lining the roadside. It was here that we decided to have our lunch with our final portion of food and work out more firmly what to do next.

Our aim was to get to the Chamonix-to-Zermatt Haute Route, which we'd then follow back towards our motorhome in Zinal. From the Haute Route guidebook on Esther's phone, the closest place that we knew we could pick up the Haute Route was a town called La Châble at about 800 metres altitude, more than a kilometre below us and somewhere along the road that we were sat on. Unfortunately, without a detailed map at this stage, we had no idea how far away La Châble actually was. We guessed it was about 20 kilometres, but that was only based on the fact most mountain roads tend to be 5-6% average gradient. For all we knew, it was actually a lot further.

It was almost certainly too far to walk anyway, and because it was mid-afternoon that meant we'd have to hitchhike or find a bus. We were now out of food, so we had to go down one way or another.

Whether it was due to tiredness, the heat or just the sudden busyness around us, it felt a little overwhelming all of a sudden. For example, in daily life it's easy not to notice the 'smell' of cars very much. Unless an especially smoky heap of junk appears, the undertone of exhaust fumes is usually just another part of the aromatic assault created by urban environments, an assault the body naturally adjusts to because that what our bodies do. They adjust, they adapt. It's why our flimsy human frames are so incredible.

After almost three weeks in the mountains, however, our experience is that even a single car is hard to ignore. Like a single cigarette being lit in a sterile hospital ward, the smell just sticks in the back of your throat like a noxious film. It only takes a few hours for the body to acclimatise again, which probably isn't a good thing, but for those first few blessed hours after revelling in the more natural dirt of the outdoors, urban environments might as well be alien worlds for the senses. The sounds, the lights, the smells, the plastic surfaces. We actually find it a difficult readjustment, though a powerful one because it allows us, for just a short window of time, to see the world with fresh eyes. To question, is this really how it needs to be?

Which is precisely what it felt like when we arrived in the town of Sembrancher just an hour after deciding not to worry about how we'd get down the mountain. This is what happened. We were sitting in the sun eating pasta, when we fell into conversation with a German couple who told us they were going to cycle up to Cabane de Chanrion on their mountain bikes. They asked what we'd been doing, so we gave them a short summary of our route and where we were heading next. Five minutes later another man approached us and told us he'd overheard our plans and was driving to La Châble, right then, if we needed a ride. It was that simple.

Our Good Samaritan was called Alan, an American who'd moved to Switzerland with his wife a few years earlier. He was an outdoor sports guide, skiing particularly, and after several years working in the Rocky Mountains around Colorado they'd decided to move to Europe. He'd just spent the day cycling with his daughter around the Lac de Mauvoisin and was now heading to their house on the outskirts of La Châble.

Alan was really relaxed, funny and easy to talk to, but his daughter was funnier without even knowing it. While I sat in the front chatting with Alan, Esther sat in the back with his daughter who was playing quietly with some dolls. At one point Alan's phone rang and he ignored it. A few seconds later his daughter called out "Daddy, why didn't you answer your phone?"

"Because I'm driving and it's not safe to use the phone while you drive" he replied.

"But…but….but you always use the phone while you're driving" she said. Alan didn't say anything but continued to drive, his eyes fixed firmly ahead.

A few minutes later she also asked him, "Daddy, why are you driving so slowly. You normally drive really fast. Especially around corners." Again, Alan didn't say a word. I love kids!

We explained to Alan that our main priority was getting some food before finding a place to stay. As a result, Alan had very kindly driven us an extra five kilometres beyond La Châble to drop us at the larger supermarkets in Sembrancher (which is also on the Haute Route by the way, just an hour of flattish valley walking before La Châble).

Unlike our other dips into civilisation, such as at Saas-Fee and Breuil-Cervinia, there was something different about being down here in Sembrancher. Why was it so overwhelming all of a sudden? Then we realised. It was 36°C. At just 717 metres altitude, it dawned on us this was the lowest altitude we'd been for almost 4 weeks (if you include the days we'd spent preparing in Zinal). This wasn't the busyness of a mountain village full of visitors, but the busyness of a main thoroughfare at a popular valley junction.

Ravenous for something soft and full of sugar, Esther dipped into the Migros supermarket and came back quickly with a batch of non-dairy yogurts which I inhaled, one after the other like I was doing shots, and with hardly any pain. They weren't exactly very calorific, but after the previous few days of slow chewing and tentative gulping, it was nice just to put something in my mouth and pretend it was normal. After that, we did a more robust stock-up.

Food on board, the next thing we had to do was find a place to stay. Booking.com revealed nothing available in Sembrancher at all, but there were a few places back up the road in La Châble. Walking was an option, it being part of the Haute Route and everything, but we just didn't feel like it.

Instead, we walked our 'full-food' packs to the train station and caught the next train back to La Châble, the end of the line. We were too tired to even think about hitching at this stage and since it was only 4 francs for a ticket, it didn't seem worth the effort anyway. Arriving in La Châble armed with a shortlist of possible hotels and rooms, we walked around in the heat trying to find the one we thought would suit us the best. First we tried an anonymous looking hotel building, but when we discovered that it was a directly above a bar and the manager kept us waiting for over ten minutes because she was serving drinks, I lost my cool and stormed out. The heat and the fatigue, the crowded bar and my endless hunger just all came to a head in that instant and I just couldn't be around anyone.

"Why the hell didn't we just book something two fucking hours ago outside the supermarket and save all this fucking about" I demanded, blaming Esther only because I had nobody and nothing else to direct my anger at (well, I did throw my bag on the floor, but all that succeeded in doing was bursting three yoghurts).

"It's six o'clock, we should be clean and rested, not walking around in this bastard sauna town just to try and save a few quid or find the softest bed."

Esther stayed calm, as usual, as I blew my frustration out. I was just tired. I'd been ill. I'd been hungry. And now I was painfully hot. I wanted a room so badly I could taste it but the energy required to get to one just seemed beyond me.

We took five minutes to sit still and breathe and then started walking again, very slowly, towards a completely different sort of accommodation option. It was a room in the house of an elderly lady, Madame Elizabeth, who kept two doubles and a single room available in her own home. The reviews online were all 9 out of 10, but I'd initially been reluctant to try staying in someone's house, preferring the idea of hotel anonymity. I couldn't have been more wrong.

Mme Elizabeth greeted us like family and showed us into a cluttered but clean and homely room on the ground floor of her house. The walls were lined with books and teddy bears, but there was enough space for our stuff. She asked us politely to leave our boots outside but was happy for us to handwash any clothes that we liked in the bathroom, even providing a plastic tub for us to use. She gave us a brief tour of her garden and encouraged us to help ourselves to as many plump blackberries as we could eat. Then she was gone. We didn't see or interact with her again until she served us breakfast in the morning.

It was such a quiet, family home with an amazing and secluded garden, that we were immediately overwhelmed by the contrast with the busy, anonymous bar-hotel we'd initially tended towards. In hindsight, this was much more suited to our personalities.

I got showered first and then handwashed our hiking clothes before getting into bed just after seven. Connecting to the internet on Esther's phone, I just chilled out by watching old episodes of Hornblower on YouTube, which was what I needed to unwind after my little explosion earlier.

Esther continued to give me space, unwinding in her own way by feeding the guinea pigs, eating blackberries and chatting with a fellow guest. Alana was an Australian lady travelling alone and who was about to start a seven day Haute Route tour herself, having just completed the Tour du Mont Blanc a few days earlier.

Spending so much time together as a couple, so intensely, for weeks on end, often with decisions to make in a state of physical tiredness, we'd come to expect and plan for needing a few hours apart now and then to relax in our own ways. On the hills, in a tent, it wasn't often possible, so this night in La Châble was just what we needed, in more ways than one.

By the time I was ready to sleep and Esther had done chatting at about ten o'clock, we spent a little time together choosing some of the photos we'd taken since Breuil-Cervinia. As per usual, since we had a solid roof over our heads for the night, it began raining heavily outside. It was so normal at this stage we hardly even remarked on our continued good fortune.

And then, quarter of an hour later, when the rain turned into a storm and started to rattle the window shutters, we simply turned off the bedside lamp and rolled over in duvet-wrapped comfort.

Vital Statistics – Day 22
Start Point: Piotrek's Hut
End Point: La Châble
Distance Hiked: 10 km
Hiking Time: 5 hours
Ascent: 230 metres
Descent: 650 metres

Verbier

Thanks to the slow but continued improvement in my mouth, breakfast was a much more abundant affair than it might have been. Mme Elizabeth welcomed us to her small kitchen table where our fellow guest, Alana, was already making a start on her Weetabix. With home-made bread, jams and fruit juices available alongside cereals, meat and cheese, it was a cosy little scene, the three of us helping ourselves to tea and coffee by the kettle and talking about everything from our adventures to our hopes and dreams for the future.

Alana was a nurse back in Australia and was in Europe for four weeks, reasoning that if she was going to come all of this way she might as well do it properly. She'd wanted to try some walking in the Alps so had joined a couple of tour groups. The organisers, she explained handled the logistics of reserving beds in refuges, providing daily maps and moving the bulk of her luggage between overnight accommodation, leaving her free to just enjoy walking.

"And do you know the people you're walking with?" we asked.

"No, you meet them on Day 1. That's what I'm doing in about an hour at the ski lift. There will be fourteen of us in total, doing seven days on the Haute Route together." Alana explained.

"Do you all have to walk as a big group?"

"No, not closely. On the Mont Blanc Tour we got paired with someone to buddy with, and the group tended to stay generally together, but you didn't have to walk side by side all day."

It sounded like a good way of doing things for someone on their own, who wasn't familiar with an area and who also wanted a level of social time on their adventure. We had to admit that part of the reason we'd just felt able to just take off into the Alps, without a firm route or timeline, was because we were in a region we'd spent time in before. Not that we knew the specific areas we'd visited, because apart from a handful of exceptions it was all new to us. But we still felt comfortable in the region. Comfortable enough to know that help was usually on hand, one way or another, and familiar enough to have a sense of which direction we were going.

Alana was a fun breakfast companion and we enjoyed chatting with her. I was also very happy to be eating more normally again and not to be eating Esther's overnight oat bran (as lovely as it is). Mixing my remaining unburst yoghurts with oats and honey, I was eating a richer, creamier and more solid meal than I'd had in almost a week, since starting to lose my appetite before reaching Breuil-Cervinia. I even managed a couple of Weetabix, soaked into paste using my portion of Mme Elizabeth's home-made pear, apple and blackcurrant juice.

Unfortunately, during my week of living on starvation rations, my stomach seemed to have shrunk to the size of a pea (a small one), so as I carefully manoeuvred the food around my mouth I was aware I couldn't eat nearly as much as other parts of me wanted to. The last thing I needed was to spend the rest of the day staggering around with a belly ache.

The Cicerone guide to the Haute Route suggests a relatively short stage out of La Châble, covering just nine kilometres but which takes an estimated six hours due to the 1636 metre height gain. The destination, as usual in the guidebooks, is a refuge, the Cabane du Mont Fort at 2457 metres.

Fortunately for us, and surprisingly, our room for the night came with a head start. At breakfast Mme Elizabeth asked if we would be needing a lift pass for the day, one of which apparently came included with a tourist tax portion of our room fee. We all said "yes", naturally, and a short while later Mme Elizabeth returned with a personalised pass for each of us and an overview map of the available lifts we could now use.

It was called the "Verbier Infinite Playground" pass and wonderfully entitled us to use most of the lifts and local buses in the surrounding area. It would be hard for us to turn down a free ski lift, especially one that would enable us to get quite so high and avoid many hours of uphill walking. Our total climbing to this point was just over 20 vertical kilometres, so dodging an extra kilometre was a very welcome prospect. If we wanted to, we could even go right up to 3328 metres at the summit of Mont Fort, although it wasn't strictly on the main Haute Route.

Back in our room with full bellies, we formulated a little plan for the day. The overview map Mme Elizabeth had provided showed us where all the ski lifts and stations were in relation to a collection of coloured hiking routes. Comparing this to the Cicerone guide, we could see that one of the relevant cable car stations was quite close to a Haute Route variant for the following stage, i.e. the stage beyond Cabane du Mont Fort.

The plan we came up with was this, to visit the very top of Mont Fort via cable car (just because we could), spend some time enjoying the view and then, in the late afternoon, catch a lift back to the lower station and start following that variant. It would mean skipping an entire stage of the Haute Route guide between La Châble and Cabane du Mont Fort, but so what. We'd be back in the high mountains and we'd almost certainly be able to find a nice place to pitch our tent.

We said our goodbyes to Mme Elizabeth shortly after ten o'clock and made our way down to the lift station, which was directly opposite the train station in proper Swiss efficient style. Noticing Alana in a huddle of people all saying hello to each other, we wished her well again and wondered if we might see her somewhere up there?

The first lift carried us gently up to the resort town of Verbier at 1522 metres, followed by a second lift up to Les Ruinettes at 2200 metres. Along the way we were surprised at just how big Verbier was. It was huge. A sprawling mass of mostly brown houses completely hidden from the valley floor, but once we were up there it looked enormous. It was also massively busy. Stepping out of the first car at Verbier, we had joined the back of a huge press of people shuffling into the Les Ruinettes lift station. It was like trying to get on a commuter train at rush hour, only with more smiling faces. We edged forward slowly, swallowed into the mass of people, packs and mountain bikes, until we eventually got spat out at the front of the huddle, almost shoved into the waiting plastic bubble.

We began walking when we reached Les Ruinettes, picking up a nearly flat traverse towards the next ski station that was open, La Chaux (2266 m). The route itself followed a gravel access road between the two stations, with an occasional shuttle van ferrying people between them. But we didn't feel like queuing for the shuttle, not when the whole world was spread out before us.

It was another beautiful summer's day and as we followed the gently rising trail we found ourselves on a balcony looking west at the combined beauty of both Mont Blanc and Grand Combin, each rising clear and proud above the landscape around them. Separated by what seemed like just a short span of air, these two glaciated, snow-bound giants were framed between the perfectly blue and cloud-free sky above and by the purple flowers swaying on the hillside at our feet.

This was the perfect angle from which to appreciate the dome of Mont Blanc's summit and how it rises above the huge but not quite as tall spires and ridges that surround it like an honour guard. We remembered that when walking around the Tour du Mont Blanc, the perspective changes and the highest point seems to be ever-changing depending on where you stand. But from here, the Big Daddy in the centre was unmistakable.

It was also by far our best view of the Grand Combin so far, its characteristic covering of brilliant white snow on the north face looking right at us, like thick icing on a Christmas cake. With each step we took, we drew closer to that magnificent summit, staring as glacier flows crept into sight and the top seemed to grow further towards the sky.

But even these two monumental mountains were just a small part of the wider scene. Beneath us, the cavernous void of the Val de Bagnes curved in a graceful sweep between the Lac de Mauvoisin and Sembrancher, splitting at its mouth between the Rhone Valley on the right and up towards La Fouly on the left. Beyond that, countless other more distant folds of earth vanished away from us.

Passing a handful of art installations, most notably a ten-foot-tall wooden penguin facing the Grand Combin (we didn't know why, but it worked), we reached La Chaux. From here we caught a crowded gondola over the Cabane du Mont Fort up to the Col des Gentianes (2894 m), followed by an equally crowded one over the Glacier de Tortin to reach the summit of Mont Fort (3328 m). With mountain bikes, children, dogs and everything in between, it was practically cheek to cheek in those gondolas, but once we stepped out on top it was totally worth the crush.

It was still busy, this being only a small viewing platform with a snack bar claiming to offer the highest fondue in Europe. But next to the cheese-vendor was the start of a carved pathway which rose another fifty metres above the station, reaching the very summit of Mont Fort where a metal cross marked the apparent top of the world. That was what we had come up here for, not the noise and the smell of melted cheese.

Lakes, mountains, glaciers and valleys. Mont Blanc, Grand Combin and the Matterhorn. Snow, ice, rock and pasture. It was all laid out before us like a feast for the eyes. Everywhere we looked was a new wonder, a new glacier to point towards, a distant reservoir, a summit or a valley we knew we'd walked along. From here we could, quite literally, see the entire region through which we'd spent three and a bit weeks walking. It was magnificent. It was enormous and it was humbling. Who were we in this universe of wonders? Just two tiny grains of sand tumbling up and down mountains in search of….what? It felt so right to be here and yet, it's hard to explain why? Is it perspective we seek up here? Meaning? A feeling of aliveness? Togetherness? Solitude? All of the above? Or just a damn fine view? "Yes" is the only answer I can give.

We spent time with each landmark and direction, zooming in closer and closer to appreciate the intricacies of the ridges and spires and then zooming out again to appreciate the whole effect. Our heads were, in both a literal and figurative sense, spinning with it all. We began tracing out the route ahead of us, over there, around that, next to those, daydreaming at the new wonders we might see. This really was a majestic place to pass the time, so much so that we almost forgot about the hundreds of others coming and going around us.

We stayed at the top for an hour. We might have stayed longer but it was cold and we still had a little walking planned for the day. We had lunch back at the Col des Gentianes station, one gondola down, leaning against a wall in the shade of a restaurant and looking across at the smooth curve of the Glacier de Tortin beneath Mont Fort. At some point we must have dozed off (surprise, surprise), only to be woken by the sensation of an army of Orthodox Jews stepping over our prone bodies.

Perhaps it was a bus tour or an extended family on holiday, but we opened our eyes to the peculiar sight of a few dozen men in dark suits, dark hats and all with payot nodding and smiling down on us. They were all very nice about it. Blinking in the sun, we waved quietly back. It seemed they were off to try sledging on the edge of the glacier, using bin bags and plastic trays to slide down the short slope close to the restaurant. It was a strange sight, grown men in their Sunday best slipping on their bums, but everyone looked so happy that it lifted our own spirits further still.

It was half past three and time to get moving. We had a few hundred metres downhill to start with, followed by a climb back up over the 2940 metre Col de la Chaux. This was the Haute Route alternative towards the next col, the Col de Louvie, and is described in the guidebook as possibly "safer under certain conditions". Well, I can't imagine what those conditions are because as we followed the blue-and-white markers up the steep and stone-studded glacial ice towards the top, we couldn't help thinking it was one of the more demanding short climbs of our entire tour. Away from the ice-encrusted and snow-packed sections, the stone trail was dusty and crumbling, sliding away beneath our feet and sending pebbles skidding across the exposed ice around us. It was exciting, but it didn't feel like something we could ever call "safe".

We crossed the col intact to find another bowl of scree awaiting us on the other side, this one a little bit steeper and looser but without the added ice. It was like walking through the aftermath of a huge landslide, which could very well have been what it was. At one point the markers led us on a traverse of a long cluster of boulders, all about the size of a small car, one of which fell away just after I'd stepped off it, crashing down into a swathe of smaller stones below. This did not feel like an easy place to be and Esther found herself experiencing vertigo for the first time of the entire tour. Considering what had come before, it says a lot about how unstable it all felt in this "safer" section. Then again, guidebooks can only mark a single instant in time, though the mountains are ever changing places to be.

Any drama soon came to an end when the gradient levelled off. It was still rocky and technical, but with less risk of falling to our deaths. Three quarters of an hour after leaving the top of the col, we began to walk along an ancient grey moraine. That's when I spotted a flat, green site just beneath us on our right side. Facing south-east, directly towards the Grand Combin as it was, I knew instinctively that we'd just found our spot for the night.

It was perfect, both in terms of the nature of the site and the timing at which we'd arrived. The route further ahead held no promise of a good pitch, since everything else that we could see nearby was either steep or rocky, or both. In contrast, this little oasis was like a private terrace garden, a garden that just happened to be overlooking one of the Alp's highest and most stunning mountains. It was only half past five, an early stop for us, but we didn't hesitate to get our tent out immediately. We reckoned we were still close to 2800 metres and were tucked away on a high shelf, far above the green hanging valley beneath us. We also hadn't seen another soul since we began our climb to the Col de la Chaux and although we thought we could make out a building by a lake many hundreds of metres below us, we felt confident that the only people who might see us before morning were those flying helicopters.

We ate our simple dinner perched on the edge of a rock looking directly at the Grand Combin.

"You take me to all the best restaurants" smiled Esther.

"You deserve it. Make sure you thank the chef" I smiled back, revelling in the simple comforts of life on the sunny hillside. We had shelter, food and it was warm. What more did we need? Only water, but I found a source a couple of hundred metres below us and made a round trip to fetch five litres that would easily see us through the night and into the next day.

When the sun did dip behind the mountain on our right, we dressed in all of our layers and continued to watch as the white summit of the Grand Combin began to shift through all the colours of the rainbow. Then, as evening faded into dusk, a group of male ibex appeared, roaming about on the steep grassy banks below our tent. We counted eight of them grazing in companionable tranquillity.

We'd spent a lot of nights on the mountain over the previous few weeks, but none any more perfect or peaceful as this moment right now. What more could we ever hope for than the deep feeling of calm that was washing over us, together, in this magical place with the priceless view.

We stayed outside until the blue sky faded to black, revealing more stars than we had ever seen before in our lives. We'd seen beautiful night skies many times during this adventure, always dazzling in the way that only a clear mountain sky can be, but coming at the end of such a perfect evening these stars seemed brighter than ever. The Milky Way stretched across the sky like an arch of tiny candles, millions of pinpricks of light creating the ceiling to our world. This was our home for the night. We felt like the luckiest humans on Earth.

Vital Statistics – Day 23
Start Point: La Châble
End Point: Below Becca d'Age
Distance Hiked: 3 km
Hiking Time: 2 hours
Ascent: 240 metres
Descent: 330 metres

Tomato Sauce

Rays of gentle sun were already falling across the grass when we poked our heads out of our tent the following day, immediately overawed once more by that majestically powerful panorama. The sun had reached our high-altitude pitch early and was already drying the overnight condensation from our tent as we slipped into our boots and began preparing for another day of adventure.

It was a difficult place to leave, so we packed slowly, lingering over the gleaming view of the Grand Combin, its entire bulk exposed and shining in the morning sun. Bags packed, we fuelled ourselves with some remnants of overnight oat bran. We'd been more cautious with our breakfast since our last camping portion had mysteriously vanished a few days earlier, making it in our metal saucepan this time and leaving a heavy rocky on top of it overnight, only for me to go and kick it across the grass by accident while packing our gear. We'd salvaged what we could, but it was tricky to distinguish ibex droppings from raisins so we erred on the side of caution. No-one wants second-hand grass for breakfast. I did my best to reassure Esther that I had nothing against her overnight oat bran, even after three and a half weeks, but I'm not sure she believed me.

Our route today would take us back up to the top of the nearby grey moraine and then climb north-east towards the Col de Louvie. We set off just before ten, tackling a basin of large rocks beneath the tip of the moraine before beginning our traverse along it. A short while later the path began to dip towards a hidden lake, bright blue in the morning sun, before climbing on less stony paths towards a notch in the ridge above of us.

We reached the 2921 metre Col de Louvie in only half an hour, a flat, bare col overlooking the rich and varied flanks of the Grand Combin and more distant Mont Blanc, both visible behind us, while ahead of us was the seemingly barren wastes left by the retreating Grand Désert glacier. In the Haute route guide this scene is described in terms such as "a bewildering landscape of dying glaciers" where "the mountains are dying, falling apart, and to wander through their scenes of destruction is a sobering experience." It's certainly poetic, but not at all what we saw as we began the long traverse towards the next col, the Col de Prafleuri. (2965 m).

Descending close to the tongue of the much-diminished Grand Désert glacier, then rising steadily through a long and uneven series of boulder fields and craggy bedrock, we could understand why this might seem a desolate landscape compared to the vibrant green pastures in other valleys. But to us, this wasn't 'sobering', it was simply another facet of the mountains. It's a scene that appears in countless places throughout the Alps, places where the almost vanished remains of ancient glaciers cling on, surrounded by scree fields and rocks slides while the smooth crags extending before them provide proof of their once former majesty. It's all part of the life cycle of the Earth. Some mountains fall while others rise, not so much dying as recycling themselves, albeit on a timescale we find hard to comprehend against our own infinitesimal blinks of life.

The sobering part, for me, is the acceleration of that process due to human action. Not hiking boots on the ground, although in places people really should respect the paths more. Not even litter, although why some of the people inclined to walk a thousand metres uphill for a nice view still drop litter on the floor is beyond me. But the human action caused by global pollution. A good friend of mine, a meteorologist his entire career, puts it like this: "There really isn't a 'climate debate' any more and there hasn't been for years." In other words, the majority of climate scientists, those who focus on the climate rather than having a passing interest or loose connection, agree that the warming we see is hugely accelerated above any sort of natural level that can be justified by historic cycles. The media might be able to dig up a few dissenters and give them air time in the interest of 'balanced reporting', but when they're in such a huge minority it isn't really balanced to split it 50-50.

Some people argue it's all a big con to raise taxes, but if there is an agenda here I doubt it is the sneaky chance to tax the little people using a climate hoax. The agenda is far more likely to be mega-rich stakeholders, such as those who own oil-based and petrochemical dependent industries, creating the illusion of confusion in order to slow down legislation and other changes that would actually affect their investments and bank balances. They used the same tactic with smoking, the harmful effects of which are now accepted as an established fact.

But as long as enough people keep thinking "it might not be real" or "they're only trying to tax me harder", then change will be slow at best and possibly even stall completely. That's what I find sobering when I see glaciers diminishing. As I questioned earlier in this book, will the glaciers even still be here when my nephews and nieces grow up? Or will glaciers be a forgotten memory while countries go to war over clean drinking water? It sounds like a left wing conspiracy theory, but the data, the facts, all point in one direction. And what do big, rich powerful nations do when other nations have something they need? They find a reason to go to war.

Getting down off my soap box and returning to the Alps, we continued to follow the red-and-white markers towards the Col de Prafleuri. From afar and on paper it had looked like an almost trivial ascent, gaining just a few hundred metres over the distance, but up close it was surprisingly hard work. With uneven footing throughout and hidden dips in the terrain, it took us almost two hours to make our way between the two cols.

The Col de Prafleuri at just under 3000 metres is a very narrow saddle, just a few metres wide, that forms part of the ridge that divides the Grand Désert Glacier face of the Rosablanche summit from the Glacier de Prafleuri face. Scanning from side to side, we could look over the gravelly wastes we'd just traversed, watch the land rise up towards the ridge and then fall away sharply again towards another gravel plateau, one which we'd soon be descending towards.

It was just after midday, so we decided to have some food and our obligatory doze. Yet it was also very hot and we struggled to find a comfortable patch of grass or rock to settle our sweaty bodies onto. Everywhere we tried we found a new lump or bump to dig into a shoulder or a hip, and before we knew it we were having an argument. Five minutes earlier we'd been holding hands and smiling, now we wanted to toss each other off the mountain.

Typically, I can't actually remember what we argued about. The underlying issue for me, the reason I was grouchy in the first place, was that despite being able to eat more normally now I wasn't actually feeling any increase in my energy levels. I still experienced a nice energy boost when I ate, but between meals I was scared by the fact my lethargy and light-headedness was actually getting worse. My sore throat and headaches were still long gone, so I didn't think I'd had a relapse of what had happened in Breuil-Cervinia. I just felt totally worn out. And that scared me.

Which is why, feeling a little sorry for myself, I accept that I precipitated an argument. Esther, I remember saying, was a slave-driving, unfeeling, obsessive hiker who wouldn't stop no matter how ill I felt. From her side, I recall being called a melodramatic, attention-seeking bully. We argued for a brief while, I stormed off and declared she was on her own. Five minutes later we gave each other a hug and an apology.

There was probably a grain of truth in what we'd shouted at each other, but it was being blown out of proportion by fatigue and fear. We were in this together, whatever happened, and we were both on board with the plan. The fact I hadn't actually communicated how rough I was still feeling also became clear, as usual, and I resolved to try and be more open about my energy levels for the rest of the trip.

We made our way down the dusty trail to the gravel plateau beneath the Glacier de Prafleuri, with a beautiful panorama of the Aiguilles Rouges d'Arolla ridge visible above the Col des Roux in front of us, which is a mouthful to say but a delight to look at. At the end of the gravel plateau we dipped again, this time into a slightly greener glen containing the Cabane de Prafleuri.

The guidebook describes this little glen as "gloomy" but we couldn't see it that way. We even began to wonder if it had been raining when the author passed through this stage? Guidebook authors have a huge influence over expectations, so while realism is essential, I'm not sure despondency is a helpful trait. Or maybe they were just sick of saying how amazing it all is?

This refuge was recommended as the end of a stage, but we wanted to continue in search of a place to camp, so we refilled our water bladders before starting the short 200 metre climb to the Col des Roux. The guidebook stage we were now starting was described as "a delight", so the author must have been having a better day.

We had no intention to do much of the stage though. We'd already been walking for about five hours and I wasn't sure I could go too much further. Even this little climb felt like Everest all of a sudden. My feet were dragging in the dirt and I think if I'd sat down I'd have been asleep in sixty seconds.

We reached the col after what felt like three hours to me but was actually just twenty five minutes. It was a great view though. Spread out before us was the magnificently enormous Lac des Dix, the gigantic five kilometre long reservoir I mentioned earlier. The one that receives water from over thirty-five glaciers via a series of tunnels and pumping stations in order to produce 2 million KW of power! Beyond the lake, at the head of the Val des Dix, was the graceful curve of the Glacier de Cheilon reaching down from the pyramidal summit of Mont Blanc de Cheilon (3870 m), flanked by a broad ridge with a streaming cloud flowing from its eastern edge. It was a gorgeous scene, with the cloudy blue lake, green valley sides and white mountain beyond.

The trail continued down towards the lake, winding in long zig-zags before straightening to pass along the mouth of a minor valley. Our camping plans took a knock when a sign specifically informed us that camping anywhere near the lake was strictly forbidden. But it was a setback that didn't last long since we soon passed a small refuge, the Refuge des Escoulaies, which is named for the small glacier at the head of the little valley.

Ducking inside to check it out, we found a long single room containing two tiers of bunks on one side facing a long wooden table on the other, a locked area with more bunks above it at the far end and a small kitchen just inside the door. A sign explained that a guardian was resident at weekends only, but that the rest of the time it was only 11 francs a night to stay. We were the only people here and it felt very quiet and peaceful. The only minor downside was that the toilets were locked.

I wanted to stay immediately. I was dizzy and my limbs felt heavy, but Esther said she wanted to check out the other nearby, unmanned refuge first, which she did on her own, jogging the 100 metres downhill to check out the Refuge de la Gentiane la Barma. She came back to say that it was also nice, without any other people yet and that the bedrooms were perhaps a little more private because they were in small bunk rooms, but there was no benefit in moving unless a noisy tour group showed up here.

So we made ourselves at home. A shelf containing food left by previous guests turned up a quarter of a pot of Ovomaltine Crunchy spread, something I'd never tried before but was like Nutella with crunchie bits. A few spoonfuls of that and I felt a lot more human, at least for a few minutes. We'd never normally buy something like that, especially as it undoubtedly has dairy in it, but in the state I was in I was temporarily beyond caring about e-numbers and other additives. I wanted sugar. Lots of sugar! Then it suddenly struck me what else I might be missing.

"Salt" I said to Esther. "I've hardly been eating any food and none of our food is very salty. We get enough when we eat normally, but I haven't been eating normally. I've been sweating for days and I can't think of anything I've eaten with more than a trace amount in."

"You could be right" she said, pointing out the tomato ketchup bottle and stock cubes on the shelf. "Put some of those in your dinner".

I had rice with tomato ketchup that evening, which to be honest I didn't enjoy very much, but it was like a magic elixir. It was as though a fog was lifting from my brain with each spoonful and this time, unlike the sugar hits I'd been relying on, the fog didn't come back twenty minutes later. I was so happy, not to mention relieved. Common symptoms of low blood sodium levels include fatigue, weakness, confusion and irritability, all of which I'd been experiencing for several days. Most people actually eat far too much salt in daily life and because I'd never once had to think about whether I get enough salt before, it hadn't crossed my mind sooner.

Esther went outside to do some stretching while I discovered a 12V charger inside and a speaker I could plug her phone into. By the time Esther came back in I was dancing around the room and singing to Katy Perry music for no other reason than I felt so bloody good. In a totally masculine way, naturally!

We then danced together for a while, revelling in the freedom of the mountain and the fact we had this wonderful, rustic shelter to ourselves for the night. Either that, or I was still high from the Ovomaltine Crunchy paste.

With artificial lights and music to keep us busy, we stayed up a little later than usual enjoying the party feeling, not turning in until almost eleven o'clock. We still used our own sleeping bags, since the refuge blankets were thick but itchy beasts that felt like they might come alive in the night and wander off.

It took me a while to fall asleep that night. I suppose it was dawning on me that we were just a few more days away from our motorhome and the potential end of the adventure. There was still plenty of distance to hold an abundance of unknown thrills, but then what? What came next? That was the thought that I found myself drifting away with as sleep finally overcame me.

Vital Statistics – Day 24
Start Point: Below Becca d'Age
End Point: Refuge des Escoulaies
Distance Hiked: 11 km
Hiking Time: 5 hours
Ascent: 540 metres
Descent: 780 metres

The Glacier

A purple sky and a glowing sliver of crescent moon marked the beginning of our 25th day of adventure. It hadn't really struck us until now, but during the last three and a half weeks the days had been gradually shrinking on us. What would have been daylight at the beginning of August was now the tail end of dawn. Was summer really on the way out?

Of course, it's all relative and summer is what you make of it. As long as the sun was shining and the nights weren't too cold, that was enough for us. We had another exciting day in store, with a plan to follow a Haute Route variant from the end of the Lac des Dix, climbing up to the Cabane des Dix at 2928 metres (the one Isabelle had recommended we visit way back in Zermatt) before crossing our first real glacier on our way towards Arolla. It would be a long day, at least six hours of walking with a good amount of climbing, but after a breakfast that included more rice and ketchup, I felt ready for anything.

It was while we were packing up our bags and preparing to leave our homely bunkhouse that we first noticed a large tour group skirting across the hill a couple of hundred metres away. There were about fourteen of them, which got us wondering how Alana was getting on. She was probably ahead of us by now, we assumed, since she'd told us the itinerary of her group was a fast moving one, intended to reach Zermatt from La Châble in just a week. But then we noticed a familiar looking purple rucksack over a blue coat.

Esther dashed across to the stragglers and asked them to pass on our good wishes to Alana when they came back together, but instead the message carried quickly forwards in a series of long distance shouts along the path. A few moments later Alana, who was more than 500 metres away from us, began doing star-jumps, which we returned in a sort of athletic semaphore.

It was a fleeting moment, and with a person we hardly knew, but it was a moment of connection which made us smile. Hiking in the hills is a great leveller. It brings people together, irrespective of the material comforts they might have at home or the size of their bank balance. You might be able to afford a more expensive bed for the night, but out on the mountains we all have our arms, our legs and each other to fall back on. Maybe that's why smiles and waves are such a powerful currency out here. Collecting smiles has long been a hobby of ours while walking and it's one that never gets boring.

We set off soon ourselves, loping down the grassy hill towards the shore, reaching the other empty refuge at nine o'clock before turning south and setting a brisk pace along the lakeside trail. About halfway towards the southern tip of the water we passed an American couple and bagged another couple of smiles for our collection.

The view south along the lake continued to be excellent, although we were slightly disappointed not to have seen the dam at the northern end, the Barrage de la Grande Dixence, which is the world's highest gravity dam at 284 metres tall. A little bit of engineering here, but a gravity dam is one that relies on the brute strength of the concrete to hold back the water, in this case over 400 million cubic metres of the stuff! An 'arch dam', on the other hand, is curved so that the pressure of the water actually strengthens it. The tallest one of those, indeed the tallest dam in the world, is the Jinping-I dam in China at 305 metres, so the Grand Dixence isn't too far off the top spot.

At the end of the lake we found a much narrower track that climbed as it snaked further up the valley. While walking along the lake a light covering of wispy cloud had dulled the sunshine slightly, lending an overcast feel to the morning, but that was now dispersing rapidly to leave a mottled pattern of shadows on the vast surface of water behind us.

For the first couple of hundred metres of ascent the path was surrounded by grassy slopes, but gradually the green faded away until we joined the end of a long and battleship grey moraine ridge. At about 2600 metres we reached a fork in the trail, left towards the Col de Riedmatten and the 'standard' Haute Route, or straight on and further up the moraine for the Cabane des Dix. We continued straight with the towering pyramid of the Mont Blanc de Cheilon ahead of us all the way. To our right the ground dropped just a short distance into a narrow gulley with a stream thundering through it, while to our left the ground fell away much more steeply onto a plateau of glacial debris. Beyond that plateau, the deep notch of the Col de Riedmatten was silhouetted clear against the sky, perfectly framing the unmistakable point of the Matterhorn cupped within it.

Towards the end of the moraine the path dipped right, down into the gulley before climbing through loose stones and scree onto the shoulder of the 2980 metre Téte Noir. During that small ascent our view was largely blocked, but as we stepped onto the shoulder it all came flooding back. A direct, close-up and unimpeded view straight towards the triangular rock wall of Mont Blanc de Cheilon, with a cascade of ice mountains tumbling down the left-hand side before merging into a graceful, debris studded curve in the form of Glacier de Cheilon. Away to our left, in front of the glacier and raised on a rocky promontory, was the Cabane des Dix itself at 2928 metres.

We made our way down and across to the refuge, stopping only momentarily to buy an orange (which I could now eat without setting fire to my mouth) and ask the guardian about the glacier crossing that stood between us and the continuation of the Haute Route. It was an impressive refuge with a fantastic outlook, miles away from anything else you might describe as civilisation. This was a truly remote refuge, unseen until you are almost at the door. The original wooden hut was built in 1908 at a lower location, but was moved in 1928 and then replaced with a stone version in 1936, so it has a rich and beautiful history.

Outdoor furniture made from wooden pallets was the theme on the terrace and surrounding crags, with an outdoor shower positioned next to a sign warning visitors that using "this product can cause a state of extreme relaxation, satisfaction and the desire to return", which we thought was lovely.

Having turned away from two glacier crossings already, the reason we'd decided to bite the bullet and cross this one was partly because it looked fairly flat and not too wide on the map, but also because it was another way of slowly peeling back our boundaries. Because we'd be traversing it side-to-side instead of climbing it, we hoped it wouldn't be too challenging without spikes. Also, it was in the Cicerone guide which gave it a degree of respectability. If it was that bad, we reasoned, it wouldn't be an alternative stage in a major guidebook, would it? It was even described as an "easy crossing with practically no crevasses", although it was "important to follow the precise line shown by the markers".

The guardian pointed us in the general direction of the descent to the glacier. From above it looked like a short descent and a brief traverse over scree before stepping onto the ice itself, but the reality proved to be quite different. It was indeed a short descent, but we soon realised that what we were walking on wasn't just scree but a thin covering of stones on top of the glacier itself.

We were doing our best to follow a series of faded red dots, but kept losing sight of them as we tried to negotiate the vertigo-inducing cracks and caves in the ice alongside us as we walked. It's one thing descending into a five metre dip in a boulder field, but when you get down into the dip and realise everything around you is really ice and there's a gaping cave opening just a few metres away from you, it feels suddenly much more unsettling. As though you can feel the pent-up power of millions of tons of ice desperate to surge forward.

After getting lost quite a few times, we did manage to make it to the edge of the uncovered ice. The good news was that it was very easy to walk on without spikes. The sun and millions of tiny pebbles had done their work to create a surface riddled with tiny indentations, more than enough for our boots to grip surprisingly solidly. It was ice, but ice that felt like it had gripper strips built into it. We felt in no danger of slipping at all. The bad news was that what had looked rather flat and continuous from above was really a series of frozen waves with several deep channels of water sluicing through it. The ice was easy to walk on, but first we had to cross the two metre deep, two metre wide torrent of glacial water blocking our path.

Fortunately, it really wasn't a very steep glacier, which made it easy to walk a couple of hundred metres up-ice to a place where the channel was narrower and a rock had created a natural stepping stone. And then we were really on it, striding across the humps and frozen bumps of ice, surrounded by white and loving every moment. We were really doing it, crossing an actual glacier at almost 3000 metres in the Swiss Alps. It may have been an 'easy' crossing. It may have been a stable glacier. But it was a step beyond what we were used to and it was totally exhilarating as a result.

We had no idea where the markers were any more so simply moved in what looked like the general direction of the Col de Riedmatten. We had to cross 150 metres of ice to reach an interglacial moraine, a thicker covering of stones created when two ice flows meet and tear off lumps of rubble from the land between them, and then another 100 metres or so of bare ice to the far side. But that was directly across, whereas we were heading down the glacier in search of the trail up to the next col.

After a while we did start noticing some orange dots painted on the larger stones and were relieved to discover we weren't entirely lost. Another wide water channel marked the exposed ice boundary, which we crossed with a leap onto a huge, wedged rock. We'd been on the exposed ice for only half an hour but it felt like even less. Time had flown by and we gave each other a big hug to celebrate before turning our attention to the climbing ahead of us.

We knew from the guidebook that there were actually two adjacent cols we could choose to cross next, the Col de Riedmatten (2919 m) and the slightly more southerly Pas de Chèvres (2855 m). While the Riedmatten choice was the higher (our usual preference), the Pas de Chèvres was closer to us and featured a couple of laddered sections which we thought would be cool to try, so we decided to go that way.

The orange markers led us from the edge of the ice through a chaotic mass of boulders that often required us to use both hands to keep moving forward. The closer we got to the slope beneath the ladders, the less and less it seemed that there was a path leading up to them. It actually looked more like a landslide. But we trusted the markers and kept on going, one scramble at a time.

I can't say that what we were going through at this point was really hiking. It was an observation that was succinctly expressed by Chrissie, the female half of the American couple we'd met briefly earlier and who we passed among the rubble piles.

"If I'd known this route involved actual climbing, we'd have picked another one" she puffed at us when we stopped to chat. To put it mildly, she was not an athletic lady but she was determined and we were inspired by her courage. We'd actually see them a couple more times during our last few days, always moving and never giving up.

When the path finally forked towards the Pas de Chèvres we branched right, shuffling along a somewhat precipitous ledge towards the base of the first ladder. It wasn't too long, maybe only 7 or 8 metres tall, but it was almost vertical and hung over an equally steep and much longer drop into a mass of sharp rocks. The second and third ladders actually were vertical, which was even more exciting, with the glacier tongue beneath us and a wonderfully far-reaching view directly along the length of Lac des Dix to our left.

We stood on the Pas de Chèvres feeling a great sense of accomplishment. It was only two o'clock and we'd just done something we'd never done before. Looking back to the west, we could see the breathtaking landscape we'd spent the day walking through, glacier and ice mountains dominating the outlook, while in the east was a tantalisingly high and fiercely sharp ridgeline beckoning us forward.

The subsequent descent into Arolla was rather tame in comparison, following well-trodden grassy slopes for the entire nine hundred metre drop. It was a pretty descent, with various viewpoints worth lingering over, but even pausing for a late lunch and a doze we still found ourselves in Arolla by five o'clock.

What should we do now? The Haute Route continued north along the slowly falling Val d'Arolla towards the village of Les Haudères, so perhaps we should just carry on going and find a place to camp in the wild we thought. But then we'd be racing straight out of one of the most scenic areas on our adventure, simply to rush back to the motorhome when we didn't really have to. If we wanted, we could probably even get back by the following evening. But why?

Much dithering ensued. I was tired and wanted to at least agree a boundary to our adventure. I could almost sense my own bed just a couple of valleys away and didn't want to start making up detours just to try and extend the tour for the sake of it. Spectacular detours, yes. Trying to put off the end with unnecessary additions, no. Esther was also tired but feeling a sadness now that we were nearly back.

In the end it was chance conversation that made our minds up. Chatting to a lady in a hiking store, she told us that a nearby refuge, the Cabane de Bertol (3311 m), was stunning but required a short ice crossing high up. The week before someone had been seriously injured in the ice and had to be airlifted out, she explained, so crampons were essential.

"But we don't have any with us unfortunately" we said.

"That's okay, we rent them here. Just 12 francs a day".

That sealed it. Enthused by our first proper glacier crossing that same day, I asked Esther to hand me one of her boots, rented us both a pair of crampons (something that we'd never worn before) and told her we were staying on the Arolla campsite for two nights so we could attempt a day hike to this apparently amazing Cabane de Bertol.

It was an ambitious plan but an exciting one. It definitely surprised Esther when I came up with it. It was usually her job to come up with magical mystery detours, but now I'd come up with my own. I suppose I saw it as the cherry on the cake now that we were within striking distance of Zinal and the end of our trip. It would be one final high-altitude spectacle before we began the more practical business of actually heading home.

Being able to stay on a camping was a nice treat, especially with the knowledge that we wouldn't be moving the tent the next day. Every other camping experience in the past month had been a one-night job, arriving late and leaving early. This was going to be extravagant compared to that. I even treated myself to some potatoes for dinner instead of lentil pasta, well-boiled so they were nice and soft. Talk about spoiling ourselves!

We turned in at ten with an early start planned for the morning. Today we'd crossed our first glacier. Tomorrow, we planned to try and climb one!

Vital Statistics – Day 25
Start Point: Refuge des Escoulaies
End Point: Camping Arolla
Distance Hiked: 15 km
Hiking Time: 6 hours
Ascent: 750 metres
Descent: 1300 metres

Ice Climb

We set out before dawn, nervous and excited about the new experiences that lay above us. It was a long time since I'd felt butterflies in my stomach at the beginning of a day of hiking. Anticipation, yes. Happiness, definitely. But nerves, not for a long time. In my pack I could feel the reassuring solidity of our rented crampons, their heavy frames with triangular spikes holding the promise of adventure. How would it feel as they bit into solid glacial ice? Would I feel anxious? Frightened?

It's not always possible to know if something will scare you until you confront it. I remember a fairground ride Esther and I tried once, a roundabout of swinging chairs that lifted up to about thirty metres off the floor. Considering I'm supposed to be the one with a head for heights, I was shocked by how terrified I was as the flashing central pillar lifted us higher and higher off the ground. As we spun, the chairs began to stretch further and further out above the rooftops of the village we were in. With my feet swinging over thirty metres of thin air, bricks and tiles, I couldn't stop staring at the six flimsy steel cables attaching our flying double seat to the frame above us.

If it had been a more robust ride, say a chunky metal framed roller coaster with heavy duty shoulder straps, I would have been fine. But I couldn't believe how exposed and fragile this felt. I was petrified, my stomach turning circles at the thought of the spinning void beneath me. Esther, sat right next to me, wasn't scared at all. I remember being hugely relieved when it ended, but excited at the emotions I'd just experienced. After years and years of enjoying, but not fearing, rides like that, I'd actually felt the terror. I kind of liked it, so I insisted we did it again straight away.

Today was another big chance to do something entirely new and I was eager to get on with it. I was slightly worried that it might not go very well and I was also conscious that we'd need to be very sensible once we got into the high stuff. We had to let go of any attachment to an outcome. The biggest mistake we could make would be pushing on if we felt uncertain. That was something we'd talked about and agreed upon the night before, that it didn't matter how far we got, if either of us didn't feel good then we'd turn back. No questions. No arguments.

In the dull pre-dawn light we completed the initial 100 metre climb from the camping back up to Arolla village, before setting out on the long plod south. The first few kilometres of hiking would be very easy, with almost no height gain at all as we followed first a tarmac road, then a gravel track which carried us towards the head of the Val d'Arolla. In the centre of the scene was Mont Collon, dividing the valley in two. To the left (as we looked at it) was the Haute Glacier d'Arolla, the glacier we would have traversed if we'd followed the Matterhorn tour suggested on our map. To our right was the much broader, more expansive bulk of the Glacier du Mont Collon. However, we could see very little of either glacier yet since they were tucked away high in their respective valley arms.

Filled with the energy of the morning combined with revitalised legs after a good night's sleep, we soon ate up the kilometres, crossing the river close to the valley head and beginning our ascent through the glacial debris on the eastern flank. The sky remained overcast, throwing a dim, cold light over the scenery which emphasised the grey scree, dark glacial detritus and pale blueness of the few visible patches of ice. It seemed a harsh, inhospitable environment to be walking into, but an alluring one with Mont Collon and its crown of snow ever present directly ahead of us.

We climbed swiftly, two tiny dots moving through the rubble, reaching the point at which the trail split. Straight on towards the Haute Glacier d'Arolla and the Swiss-Italian border, left to continue climbing towards the Cabane du Bertol. We went left, entering a series of dry, dusty switchbacks which took us onto a shoulder with a small, dilapidated hut at 2600 metres. It was here that we got our first glimpse of our destination.

Seven hundred metres above us was a tiny, angular irregularity on an an otherwise jagged triangle of rock. That was where we were going. Beyond the dusty track and pale stones, beyond the sharp grey moraine and beyond the chaos of apparently vertical scree and ice beneath the refuge. From where we were standing, the route ahead did not look like something you could describe with the word 'hike'.

We got out our map to compare what we could see with its contours. That angular irregularity was definitely the refuge, constructed improbably on the right-central downstroke of a sharp 'W-shaped' ridge which ran across the top of the valley. On this side of the ridge the ground dropped sharply into a jungle of rocks, that was what we had to climb, while on the other side of the ridge a huge sea of glacial ice stretched away eastwards for more than five kilometres. Not that we could see much of that ice yet, just a couple of small patches which spilled through the dips in the 'W'.

"Perhaps we walk up one of those then" we guessed. "Although the lady in the shop said we'd only need the crampons for a short distance, and they don't look like short distances?"

We resumed our ascent, zig-zagging up the steep side of the hard-packed moraine and then walking along its crest until it was swallowed up by the mess of stones tumbling down the mountainside. We were close to 3000 metres now and had been following red-and-white markers to reach this point, but a blue-and-white stripe on a distant, truck-sized chunk of rock foretold that things were about to change.

From now on there was very little that could be recognised as a trail, certainly not in terms of a track on the ground. Usually it's quite easy to follow a trail, even when the ground is hard, because there are usually indications that other feet have come this way. But here, in a rockfall, with nothing but bare stones heaped into loose, shifting piles, there was no sign at all that others had come this way.

At first, there had been a couple of blue stripes painted on the rocks, but we could no longer see any of those. We thought we'd maybe gone the wrong way, except there wasn't really anywhere else we could have gone and nothing we could see nearby that looked any more 'trail-like'. There were a few cairns dotted around, just visible in the middle-distance, but they were scattered on both sides of the shallow gulley we had climbed into, so they couldn't all be marking the same route.

In the end we just went up, using gravity as our compass as we grunted and hauled ourselves between the most apparently flat surfaces on the ever-steepening slope. Already we were rising at a 50% gradient and it was only getting harder. Fairly soon we realised that this wasn't just a rock pile at all, but an increasingly thin covering of rocks embedded directly in the glacial ice. What we had seen from afar as a small glacial tongue spilling over the ridge was actually a much more extensive ice slope, flowing down the valley beneath us and buried in a variable coat of rubble. With a few hundred vertical metres still left to climb, we were now stepping from stone to stone with bare ice visible between each one.

Unlike the white, mottled and grippy ice of the Glacier de Cheilon the previous day, this ice was almost clear, totally smooth and as hard as granite. At one point we had to traverse sideways across the slope, right at a point where the stones were so spread out that we had to jump between them as though fording a frozen waterfall. After a time, we came to the first of several long snow patches and decided to give our crampons a try, reasoning that going straight up in spikes might feel less precarious than hopping over icy gaps.

Pausing to slip the evil-looking spikes from my pack, I talked Esther through putting them on in the same way that I'd been shown for the first time the previous evening, using my best 'relaxed and confident' voice. Then I led the way, stamping my enhanced footwear into the deep snow and leaning forwards into the slope.

It was a strange sensation to be wearing crampons for the first time. I felt both stable and unstable simultaneously. Stable, because I could feel when the spikes were biting into the hard portions of snow and holding me firmly as I swung my trailing leg forward. But unstable because the marginally increased weight and resulting shift in the balance of each foot was such an alien sensation. As was the grating, scratching, grinding feeling when a spike hit bare rock. It was totally cool though. We were at 3000 metres on a steep glacier wearing crampons and there wasn't another soul anywhere to be seen. How awesomely wild and thrilling is that?

I could see Esther plugging away below me. She wasn't saying much and I knew that this was even more out of her comfort zone than it was for me, but I could also see the steely resolve on her face and knew she was determined to master this new skill. And, although this was our first time in crampons, we at least had a lot of other hiking experience to draw on. We weren't just novice cowboys visiting the Alps for the first time. We were in an alien and dangerous environment but we did have a good awareness of our bodies and their limitations.

The snow crossing brought us to the foot of a vertical cliff, still about 200 metres below the refuge. Above us was a ladder and a series of cables, so we removed our crampons, stowed our trekking poles and began climbing. The first ladder was about ten metres high, followed by a series of metal D-rings and chains hammered into the crags which came next. Mostly it was the kind of thing we had done before, although always at much lower altitude and not surrounded by so much glacial debris and ice. There was only one especially tricky part, a long step out above a ten-metre vertical drop, balanced on a couple of small D-rings. Once stood on those D-rings there was nothing but void below, and the supposedly helpful chain nearby was so slack that it actually unbalanced us rather than assisted. But we made it across.

  That first section of cables and ladders bought us to another twenty-metre section of bare ice, which we had to cross to reach the final ascent, a series of three long ladders up a fifty-metre cliff to the refuge. Donning our crampons for a second time, we stepped out onto the ice, doing our best to make sure all the points contacted at once and taking small steps, as per the advice I'd watched on YouTube the night before. This bare ice section wasn't as steep as the snow climb, in a vertical sense, but it was shaped like a saddle meaning that the ice fell away sharply on either side. If we slipped left it would mean a fifty-metre fall into rocks. If we slipped right it would mean potentially hundreds of metres of sliding down the main glacier, also ultimately into rocks. Neither seemed like a good idea, so we went slowly and cautiously.

  That the lady in the shop had warned us about the ice but not mentioned the fifty metres of near-vertical ladders seemed odd when we reached the base of them. And when I say 'near-vertical', I mean tilted forward by just a few degrees. If we fell then there was no doubt that we'd be falling the whole way down. This was a smooth cliff and apart from the ladder, there was nothing else to cling to. Whether we fell from five metres or forty-five, the outcome would be the same. A painful and possibly fatal landing on glacial rubble. We were so close, but did we really want to attempt this final step?

Esther went first this time. Gripping the solid metal rungs and climbing steadily to the top of the initial five-metre ladder, she cautiously sidestepped directly onto the adjacent twenty-metre ladder, whose end hovered in thin air, and then continued steadily towards a half-way platform. I started a minute later, pleased to feel the firm solidity of the metal clenched in my gloved hands. Holding my body close to the ladder, I used my legs to step upwards, always keeping three points of contact as I moved. The side-step, which I'd seen Esther perform, was quite fun to do, shifting between ladders over a drop.

Ten metres from the ground and I could already feel my legs and arms aching from the effort of the climb. At the same time, I was increasingly aware of my pack pulling me gently but incessantly away from the ladder. By fifteen metres from the ground I suddenly became aware of an unfamiliar sensation. I was a little bit scared. Doing what you're not supposed to do, I looked down, and while part of me thought "this is brilliant, how cool is this?", another part simply said "fucking hell, don't fall!".

I couldn't remember getting vertigo on a mountainside before. I'd seen Esther get it and I'd heard it described as an uncontrollable loss of coordination and focus. Not just a fear of heights, but a dizziness and weakness that simply overrides motor control and you can't help it. But I'd never actually experienced it before, until now. My knees were feeling wobbly and there wasn't a lot I could do about it.

I steeled myself to complete the first portion of the climb, focusing on gripping as tightly with my hands as I could until I arrived onto the halfway platform with some relief. Esther was already tackling the second, slightly less vertical ladder section and I watched her with deep admiration. I was supposed to be the sure-footed one. The one who didn't mind heights and could walk across a board spanning a yawning chasm as though it was a pavement in a town centre. But if I felt the fear up here, what was Esther feeling?

"You're amazing" I called out. "Looking good. Doing great". I didn't mention that I'd got the willies just now. What good would it have done? I'd tell her later, probably.

The second portion of the climb wasn't so unnerving, though climbing a ladder tilted forward 20 degrees from the vertical has its own challenges. But just a few minutes later, it was done. A final series of metal staircases led away from the top, ascending past shuttered windows on the side of the refuge. We climbed them together and arrived into a world of ice.

Standing on a square-mesh platform outside the upper floor of the refuge, we could now look straight down between our feet to the surface of a glacier more than a hundred metres directly below us. Allowing our gaze to rise slowly, the ice simply continued and expanded in every single direction until it grew into a sight like nothing we had ever seen.

With the still overcast sky seeming to mirror the scene below, what we were looking at was like an expanse of frozen sea, rising, falling, splitting and merging in one powerful mass of blue-white enormity that completely filled our vision. Our map showed various names for the different sections flowing down from the different peaks we could see, but to us it was all one. It totally stopped us in our tracks and before we could even think of going inside the refuge or looking around the other side, we literally fell back onto a wooden bench and stared open-mouthed at it all.

It took us a while to recover our wits I suppose. It was hard to believe how the day was turning out. We'd just climbed a glacier, worn crampons, scaled a vertical, laddered cliff and now we were, literally, hovering above what looked like a mini ice age. I'd often tried to imagine what it must have been like when the glaciers we'd visited over the years had been a thousand times larger than they remain today. What it would have looked like when they literally filled the valleys that they carved and only intermittent stone spires emerged from the ice. Well, now I'd seen it. Ice that filled the world. Only peaks were visible above it, including the Matterhorn in this case which poked out on the eastern horizon.

 We did look around the refuge eventually, briefly dipping inside where the enticing warmth and smell of baking almost had us ordering cake and a cup of tea, but it was outside where we really wanted to be. It looked like quite a large refuge, with a warren of dormitory beds downstairs and the dining room and kitchen on this upper floor. It was incredible to learn that a hut had first existed up here as early as 1898, though it's obviously been expanded and rebuilt significantly since then. The modern refuge has eighty beds available on four different levels.

 Continuing round onto the other side of the terrace to look out over what we'd climbed, we found ourselves suspended directly over the bowl of ice and rubble with fantastic views over the distant ice plateau of the Glacier du Mont Collon. Alongside the ice a host of other white-capped summits were now almost at our eye level. Four and a half hours ago, when we'd set off, those peaks had towered over us, their glaciers and snow-drifts hidden from sight.

 Over the next half an hour we alternated between sides, though mostly gazing out over the ice world which we would soon have to say goodbye to. Regretting slightly that this was an especially long day hike, so we couldn't hang about, we resolved that if we ever did anything so long and high again we'd probably plan to spend the night in the refuge. But today that wasn't the case and when a light drizzle began to fall, we knew we had to get going soon. We didn't want to push our luck. If the darkening clouds above us really started to unleash their fury then we didn't want to be hanging from ladders or slipping down rubble-encrusted glacier ice at the time.

We left just forty-five minutes after reaching the top, during a brief break in the rain. It was a sad farewell. We both knew that something special had just happened. That what we had just achieved was right on our current limits of ability and experience, with an enormous reward as a result. Other hikes might have better views while others might be slightly harder and more frightening, but this had been the perfect combination of technical demand, risk and reward for us. From the moment we'd left the red-and-white trail below we had been able to forget everything except the placement of our feet and lose ourselves in this magnificent mountain bubble, and that sort of focus is a rare gift in a hectic world.

Still, it wasn't over yet and I could already feel butterflies again at the prospect of going down those ladders. One more look over the ice sea and we began, one rung at a time. Ladders and crampons, crags and D-rings, rubble and ice. There was no particular incident or event that scared us, just a steady series of slips, slides and shifting boulders that kept us alert to the dangers of the descent. At the long snow crossing, we passed a group of six men ascending with a better-equipped guide at the head of the group, confidently ascending using the same route that we had.

As we approached the final stages of the ice and rubble, I started to become aware of just how tired I was. I remember reading in Bear Grylls book 'Facing Up', about his ascent of Everest, that a family friend had warned him that it was the descent that would be the "danger time", and I could feel that strongly now. All the adrenalin of the climb was suddenly fading and a pronounced lethargy was slowly taking over my body.

We stopped at the dilapidated hut for food and slept for half an hour on the grass nearby. The rain had, thankfully, fizzled out for the time being and it was even beginning to feel warm whenever thinner patches of clouds drifted over the sun.

We got back to Arolla at half past four, nine and a half hours after leaving. It had been a big day in more ways than one. We returned our crampons and thanked the assistant profusely for giving us the idea to visit that wondrous place. We could see that she also loved the mountains and we chatted for a while about other places we'd seen over the summer. Then we bought a little more food and headed back to our tent for dinner and a shower.

On the one hand, we were now just a couple of days away from finishing our tour. On the other, if our experiences so far proved anything it was that we never knew what the morning would bring. Our morning mantra of "I wonder what adventures we're going to have today" had proved so appropriate that neither of us could say with any certainty what lay ahead.

Vital Statistics – Day 26
Start Point: Camping Arolla
End Point: Camping Arolla
Distance Hiked: 16 km
Hiking Time: 8 hours
Ascent: 1310 metres
Descent: 1310 metres

Are We Nearly There Yet?

From Arolla, the Haute Route guidebook suggested taking three more days and a total of fifteen hours of hiking to reach Zinal, but we had other ideas. Although the meandering guidebook route looked undeniably stunning, at least half of it would be spent travelling through the Val d'Anniviers and specifically the western-most branch, known as the Val de Moiry, a place we were already incredibly familiar with after previous visits to the area.

As a result, neither of us had a massive desire to retrace routes we'd already hiked more than once, especially not at the end of such a marvellous adventure that had already included so many unknown and unexpected surprises. To do so, we felt, would be extending the tail-end of our trip largely for the sake of it.

For the past few days we'd been discussing, you could say negotiating, whether or not we would use the remaining few weeks before we had to fetch our dogs to attempt another shorter tour in an entirely different region. Or, alternatively, whether we would use our motorhome to simply tour around and try some new day hikes and maybe some overnight stays in refuges? Both were exciting prospects and we felt lucky to be faced with such a decision.

I leaned towards day hikes. The fatigue I was feeling after almost four weeks, especially after my illness, had eroded my resilience. I still had some soreness in the roof of my mouth and I wanted to enjoy the relative comforts of our motorhome for more than just a couple of nights. Esther leaned towards another tour. The freedom of a canvas home deep in the wilderness was her passion and she didn't want to surrender that.

In the end we'd agreed on at least five days of total rest in the motorhome while we made our minds up. It was a compromise that worked for both of us, with more new adventures in store one way or another, but with some guaranteed rest time built in. We were both now mentally ready to get back to Zinal as efficiently and quickly as we could.

    Why am I telling you all this now? Because I want to try and explain why we tore out of Camping Arolla at nine o'clock in the morning and began a firm-paced march down the road towards Les Haudères, the village at the mouth of the Val d'Arolla. Once we reached Les Haudères, taking the most direct route that we could, we would then immediately start the vertical mile of climbing required to reach the 2867 metre Col du Tsate and put ourselves above the Val de Moiry. We wouldn't continue to follow the standard Haute Route, but would instead cut the corner by going straight up towards the col using other more direct trails marked on our map. What we did when we got to the top would depend on how we were feeling, but the sooner we got there the more options we'd have, so we got moving.

    We did briefly consider hitchhiking to Les Haudères rather than walking along the road, but we only saw two vehicles the entire time we were on the tarmac, both of them commercial delivery trucks which wouldn't have been allowed to stop for us anyway. Instead we quickly reached the hamlet of La Gouille and a short time later left the road to cut down the tree-lined hillside towards Les Haudères.

    Esther had to ask me to slow down a couple of times, so clearly the carrot of a night back in our motorhome was getting my juices going a little more than I realised. We did agree to stop several times to stuff our faces with ripe wild raspberries though, so we can't have been in too much of a hurry.

    It took us just under an hour and a half to reach Les Haudères, compared to the three hours the guidebook route was supposed to take, so we felt we were making good time. On our final approach we had emerged from the cool shade of the valley into the hot morning sun, so we sat to warm ourselves for a short time in the village square, eating juicy oranges bought from the épicerie just across the street. Les Haudères seemed a picturesque and quiet village, with mostly wooden houses decorated with the conventional red geranium window boxes which characterise much of this region.

Directly opposite from the bench we were sitting on was an old refrigerator, painted bright red, with the words "Pop-up Office de Tourisme Les Haudères – Servez Vous" written on it. Inside we found stacks of leaflets and board games for everyone to make use of, which we thought was very quaint.

Signs in Les Haudères told us that the Col du Tsate was four hours away, but I hoped we could shave a little off that time. I took the lead, powering up the humid, grassy slopes and sending grass-hoppers flying everywhere. At the first 'time-check', the village of La Forclaz, I was pleased to find we'd just done an hour of 'signpost climbing' in just under half an hour, so we were going at more than double-speed. I wasn't sure Esther was quite as happy about it as I was, since she was lagging behind a little on the steepest sections.

I couldn't deny I was feeling pretty sprightly. My guess was that the weight I'd lost while ill, now that I was eating more normally again, was working in my favour whenever the trail got steep. I doubt that I was any stronger, probably the opposite was true, but I felt nimble on my feet nonetheless. As a result, I took several things from Esther's pack, just as she had done for me back in Breuil-Cervinia. We were a team and wanted to share our strengths.

As we gained height we were treated to an excellent view along the Val de Ferpècle to our right, straight towards the tongue of the huge Glacier du Mont Miné which we had looked down on from Cabane de Bertol. We could only see the tiniest tip of ice now, compared to the kilometres we had seen the previous day, but it was a nice feeling to be able to connect the dots of all the different views we had enjoyed.

We sweated ever onwards and upwards, the hillside remaining green around us as we marked an hour of brisk climbing. The sky above us was clouding up, with a dark patch sitting on our destination, and the risk of rain helped to keep us motivated as our legs started to throb. By the time we'd been moving for two hours, we were almost there.

The final approach took us through black, almost slate-like scree. That was when the rain finally arrived, driven sideways across the slope by a powerful and cold wind that tried to steal the waterproofs from our cold fingers as we layered up. With the onset of the rain coupled with exhaustion setting in, the plunging temperatures affected us more than we had hoped, turning that final approach into a mental battle as much as a physical one. But we made it, eventually, reaching the Col du Tsate (2868 m) just two and half hours after leaving Les Haudères, a climb of almost 1400 metres. Ahead of us was the hugely familiar sight of the Val de Moiry. It was a little like coming home.

It was still raining slightly at the top, but after such a sustained and fast-paced effort, we needed a sit-down and some food, rain or no rain. We still only rested for quarter of an hour though. It was coming up to two o'clock and I knew that if we could just get down into the Val de Moiry and along the long reservoir that fills it, the Lac de Moiry, we could possibly still catch a bus back to Zinal that very same day. But to make that even an option we simply had to keep moving.

We'd caught a lot of buses in the Val d'Anniviers before and from what we remembered the ones from the Barrage de Moiry, the dam at the end of the lake, stop running quite early in the day. With a sign on the Col du

Tsate telling us that the barrage was 2 hours and 15 minutes away, this was no time to stop as far as I was concerned. We could rest when we made it home.

I knew I was driving us both hard as we half-jogged down the soggy paths towards the head of the Val de Moiry. I knew I was flagging myself and I could see that Esther had run out of steam some time ago. I did my best to make encouraging noises but I wasn't sure if I was actually being a help or a hindrance at this stage. It also crossed my mind that all this hurry and fluster was totally unnecessary since we could quite easily camp in the Val de Moiry that night and get back to the motorhome the next day. Or even call a bloody taxi if we were that desperate to get back tonight. But I liked the challenge of trying to make it. It made it exciting to have a demanding goal and I suppose I had a bit of tunnel vision now that I'd locked onto that target.

The familiar sight of the Glacier de Moiry drifted into view on our right as we lost height, as did the distant Barrage de Moiry away to our left. We'd visited this place many times before and even lived in our motorhome up here for a week one September, but we'd never seen it from this particular angle.

This descent from the Col du Tsate was blessed with a very special panoramic view which swept the entire length of the valley, taking in the tumbling ice fall, the moraines at the valley head, the cloudy lakes at the tip of the glacier, the river nestled in a lush green gulley and the mirror-like surface of the reservoir. That it had stopped raining and that the sun was even threatening to return also helped keep our spirits buoyed up.

After an hour of intermittent jogging and power-walking, we finally reached the valley bottom and crossed the river that flows between the tip of the glacier and the southern end of the reservoir. From here, it was just a short climb back up to the road where the prospect of thumbing down a lift had been hovering in our awareness for some time. The problem was, there just didn't seem to be very much traffic.

"Quick, I think I hear a car coming…" I blurted out from my position ten metres behind Esther and still fifty metres away from the tarmac strip above us "…run and stick your thumb out". I watched in nervous tension as Esther's rucksack suddenly sprang to life, moving surprisingly quickly away from me to reach the road just in time to poke an optimistic thumb in front of a small white car. Mercifully, it stopped to reveal a young, smiling couple who immediately asked where we wanted to go.

"Allez vous a Grimentz ou Zinal?" Esther asked.

"Oui, Grimentz. Bien sûr." replied the driver as he hopped effortlessly out of the car and opened the boot for us. We'd been saved!

Their names were Ronan and Mauvoin, trainee lawyers from Strasbourg who studied in Paris, and who were visiting the Alps for a week's vacation. They both spoke good English and we had a happy conversation as they drove us down the beautiful valley into the waiting arms of the village of Grimentz. They also never once mentioned how bad we must have smelled, or the muddy boot prints we left in their immaculate car. We couldn't thank them enough and their casual response of, "it's natural, we're going that way and have the space" seemed the essence of communal kindness.

Standing outside the Coop in Grimentz, a place we had shopped at many times over the years, I felt like a hero returning from a victorious campaign. We'd done it. The sense that we'd just accomplished something was washing over me like a mood-boosting wave. Paradoxically, there was also a sadness beneath the elation, but there'd be more time for reflection later. Right now I just wanted food and a bus back to Zinal. In that order. As luck would have it, I'd end up with both.

We walked through the cobbled, geranium decorated streets of Grimentz to the tourist office to pay for a day's worth of tax. In return, we received the pass which would give us a bus ride home. Familiar faces behind the counter greeted us as friends, smiling and laughing at our two-minute summary of where we'd been. Then we went to sit at the bus stop, taking turns at smearing rich, creamy almond butter onto oatcakes and turning them into mouthfuls of heaven. By the time the bus arrived ten minutes later, the pot was empty, but we definitely weren't.

As luck would have it, we'd arrived just in time for the last direct bus of the day between Grimentz and Zinal. Other connections would have been available if we'd arrived later, but we'd have had to wait much, much longer and go in a different direction to pick up the connecting service. That luck continued when we entered Zinal ten minutes later. There are only two bus stops in Zinal, neither especially close to where we'd left our motorhome, yet what we didn't know was that another couple had already agreed an impromptu stop with the driver. That stop was only 100 metres away from our motorhome.

Giddy with excitement, we approached the motorhome slowly, it's reassuring shape seeming unreal after so long. Then I gave it a hug.

Vital Statistics – Day 27
Start Point: Camping Arolla
End Point: Zinal
Distance Hiked: 14 km
Hiking Time: 6 hours
Ascent: 1440 metres
Descent: 1140 metres

Glorious

Elation, relief and a warm sense of accomplishment were all mingled with just the tiniest hint of loss as I slowly and sleepily returned to the world of consciousness the next morning. Surprisingly, after so many aching, restless moments in our tent longing for our 'real' bed and our 'real' pillows, sleep had arrived tediously slowly the previous evening. Rather than falling immediately into the deep and blissful slumber I'd long imagined would greet me upon our return, events, faces, places and viewpoints from the previous twenty seven days had instead kept me awake for several hours as they jostled for my attention and kept me mentally asking questions such as "Wow, did we really do that?", and "was that really three whole weeks ago!"

Still, sleep had eventually arrived, and a solid and very welcome eight hours of it at that, leaving me feeling quite refreshed and cheerful as I stretched my legs beneath the duvet and listened to the sounds of Esther trying to slice up a melon and make a cup of tea silently on the other side of the curtain. From the almost inaudible clunks and chinks it was clear that she was trying her utmost to be silent and so let me sleep. Grateful that she was being so thoughtful, I almost didn't have the heart to let her know that I was awake at all.

"Good morning" I yawned through the curtain, resulting two seconds later in the appearance of a smiling face with a small piece of melon still sticking out of it. "What time is it?" I asked.

"Almost nine" came the cheerful reply.

We looked into each other's eyes for a moment, neither of us saying anything but both of us understanding what the other was feeling. Sadness. Excitement. Pride. Happiness. Soreness. Lethargy. Restlessness. All of the above.

"What adventures will we have today?" we said in unison, reaching out to hold each other tightly.

It was day 28. Four weeks after we'd first arrived in Zinal, 320 kilometres, 24500 vertical metres and 140 hours of walking later, and we were back.

Nothing had changed, yet nothing felt the same either. Just five days later, it would start all over again.

Epilogue

Esther sometimes likes to say that's she's made up of two different 'bugs', a 'home bug' and an 'adventure bug'. Sometimes, when the home bug gets bored and restless, the adventure bug comes out to play. Only when the adventure bug gets tired does the home bug emerge once again.

You might be tempted to think that after our four week odyssey it was time to give the home bug a few weeks of indulgence, but it was not to be.

Just five days after hugging our motorhome, we would set off again. Carrying even less gear, our plan was to attempt a much less demanding, far more conventional 'guidebook' version of the Tour of the Vanoise National Park in France. As you might expect by now, we got carried away.

Hopping across the border into Italy and tagging on a high-altitude loop of the adjacent Gran Paradiso National Park as well, our 'straightforward' little walk turned into an epic fifteen days without a rest. With glacier crossings, snowstorms, endless boulder fields, countless ibex and the company of excellent friends, our additional 'easier' jaunt ended up taking us further and higher each day (on average) than even our Matterhorn adventure. And we got to sleep in a treehouse.

The next book in this series, **Walking Through Paradise**, tells that story. Visit **www.estheranddan.com**, sign up on our Facebook page or follow us on Instagram to receive updates.

But even that wasn't enough for Esther, who at the end of September also took off into the Pyrenees with two of our dogs for 'a few days of walking'. I collected them all a month later! But that's a story she needs to tell.

Until then, happy adventures.

Thank You

Hello wonderful reader and thank you for making it all the way to the end of *Just Around The Matterhorn*, the second book in the Alpine Thru-Hiking series.

I know you could have picked countless other books to spend time with, but you picked this one and for that I am extremely grateful.

Adventures all start with a single step and I hope that, just maybe, this account of our four week odyssey has set you dreaming of your own future adventures?

If so, it would be wonderful if you'd take a few seconds to leave a review on Amazon. Your review is very important and need only take a matter of seconds.

And, if you'd like to continue the adventure with us, flick to the end of this book for more titles in this Alpine Thru-Hiking series.

Thank you.

Acknowledgements

Writing takes patience, a head full of words and, most important of all, a good story. However, left to my own devices there's a chance I might lose myself in books and forget to have adventures at all. Thankfully, I have a life partner who won't let that happen.

Rain or shine. Snow or sun. Esther has an indomitable spirit of adventure and, for reasons known only to her, keeps allowing me to tag along.

As with all of my books, this adventure and the words that have followed from it have been a joint project from start to finish.

Thank you, I love you.

Dan Colegate – 2019

www.estheranddan.com

www.instagram.com/estheranddan

www.facebook.com/estheranddan

Photos

1 – Descending from the Barrhorn (3610 metres) towards the Brunegggletscher

2 – Yoga in front of our dream home above the Mattertal (2100 metres)

267

3 – Chased by walking pom-poms (aka blacknose sheep) up a ladder at 2800 metres. I swear that ladder was bent before I stepped on it.

4 – The Matterhorn, as seen while descending from the Platthorn (3345 metres)

5 – Looking along the cloud-covered Mattertal while descending from the Hörnlihütte (3260 metres)

6 – Final approach to Rifugio Quintana Sella (3620 metres).

7 – Adventuring together on top of the world. Outside Rifugio Quintana Sella (3620 metres).

8 – A view along Lac Mauvoisin from 2500 metres

9 – Camping at 2800 metres overlooking the Grand Combin (4314 metres)

10 – Final laddered approach to the Pas de Chèvres (2855 m).

11 – Hiking up-ice on the Glacier de Cheilon (2700 metres)

12 – A sea of ice from Cabane de Bertol (3311 metres)

These are just a few images from many thousands. For more photos from our adventures, visit our website at **www.estheranddan.com** or our Instagram page **www.instagram.com/estheranddan**

Turn over for more books by the author

Also By The Author

What Adventures Shall We Have Today?
Travelling From More To Less In Search Of A Simpler Life

You've read one small part of our adventures, now read about the rest! The perfect book for anyone who has ever felt there could be more to life.

Six years ago Dan and Esther were counting down the days until their wedding and the honeymoon of their dreams. Then Dan almost died. Told to say goodbye to each other "just in case" in the early hours of a sleeting January morning, that was the moment when their lives would change forever. Three months later they drove away from their home, their jobs and everything they'd ever known in a second-hand motorhome. Friends and family asked "What do you want to see? Where do you want to go?". All they could say in response was "it's a feeling we're searching for."

At first they planned to travel for a year but as their outlook on life evolved, their priorities changed and they started to get glimpses of 'that feeling', their escape quickly morphed into a lifestyle all of its own.

This is the story of their travels for the past six years. With no plan and no purpose beyond living in the moment, their meandering adventures have taken them over mountains, under the sea, inside of pyramids and across the skies. They've crashed a hot air balloon by the Nile, adopted a dog who surprised them by being pregnant and even became organic farmers for a while, among other things. More than anything, however, they've found themselves confronting their own insecurities and limiting beliefs about how life is supposed to be lived.

This is more than a story of two people drifting around Europe, it's about looking at the world through fresh eyes, reassessing what's truly important and embracing the inevitable challenges that life throws up.

Visit **www.estheranddan.com** or Amazon to find out more.

WHAT ADVENTURES SHALL WE HAVE TODAY?

DAN COLEGATE

Turn Left At Mont Blanc: Hiking The TMB

One Couple's Inspirational, Funny & Brutally Honest Account Of Their Adventure Around Europe's Highest Mountain

The first book in the Alpine Thru-Hiking series. A hiking story that makes you want to dust off your boots and head straight to the nearest mountains.

Three years before the adventures in this book, back when Dan and Esther were even less experienced mountain walkers, they flew to Geneva with a bag full of gear, an unopened guidebook and a vague idea that they'd start by walking south.

What happened next was a life-changing adventure.

From one stunning viewpoint to another, from valley to col, from acts of random kindness to moments of unbelievable fortune, this was an adventure that pushed them to the limits of their bodies, their relationship and forced them to face up to some of their deepest fears.

And they got to spend a night in a real teepee!

Written in a light-hearted but direct manner, this is a funny, inspiring and brutally honest account of what it was like to head into the mountains unprepared, under-planned and over-geared and come out on the other side with a whole new outlook on life.

Visit **www.estheranddan.com** or Amazon to find out more.

One Couple's Incredible Adventure

TURN LEFT at MONT BLANC

DAN COLEGATE

Walking Through Paradise
A Magnificent Journey Through Western Europe's Largest Nature Reserve

The third book in the Alpine Thru-Hiking series is a light-hearted, uplifting and inspiring account of Dan and Esther's fifteen day odyssey through the French and Italian Alps, exploring the Vanoise and Gran Paradiso National Parks.

Just five days after their demanding four-week adventure around the Matterhorn, Esther and Dan set out into the wilderness once again. Their goal is simple, to enjoy a peaceful walking holiday in the Alps. However, as usual, the moment their shoes hit the trail their plans go straight out of the window and the adventure takes on a life of its own.

Driven by an inexplicable thirst to always look beyond the next summit, their initially sedate hike from refuge-to-refuge soon becomes an expedition across blizzard-ridden 3000-metre passes, tumultuous boulder fields and snow-packed glaciers, turning each day into a unique pilgrimage through some of the most remote and stunning Alpine scenery they've ever seen.

Sleeping in everything from luxury hotels to snow-covered storm-shelters and abandoned tree houses, their quest to lose themselves in the heart of the Alps becomes far more than a search for nice views and exciting stories. It's about rediscovering the solitude of the hills and the calm of the night sky, miles from civilisation and the chaos of the modern world.

A perfect book for anyone who wants to experience the awe-inspiring magic of Europe's most beautiful wilderness.

Visit **www.estheranddan.com** or Amazon to find out more.

WALKING THROUGH PARADISE

A Magnificent Journey Through The Heart Of The Alps

DAN COLEGATE

A Note On Names, Altitudes And Distances

During this adventure we would have been lost, quite literally, without a variety of maps, guides, scraps of paper, posters on tourist office walls and, more than just once, friendly advice.

Because we were passing through two different countries, one of which has four national languages, there were sometimes minor variations between different sources. The most obvious example is the mountain at the heart of our tour, the world famous Matterhorn, which actually has three different names depending on where you're standing.

It's called Mont Cervin in French, Das Matterhorn in German and Cervino in Italian. Yet despite these local variations, you might still be tempted to think 'Matterhorn' would be universally accepted. It's not. I lost count of the number of blank stares we got until we managed to pronounce Cervino just right. Or perhaps it's just a game they play with tourists?

Mostly, however, the variations were much less noticeable. For example, our Swiss-bought map called a particular Italian pass the "Col de Valcornera – 3065 m", while a leaflet we found in an Italian tourist office used the local name and a slightly different altitude, "Col di Varcornera – 3066 m". In the moment, this discrepancy didn't change our lives one iota. To be honest, until I wrote this book, I hadn't even noticed it.

In terms of which names and altitudes to include here, I was initially going to use only local names. Then I realised that there was sometimes more than one 'local name' to choose from. So instead, I've mostly used the version given on the maps we personally used.

In terms of distances and the altitude gains/losses given at the end of most chapters, this is simply my best estimate made from those same maps, leaflets and guidebooks. I have no way of knowing if we walked for precisely 14.8 km on a particular day, or 15.6 km, or possibly even 16.1 km? Similarly, if we started at 2000 metres, climbed to 3000 metres and descended to 1500 metres in a day, I've written down a height gain of 1000 metres and a loss of 1500 metres. I haven't even tried to take into account all of the little variations.

In short, if you plan to try and reproduce any of these walks, please don't take the names, distances and height changes in this book as an exact guide. Instead, grab hold of a map and lose yourself in the contoured splendour of the great outdoors. A map, I find, is like a window into an adventure.

Happy exploring.

Printed in Great Britain
by Amazon